To Sister
Joel and all the
folks at Alverno College
in friendship from
people of Saint Paul.
Best Regards,
George Latimer
May 1987

SAINT PAUL

Picture Research by Rosemary Palmer
Corporate Profiles by Dick Schaaf

Produced in cooperation with the
Saint Paul Area Chamber of Commerce

Windsor Publications, Inc.
Northridge, California

A Modern Renaissance
SAINT PAUL

VIRGINIA BRAINARD KUNZ

Windsor Publications, Inc.—History Book Division
Publisher: John Phillips
Editorial Director: Teri Davis Greenberg
Design Director: Alexander E. D'Anca

Staff for *Saint Paul: A Modern Renaissance*
Senior Editor: Gail Koffman
Director, Corporate Profiles: Karen Story
Assistant Director, Corporate Profiles: Phyllis Gray
Editor, Corporate Profiles: Judith L. Hunter
Production Editor, Corporate Profiles: Una FitzSimons
Sales Representatives, Corporate Profiles: Joseph Belshan, Henry Hintermeister
Editorial Assistants: Kathy M. Brown, Laura Cordova, Marcie Goldstein, Marilyn Horn,
  Pat Pittman
Proofreader: Susan Muhler
Design and Layout Artist: Christina McKibbin
Assistant Layout Artist, Corporate Profiles: Mari Catherine Preimesberger

Library of Congress Cataloging-in-Publication Data

Kunz, Virginia Brainard.
  Saint Paul, a modern renaissance.

  Bibliography: p. 233
  Includes index.
  1. Saint Paul (Minn.)—History. 2. Saint Paul
(Minn.)—Description. 3. Saint Paul (Minn.)—Industries.
I. Title. II. Title: Saint Paul, a modern renaissance.
F614.S4K85   1986   977.6'581   86-24670
ISBN 0-89781-186-0

Facing page: *Landmark Center and Rice Park, with the
Ordway Music Theatre on the
left, appear in this aerial photograph by Steve Linder.*

CONTENTS

To St. Paul's leaders
past and present
Who laid the foundations for their
city's renaissance and then made it happen

ACKNOWLEDGMENTS

This was a difficult book to write, in good part because the record of contemporary events, unlike those of history, often fail to keep pace with the onrush of the events themselves. The task was eased greatly by the members of the Readers Committee who demonstrated once again that few books are the work of any one person. This is particularly true of this one. It could not have emerged into print without the wise counsel, guidance, and advice of five of Minnesota's best-known and widely-respected leaders: Ronald M. Hubbs, retired chairman of the board of The St. Paul Companies; Robert Orr Baker, retired St. Paul Companies executive and St. Paul's unofficial historian and past chairman and president, Ramsey County Historical Society; Charlton Dietz, vice president for legal affairs and general counsel for 3M, and past board member of the Ramsey County Historical Society; Frank Marzitelli, whose many civic leadership roles helped bring to pass much that is described in the following pages, and a current board member of the Ramsey County Historical Society; Amos Martin—and especially Amos Martin—who entrusted to me once again the task of writing about St. Paul. His two decades of leadership of the Saint Paul Area Chamber of Commerce have earned him a reputation as one of the outstanding Chamber executives in the United States.

Cheerfully donating hours of their time in reading through four and more drafts of this manuscript, each brought to this project a strong sense of history as well as invaluable criticisms and insights drawn from his own participation in the community and its renaissance. They helped me keep pace with St. Paul's changing business and economic landscape. No writer could have had a finer group of editors.

A special thanks goes to Philip H. Nason, retired chairman of First Bank St. Paul who loaned me his scrapbooks and graciously gave of his time to talk with me and to read and comment on the first section of this manuscript. I am indebted also to Mayor George Latimer for sharing with me his own perceptions of the linkages of events, and to many others who took time from their crowded schedules to meet with me, to share reminiscences, to clarify events, to provide significant information, to review sections of the manuscript: Robert E. Hess, Richard T. Faricy, Richard T. Murphy, Wayne Winsor, Laurie Murphy, John Pfaender, Jack Nichols, Larry Culligan, Coleman Bloomfield, Malcolm McDonald, William Hickey III, Robert Van Hoef, Richard Broeker, James H. Bellus, James Stolpestad.

I am indebted to my colleagues on this project, to Rosemary Palmer, widely-respected historian and researcher who spent countless hours locating and assembling the photographs that illustrate and extend the text, and to Dick Schaaf, well-known business writer, for his understanding of my role in preparing the text as he pursued his own separate and independent assignment of researching and writing the business biographies.

I am most grateful to the staff and board of directors of the Ramsey County Historical Society for bearing with me through eighteen difficult months of research and writing, and to the Board of Ramsey County Commissioners whose support of the county's cultural institutions, including the Ramsey County Historical Society, makes it possible for all of us to present the programs which have added so much to this community's quality of life. And few writers could have had a more understanding and skilled editor and publisher than Gail Koffman and John Phillips at Windsor Publications.

But in the last analysis, all credit must go to the leadership, private and public, of Ramsey County and St. Paul, whose enlightened collaboration has made possible the renaissance this book describes.

FOREWORD

The post-World War II period marked a dramatic change in American cities. Many cities geared up to meet the postwar economic boom and to make sure their communities were part of the action. When shopping and office centers moved to the suburbs, many cities were left with older, decaying downtown areas.

This period also marked a dramatic change in the role of the private sector in addressing community development. In many cities, chambers of commerce abandoned their "boosterism" emphasis and returned to the Chamber's traditional role of job creation and economic development—with special emphasis on rebuilding aging and decaying downtown areas. The Saint Paul Area Chamber of Commerce was in the forefront of the nation in heralding this change, in assuming a leadership role in the renaissance of St. Paul, and in developing the public and private partnerships that made it happen.

The Saint Paul Area Chamber of Commerce and its participating member firms are sponsoring the publication of *Saint Paul: A Modern Renaissance* to help the community understand the sometimes unrecognized role that business plays in society. St. Paul serves as a "showcase" of what the country's free enterprise system can provide. We hope this book will underscore the importance of volunteer business involvement and private entrepreneurial spirit in the economic development of an area.

In St. Paul, the entrepreneurial spirit has fostered an exceptional combination of forces which date back to the city's inception. Today this private and public partnership is recognized nationally for the role it has played in the city's renaissance and presents a model for the future. As the country's political system moves toward more reliance on the individual, business volunteer organizations and other citizens' groups must take the lead.

The Saint Paul Area Chamber of Commerce and its business and professional members believe *Saint Paul: A Modern Renaissance* will provide an important overview of what the city has become and how it got there. We invite all citizens in this region—natives and newcomers alike—to join in our efforts to make the remaining years of the twentieth century as successful as the renaissance era we now celebrate.

Joseph T. O'Neill
Chairman
Saint Paul Area Chamber of Commerce

Landmark Center is a tribute to the collaboration of private and public forces. Courtesy, Saint Paul Area Chamber of Commerce

INTRODUCTION
A LEGACY OF LINKAGES

In the long line of St. Paul mayors that stretches back to the 1850s, only a few have left so faint a mark on their years in office as to be imperceptible. Most have been cast in the individualistic, driving mode that has been characteristic of St. Paul's often rambunctious political arena. Many have served longer than the two years the city allots to its mayors. None has served as long as George Latimer, who is now in his sixth term of office, which has as much to do with St. Paul's remarkable renaissance of the past decade as has any other single factor.

While Latimer fits neatly into the classic mold of colorful St. Paul politicians, he also departs from it. Sophisticated, well-educated, he's a sparkling man. Not a native, he nevertheless has a strong feeling for the city he has led since 1976. Born in upper New York State into a Lebanese-American family, a background that leads him away from the Irish-Catholic tradition of political leadership in St. Paul, Latimer holds a law degree from Columbia University and began practicing in St. Paul in 1963. He has been a regent of the University of Minnesota, president of the National League of Cities, and chairman of the Minnesota Tax Commission—appointed by Governor Rudy Perpich in 1983 to conduct the first comprehensive review of the state's tax system in thirty years.

There are those who feel that St. Paul's renaissance years should be labeled the Latimer Years, but Latimer is the first to cite the achievements of his predecessors and his peers. In the following introductory essay, he looks back over the past few years to identify a number of linkages in the transformation of the city.

We all stand on the shoulders of those who came before us. During the six years after 1960 when George Vavoulis served as mayor, he forged a partnership with the business community that became the foundation for the redevelopment that followed. This was the first link in that chain of events. By 1970 some of the economic tools were in place that were essential in the continuing redevelopment of the city. Under

Sunrise breaks over St. Paul's multi-faceted skyline. Photo by Leighton

The World Trade Center, scheduled for completion in 1987, will renew St. Paul's role as an international trading area. Photo by Leighton

Tom Byrne, mayor during the later 1960s, the public resources that would combine with private investment to fuel our downtown redevelopment efforts were beginning to assemble under the Capital Improvement Budget Program. This was a commitment by the state legislature to grant St. Paul the right to spend $6.5 million a year to improve its capital structure without legislative approval or referendum. Out of that grew an elaborate community participation process that in the early 1970s was combined with the Community Grant Program, an intensely democratic process. Money was appropriated only after projects were reviewed by a citizens task force representing all city neighborhoods. Today some twenty million dollars is spent annually through these two programs, another sequence of footprints that linked one event to the next.

In the meantime, the private sector was hard at work, led by nearly every corporate leader in the city. In the 1960s the Saint Paul Hilton went up, the first new hotel in downtown St. Paul since the 1920s. In the early 1970s the Civic Center was built, and the redevelopment of a dozen downtown blocks was under way as part of a plan drafted by the Metropolitan Improvement Commission—reorganized later as Operation 85. This created Osborn Plaza and made the next link possible, the filling in of "Super Hole," a block that had been empty so long that it was eligible for historic designation. And this became Town Square, the first use in St. Paul of another innovative tool, the Urban Development Action Grant, a federal program St. Paul leaders helped design during the early years of the Carter Administration. Congressman Bruce Vento was one of the authors of the UDAG bill that grew out of a program developed by a Conference of Mayors. St. Paul has had sixteen UDAG projects totaling more than fifty million

dollars and leveraging another $300 million. At least half of these grants were for redevelopment projects in the downtown district.

By this time another link had been forged that would make St. Paul's redevelopment a reflection of its own history. Nearing completion on Rice Park was the restoration of the Old Federal Courts Building as Landmark Center, a home for arts and cultural agencies. This was a step taken by a creative group of public and private citizens and supported by $13.5 million in private philanthropy in partnership with Ramsey County, which owns the building and supports its maintenance.

When the folks led by Sally Ordway Irvine and her family decided to help build the newest jewel in our city's crown, the Ordway Music Theatre, it was only logical that it be built on Rice Park. It's intriguing how often politicians view the historic preservation movement as something they either separate from urban development, simply tolerate, or view negatively. In fact, $100 million-plus in new development has taken place in St. Paul because of historic preservation. This is a classic example of the positive domino effect, the use of such other economic tools as the federal tax credits that encourage historic restoration, and the extraordinary resources of the Port Authority of the City of St. Paul, which has been brought into our development efforts. Much of the building of the last ten years would not have been accomplished without the innovative financing of the Port Authority. Town Square Center, St. Paul's first UDAG grant, wouldn't have been possible without these programs.

Town Square Park is the largest enclosed park in America. It is used by people from every walk of life, and it helps give the city a special flavor. St. Paul has been called the Boston of the Midwest, the last city of the East, but it also resembles a European city with its remaining nineteenth-century buildings blending with its glittering new towers.

It also is one of the fortunate few American cities to possess five National Historic Districts and at least a hundred individual National Historic Sites that enrich the older sections of the city. Rice Park, an American version of Europe's inner-city squares, is surrounded by the castle-like Landmark Center, the classic seventy-year-old Saint Paul Hotel, the contemporary Amhoist Towers, the art-deco Northwestern Bell Telephone tower, the Florentine palazzo that is the St. Paul Public Library, the venerable Minnesota Club, The St. Paul Companies' modern structure, and the sparkling new Ordway Music Theatre, itself in the best European music-theater tradition. Over it all loom the baroque St. Paul Cathedral and the serene white marble state capitol.

Today, St. Paul, which was founded as a riverport, remains the largest riverport in the Upper Midwest, serving a hinterland that stretches between Chicago and Seattle. This is a role that will be greatly magnified when the World Trade Center opens in downtown St. Paul. It will mark a return to a vision nourished by empire-builder James J. Hill almost 100 years ago when his rail lines reached the Pacific and he set out to establish trade with the Orient. Even Hill was not breaking new ground. During the earlier years of the nineteenth century, shipping of furs down the Mississippi toward Europe for the Hudson Bay Company had already made St. Paul a world trade center. This brings us to a final link, the city's newest effort, the redevelopment of its greatest natural resource, its Mississippi riverfront, a five-mile stretch of winding river that flows through downtown St. Paul.

Mayor George Latimer
St. Paul, Minnesota

Mayor George Latimer with the city of St. Paul in the background. Photo by Gerald Gustafson

A PUBLIC AND PRIVATE PARTNERSHIP

St. Paul, the upper Midwestern city of 267,810 that sits firmly at the head of navigation on the Mississippi, serves many roles. It is the capital of Minnesota, the major transportation center serving the northern tier of states, and the gateway to the Northwest. It has been named an All-America city and it has won a City Livability award.

It is also a classic example of renewal and rebirth, of a city's restoration after having been gutted by the tear-it-down syndrome of the 1950s and 1960s and victimized by that most devastating of post-World War II movements, the flight to the suburbs.

St. Paul is a city of contradictions. Skyscrapers line the Mississippi River while the Jonathan Paddelford *and* Josiah Snelling, *paddlewheelers reminiscent of St. Paul's steamboat days, cruise the river. Photo by Kay Shaw*

Left: *St. Paul is at once a contemporary and a classical city, combining skyscrapers with parks and historic buildings. Photo by Herb Ferguson*

Facing page: *Viewed from beneath St. Paul's near century-old Wabasha Street Bridge, St. Paul's skyline—including Northwestern Bell towers, Amhoist tower, West Publishing (lower left), and the Ramsey County Jail (lower right)—rises above the mighty Mississippi. Photo by Leighton*

St. Paul today, and especially its downtown, gleams with new towers neatly blended with restored nineteenth-century buildings that soften the urban landscape. The city's neighborhoods, their strong cultural and ethnic identities relatively intact after more than a century of settlement, not only have survived but have also been strengthened by the distractions of expanding colleges, universities, hospitals, and the commercial centers that serve them. The suburbs, the historic villages of Ramsey County, received those refugees from the inner city and became glossy new cities in their own right.

Clearly, not all of St. Paul's renaissance has taken place in the downtown district, but it is in the city's commercial center, where billions of dollars have been spent, that the renewal has been most visible and perhaps most exciting. While this is in good part the result of an explosive five to seven years of building the new and rebuilding the old, it really began more quietly and somewhat reluctantly thirty years ago with civic leaders who forged a private and public partnership that has endured, despite changes

in leadership and philosophy on the public side, retirements and transfers on the private side.

Philip H. Nason, retired chairman of First National Bank of St. Paul, has influenced St. Paul's business and economic resurgence more than any other person. Looking out over the city from his office in the First National Bank building, Nason remembers a dormant, stagnating city of the mid-1950s.

Downtown St. Paul was in terrible shape. We'd had no new construction for twenty years, except for Minnesota Mutual, who built a new headquarters in 1955—a courageous decision, considering the state of the downtown. The tax base was ridiculously low, with taxes for manufacturing and residential properties too high and the downtown area not paying its way. First Bank's primary interest was in loans and deposits from the St. Paul area. We wanted St. Paul to prosper. When I became president in 1954, my directors and I decided that I should spend up to a third of my time on redevelopment projects that

*Mears Park provides a peaceful setting for lunch breaks.
Photo by Leighton*

would attract business to the city.

"People weren't ambivalent about the extent of the downward spiral," states James H. Bellus, director of St. Paul's Planning and Economic Development Department since 1980. "Things were so bad that an opportunity was created for private market forces to step in and invest money."

One force was led by Nason. One of its goals was a first-class downtown department store. Along with the growing shabbiness of the commercial center, the city's once-glossy retail stores had declined into third-class operations. St. Paul's shoppers were going elsewhere.

In 1956 Nason got into his car and drove across the river to Minneapolis to call on Bruce and Donald Dayton, the senior members of the family who owned the prime department store in the Twin Cities. The Daytons told him they had been considering moving into St. Paul for some time. In 1958 they bought the old Schuneman and Evans department store and opened it as their own new store, one of the early cornerstones in the redevelopment of downtown St. Paul.

At about the same time, another community force was being transformed into the sophisticated operation it is today. This was the Saint Paul Area Chamber of Commerce, still cast in its old glad-handing role, its meetings attended chiefly by its members' fourth-rank managers. The business leadership knew the Chamber had to be reorganized and that a strong Chamber needed the support of business. The result was that St. Paul attorney Joseph P. Maun, the Chamber's president, and a five-man committee hired a tough, professional, conservative executive, John Hay, from Muskegon, Michigan, who revitalized the organization. Among other moves, he merged the Convention Bureau and the Downtown Council, which had become separate organizations, back into the Chamber.

Now the city's political leadership entered the picture. George Vavoulis, elected mayor in 1960,

understood the need to work with the business community. With Vavoulis in office, the Chamber reorganized, and with Nason and his group of corporate leaders pushing the private sector, the foundation was laid for the years of rebuilding that followed.

Not all of it progressed smoothly. There was a certain reluctance in some quarters. At the time he was elected, Vavoulis recalled in a recent interview, no businessman would think of participating in government. While the city's old-money families would provide strong leadership and financial investment in the city by the 1970s, in the 1950s there was a leadership vacuum. Some business leaders whose family fortunes had been badly shaken by the Depression wanted nothing more than to stay out of politics and out of investing in redevelopment, which they viewed as chancy at best.

One project, however, captured their enthusiasm. This was the financing of a new hotel, the first since 1927 when the Lowry Hotel went up a block from the Saint Paul Hotel. Both had declined to second-class status. A few blocks away the once-magnificent Ryan Hotel, built in 1884, occupied an entire block, but its deterioration seemed to have passed the point of restoration, and it would be torn down in 1962.

To launch this high-priority item on the business community's agenda, Vavoulis' office and the Chamber of Commerce created the Metropolitan Improvement Committee, which brought together the community leaders whose commitment would be essential: Harold Cummings, president of Minnesota Mutual; A.B. Jackson, president of St. Paul Fire and Marine; Paul A. Schilling, president of Hoerner-Waldorf; Reuel Harmon, president of Webb Publishing; Joseph P. Maun; E.E. Engelbert, president of St. Paul Book and Stationery; Louis W. Hill, Jr., president of the Hill Family Foundation; the Northwest Area Foundation and Nason and his fellow bankers, Rollin O. Bishop of American, H. William Blake of Northwestern, now Norwest Bank, and Edward G. Bremer of Commercial.

SAINT PAUL AREA CHAMBER OF COMMERCE

There was a time when chambers of commerce were seen primarily as civic booster clubs. If that perception was ever valid in St. Paul, it faded away some 30 years ago in favor of a new type of chamber, one dedicated to fostering a climate conducive to productivity, profitability, and long-term stability for the businesses that give economic life to the city.

The Saint Paul Area Chamber of Commerce—the name officially adopted in 1960 to reflect its metropolitan scale—is today an innovative and involved association of the city's business leaders, now more than 2,000 members strong. Over the past 30 years the chamber has played a crucial role in the economic and civic renaissance of St. Paul.

The outlines of today's chamber began to take shape in the late 1950s, when the decision was made to professionalize the organization's activities and combine them with the previously separate Downtown Council and the St. Paul Convention Bureau. John Hay, a professional association executive from Muskegon, Michigan, was recruited as the new full-time president, a position he held until 1967, when he was succeeded by Amos Martin.

The "new" chamber's first major challenge was providing private-sector input and assistance on the 12-block Capitol Center urban-renewal project, working in association with the city and the federal government. Begun in the early 1960s, this ambitious undertaking spanned decades. Its eventual success can be measured in many ways: It spawned the skyway system, kept many major businesses in the downtown, and helped St. Paul regain confidence in itself. It also established the chamber as the vital private-sector voice in the city's emerging knack for getting things done through public-private partnerships.

Over the years that voice has

been backed by a wide variety of actions. The chamber helped sell stock and debentures to get the St. Paul Hilton (now the St. Paul Radisson) Hotel built. It recruited businesses to guarantee that the interest on the new St. Paul Civic Center would be paid through its first 10 years of operation. It pushed for the lengthening of the runway at the downtown St. Paul Airport.

In addition, the chamber cooperated with the Downtown Council, the Port Authority, the city, and the cultural, retail, and entertainment sector in developing an effective marketing program for the city and the downtown. It led a coalition of over 30 organizations that in 1985 convinced the governor and state legislature to eliminate onerous provisions of the Minnesota "superfund" legislation. It initiated, and originally managed, "Literacy 85," a program designed to focus attention on the problem of adult illiteracy.

Through the years the chamber has developed special programs to meet special needs:

*an Employer's Council for Equal Employment Opportunity in 1967 to help members meet EEO and affirmative action guidelines;

*an Urban Coalition with representatives of the minority communities in the area in 1968 to assist small businesses and find jobs for minorities and youth;

*a Labor-Business Ad Hoc Task Force with the Saint Paul Trades and Labor Assembly in the late 1960s, nationally one of the few chamber working relationships with organized labor;

*a Small Business Council, one of the first in the country, to help small and entrepreneurial firms prosper and grow;

*Project Responsibility, a specially funded program in the 1970s to encourage and publicize business' cultural and civic involvement in the city, including

When completed, the new World Trade Center will serve as a focal point of international trade and commerce for the entire midwestern region of the United States. The Saint Paul Area Chamber of Commerce, the City of St. Paul, the Port Authority, and other groups were involved in getting the World Trade Center located in downtown St. Paul.

a teacher internship program, career seminars for student counselors and teachers, and a Corporate Social Responsibility program.

Under Amos Martin, the chamber's ability to make things happen in the shorter term has been mirrored by a willingness to look at the hard question facing the city and the state over longer periods of time. Its mission has become a broad-based commitment to represent the city's businesses and their needs, helping them stay competitive and helping them stay in St. Paul, where they can continue creating more and better jobs for the people of the city.

The glittering new Amhoist tower houses the Amhoist corporate headquarters, offices, and luxurious residential units. The Saint Paul Hotel is on its right. Photo by Kay Shaw

Within weeks the group incorporated. Forty-two men sat on MIC's board of directors under the general chairmanship of St. Paul attorney Robert E. Leach, cochairman Walter Seeger of Whirlpool, and attorney Wilfrid Rumble. They hired a young architect-planner from Michigan, Robert Van Hoef, as executive director. Their mission was to help rebuild St. Paul. As one of their first tasks, these men put together the St. Paul Hilton Hotel project.

A new first-class luxury hotel of at least 500 rooms was critical to stemming St. Paul's loss of convention business, providing good accommodations for business visitors, and attracting shoppers to downtown retail stores—to say nothing of pouring an estimated seven million dollars into the city each year. Nason and Leach had been quietly lining up private financing for the project. Sometime later Bernard Ridder, Jr., publisher of the *St. Paul Pioneer Press Dispatch* and a hotel investor, recalled Nason's approach to his peers: "Put on your civic hat, boys. We need a hotel. St. Paul needs the convention business." It would not, Nason added,

make anyone a millionaire. It was a civic gesture representing "enlightened self-interest."

MIC decided to go after the Hilton Hotel Corporation. Both Nason and William L. McKnight, board chairman of 3M, were directors of the Great Northern Railroad. They were on a directors' inspection of the railroad, a trip that ended in Seattle. Nason had made an appointment with Conrad Hilton, so McKnight had his plane sent out and the two men flew to Los Angeles, McKnight worrying that Hilton might never have heard of 3M. He had.

Right: *The elegant Saint Paul Hotel is located in the Rice Park area adjacent to Land- mark Center and the Ordway Music Theater. The hotel is a favorite gathering place for pre- and post-theater events. Courtesy, St. Paul Convention Bureau*

Facing page: *St. Paul's Radis- son Hotel (formerly the Hilton) opened in 1965 with great fanfare. The Radisson's prominent position on the bluff offers magnificent views of the city and the Mississippi River valley. Photo by Kay Shaw*

In 1963 Hilton announced that his corporation would build a twenty-two story, 500-room hotel on the corner of Wabasha Street and Kellogg Boulevard. It would cost $12.5 million, with $5.5 million to be raised by St. Paul businessmen. A separate corporation, the Saint Paul Hilton Hotel Company, was formed to sell stock and $4.5 million in debentures; Hilton put in $500,000 and received a management contract. The rest came from Prudential Insurance Company in the form of a $6-million mortgage. The Saint Paul Hilton (now the downtown Radisson) opened with great fanfare in 1965, and for years most of the major community events have been held there.

By now city leaders were looking for other new routes to a vibrant downtown that would attract people who would stay at the Hilton. A convention center where they could meet and hold the trade shows that were the core of the convention business was high on the list, but so was an opportunity to attract a national-league hockey team to St. Paul. John Hay had warned the Chamber's board that major events

were leaving St. Paul because the city lacked a good auditorium. Thus the Civic Center project was born.

The proposal was to remodel and update the city auditorium on the western edge of the downtown district, add a theater section and arena that would seat 15,000 and connect them to a parking ramp on Kellogg Boulevard, all at a cost of $12.8 million. State Senator Wendell Anderson sponsored legislation that authorized the city to issue general obligation bonds if the Civic Center could generate enough yearly in- come to pay the interest. Parking and conces- sions were expected to total at least $500,000 annually. St. Paul's business community agreed to guarantee that income.

Harold Cummings, who played a major role in the center's development, later shared with the *St. Paul Sunday Pioneer Press* a vivid memory of a meeting in the basement of the Minnesota Club. Some two dozen business leaders were discussing the financing of the Civic Center. Nason offered to ask his bank for $25,000 a year to help guarantee the center's revenues

AMERICAN BAKERIES COMPANY

For travelers through the city on I-94 and visitors to the state capitol or, depending on the set of the wind, downtown St. Paul, it is as much a landmark as Landmark Center. It doesn't dominate the skyline or rival the high-tech marvels of other businesses around town. But for nearly 75 years this particular St. Paul business has been an integral part of the downtown just because it has made the city smell so good.

It's the "Taystee bakery"—officially the American Bakeries plant along the north side of the freeway, just a short walk from the capitol mall, where each week nearly one million pounds of bread and baked goods roll out of the ovens, to the delight of noses of every age and occupation.

It is also the foundation around which has grown the nation's fifth-largest producer of bakery products: American Bakeries Company, a diversified, $460-million corporation headquartered today in New York City, but tracing its ancestry back to the hard work and good-tasting products of two Twin Cities bread salesmen.

Mike Molan and Tom O'Connor left sales to start a bakery of their own in Minneapolis in 1902. It was an era of many small, competing bakeries, but Molan and O'Connor managed to survive and grow, in

1912 adding a bakery in St. Paul at the corner of University and Kent.

That same year one of the region's first large-scale, modern bakeries was built at 12th and Minnesota streets by the Foley Brothers of St. Paul. Four years later the Foleys' St. Paul Bread Company merged with Molan and O'Connor's Twin Cities operations, and the Flour State Baking Company was born.

The smaller bakeries of that colorful era are long gone, but the plant at 12th and Minnesota remains, testimony to the foresight of the builders and quality of the bakers who have operated it for nearly three-quarters of a century. Meanwhile, the firm has grown to national scale, first as Purity Bakeries Corporation, and since 1953 as American Bakeries.

Today St. Paul is home to one of 17 plants of American Bakeries. Each day the historic plant turns out more than 300 different varieties of Taystee® breads, buns, and doughnuts; Mickey® cake and snack products; and custom-baked goods for restaurants, fast-food stores, and institutional food operations.

From I-94, the "Taystee bakery" near the state capitol is a familiar sight—and scent.

In addition to bakery products for restaurants, institutional food operations, and fast-food customers, American Bakeries' products are familiar sights in area homes.

More than 300 employees—many of them members of Local 22 of the Bakery and Confectionary Workers, Locals 289 and 471 of the Teamsters, Local 70 of the Engineers, and District Lodge 77 of the International Association of Machinists—operate the giant ovens and mixing lines, and keep the plant running, sometimes around the clock, to meet the needs of institutional customers, retail stores, and restaurants in Minnesota and western Wisconsin.

Yet even though the business begun at the turn of the century has grown large, the St. Paul operation has never outgrown its pride in its local history. Only two regional managers—J.M. Tombers and now Jerry Partlow—have directed the plant's operations over the past 58 years, and most of the plant's department managers have come up through the ranks of the plant's workers. For them, the distinctive flavor American Bakeries Company brings to the city is the sweet smell of success.

WILKERSON, GUTHMANN & JOHNSON, LTD.

Wilkerson, Guthmann & Johnson, Ltd., is an accounting firm with a tradition of caring and serving. Since 1923 its highly educated and motivated staff of certified public accountants and support personnel has been assisting clients in identifying their financial and organizational needs, helping them to achieve *their* goals and objectives. The identifying and satisfying of needs has been a long standing personal philosophy of the firm's leadership.

This spirit of genuine helpfulness benefits both clients and numerous community and church organizations that have been helped on a volunteer basis.

The company's current shareholders, Howard M. Guthmann, John L. Phillippi, Roger A. Katzenmaier, Austin J. Stibbe, James V. Lewis, James G. Platz, John T. Kisch and Ronald H. Zuercher, are all recognized professional and community leaders.

All of the shareholders are members of the American Institute of Certified Public Accountants and the Minnesota Society of CPAs. The firm stresses active professional involvement and the concept of lifelong learning. Its educational program includes staying current with the latest developments in the practice of accounting

The Tax Reform Act of 1986 requires a lot of research, writing, and telephoning.

as well as areas of interpersonal relationships. It is continually seeking ways to grow and improve its collective skills in meeting client needs.

Wilkerson, Guthmann & Johnson is a people-rich firm. It's accountants can effectively serve others on a timely basis because they are backed by a highly competent support staff. By placing a premium on collaboration and team

Assistance is given to both clients and staff.

effort, the firm is able to bring both technical and creative skills to its practice of accounting on a cost-effective basis.

The company is strategically located to serve Twin City organizations through its offices in St. Paul, Minneapolis, Blaine and Hastings. In addition to providing the traditional tax and accounting services of a full service accounting organization, Wilkerson, Guthmann & Johnson assists clients with numerous management functions including organizational structures, planning, personnel, financing, data processing, etc.

Client activities include manufacturing, wholesale, construction, retail, health and welfare, education, finance, real estate, and other services both for profit and nonprofit organizations. Many of the firm's clients are individuals with special financial needs. Most clients operate only in Minnesota but some are active coast to coast.

Throughout its history, Wilkerson, Guthmann & Johnson has maintained its focus on intensive personal familiarity with the financial, tax, accounting and management needs of the organizations and individuals it serves. For more than 60 years, the firm has served with expertise, diligence, and pride.

St. Paul's circular Civic Center hosts numerous local and national events, including professional conventions, home and garden shows, and the St. Paul International Institute's Festival of Nations which celebrates St. Paul's ethnic heritage. Photo by Kay Shaw

for ten years. Donald Nyrop, president of Northwest Airlines, said his company would guarantee half of that amount.

"Then there was an awful silence," Cummings remembered. "Nobody said a word. Everybody stuck his hands under his pants and held them there. Then we all went upstairs for a drink and lunch." Nevertheless, Cummings persuaded forty-three firms to guarantee another $150,000 and, although some years of planning and negotiation lay ahead, the Civic Center was eventually built. This was a significant move, coming as it did on the heels of the business community's investment in the Hilton.

In the meantime, the Metropolitan Improvement Committee had been promoting a renewal plan called Capital Centre, a project that grew out of the urban-renewal surge of the 1950s and early 1960s. An array of postwar programs with federal dollars attached had pushed cities all over the country into projects that had more to do with the decline of the cities' commercial cores than crime, the quality of schools, or any other factor. Interstate highways, cheap gas and oil, and long-term, low-interest home mortgages encouraged people, and particularly the middle class, to move to the suburbs.

City leaders, all too aware of their decaying commercial districts where the Depression and the war had put a damper on new construction, reached for those federal dollars that were committed to housing and redevelopment programs. The result was a rush to tear down that was in some respects a destructive force. Cities were left with holes in their centers that sometimes took years to fill. Buildings were torn down that might have been preserved and restored.

Amos Martin, who succeeded John Hay as president of the Saint Paul Area Chamber of Commerce in 1967, believes St. Paul was fortunate in that redevelopment did not get under way as quickly there as it did elsewhere. As Nason put it, a conservative faction "wanted to keep downtown a nice quiet place with a little grass growing in the streets," and saw little reason to make the parking problem worse than it already was. As a result, postwar development did not start as early in St. Paul as it did in other cities. Buildings were spared that today help give the city's downtown its special ambience.

Capital Centre involved some twelve square blocks in the heart of the city that the St. Paul Housing and Redevelopment Authority was clearing of their decaying nineteenth- and early twentieth-century buildings. It was an imaginative program that drew together representatives of business, civic, and labor groups; the City Planning Board and staff; city-government officials; the Housing and Redevelopment Authority under B. Warner Shippee, and the federal agencies. Shippee had a special sensitivity toward historic structures that was unusual in HRA officials at that time. He called on representatives

from the Ramsey County Historical Society, the Minnesota Historical Society, and the City Planning Board's historic sites committee to tour buildings scheduled for demolition and determine what might be saved. The result was that fine architectural details were carefully removed for use elsewhere.

The Capital Centre project, approved by the City Planning Board in 1962, was funded by a $19-million federal grant and matched by another six million dollars from the city, which also paid the administrative costs. It spread over forty-three acres and involved more than 100 buildings, most of which were torn down. Its centerpiece was, and remains, the gracious and spacious Capital Centre Plaza, an outdoor urban gathering place where festivals and other programs are held during the warm months of

Amos Martin directed the Saint Paul Area Chamber of Commerce from 1967 to 1986. Courtesy, Saint Paul Area Chamber of Commerce

A network of skyways link downtown commercial and residential development in St. Paul. Courtesy, St. Paul Convention Bureau

Facing page: *Capital Centre Plaza is graced with this modern sculpture in its courtyard. Courtesy, St. Paul Convention Bureau*

the year. The gleaming Osborn building, built by Economics Laboratory in 1968, flanks the plaza.

Since most of the city's leadership had committed itself to Capital Centre, other buildings began going up. The Daytons invested $6.4 million in a new downtown department store and built Wabasha Court on the site of their earlier Dayton's-Schuneman's store. Farm Credit Banks built the first phase of its new building at 375 Jackson Street, Northwestern National Bank built at Fifth Street between Cedar and Minnesota, and First National Bank launched a $5.5-million, six-story addition to its building at Fifth and Minnesota.

It was at this time that St. Paul's remarkable skyway system, a Northern city's answer to the sharp cold of a long winter and the intense heat of a short summer, began to flourish. Now studied by planners from all over the world, the first public skyway in the Twin Cities and one of the earliest in the country linked the old Golden Rule department store to its parking ramp. Another extended from the new Federal Building at Kellogg Boulevard and Robert Street to the Pioneer and Endicott buildings across Fifth Street. Today the four-mile system with its thirty-three bridges linking about 125 downtown buildings is the longest climate-controlled walkway in the world.

However, Capital Centre was not the only new downtown project. Earlier in the 1950s and 1960s new parking ramps were built: Victory Ramp on the site of the massive 1884 City-County Courthouse that occupied an entire city block between Wabasha and Cedar; Garrick Ramp on the site of the old Garrick Theater at Sixth and St. Peter; and the Golden Rule ramp. In 1957 Commercial State Bank erected its building on the site of the Orpheum Theater at Fifth and St. Peter. Four years later, in 1961, there were four more new buildings: The St. Paul Companies at Fifth and Washington, Capp Towers on Ninth Street, the Degree of Honor Building at Fourth and Cedar, and the new YWCA on Kellogg Boulevard. In 1964 the Arts

SUPERAMERICA

It started in 1960 with a combination gas station and car wash on East Seventh near Sibley in downtown St. Paul. It has grown to become the pacesetter in the convenience-oriented, gas-and-goods retail business. With over 400 stores from Pennsylvania to Montana, plus fast-growing operations in Florida and other southern states, SuperAmerica has matured into a unique and successful collection of neighborhood markets that today serves more than a half-million Americans per day.

As did so many successful businesses in St. Paul, SuperAmerica began as a family-run operation, a first venture into retailing for the Erickson family that founded and operated Northwestern Refining Company in St. Paul Park. From 1939 through the 1950s Northwestern Refinery had sold its gasoline and other light oil products to independent distributors and gas stations. The founding of SuperAmerica allowed Northwestern to add retail sales of its gasolines, but it took some time to settle on the right mix of other products to sell.

The first stores were oriented to Minnesota's outdoor activities, stocking fishing and hunting gear, sporting goods, small appliances, even lawnmowers and bicycles. Food and nonfood household items were only a minor part of the business. But as the company grew, it made a point of paying attention to its customers—an enduring SuperAmerica trademark and one key to its success. New products were stocked, store layouts were expanded, additional gas islands were added, and customer convenience was systematically enhanced.

By 1970 there were 110 SuperAmericas from Ohio to Montana, and the firm was also the sole gasoline retailer at Minneapolis/St. Paul International Airport (expansion gobbled up the familiar gas-and-repair facility in 1977). But

SuperAmerica has grown from one gas station and car wash in downtown St. Paul to a successful collection of neighborhood markets serving more than a half-million Americans in the Midwest, and the eastern and southern United States. Photo by Chris Walker

Many SuperAmerica stores offer fresh bakery and fast-food items for the convenience of their customers. Called SuperMom's, many items are made fresh daily at Super-Mom's kitchen in St. Paul Park. Photo by Chris Walker

growth requires resources. In 1970 SuperAmerica and Northwestern Refinery Company were acquired by Ashland Oil of Kentucky, one of the top 50 corporations in the country with sales of more than eight billion dollars annually. Ashland's retail stations were added to the SuperAmerica family, with the result that the number of stores has more than tripled and continues to grow at a pace of 50 new outlets each year.

Under the leadership of Richard Jensen, who joined SuperAmerica as the Erickson family's general manager in 1965 and became its president in 1975, the firm has continued to pay attention to its customers and the communities in which it operates. In addition to food and gasoline, SuperAmericas

continue to be noteworthy for their large selection of nonfood items—automotive parts and supplies, film and batteries, household goods, even seasonal greeting cards and wrapping paper. Most stores are open 24 hours a day, and all are staffed by at least two clerks for fast service whenever a customer stops in.

Through the years SuperAmerica has become the one the industry watches for innovation. It was the first to offer multiple gas pumping points to make self service truly convenient, and the first to build weather-shielding canopies over its gas islands. SuperAmerica was the first to offer a bakery in its stores, supplied by the firm's SuperMom's Kitchen in St. Paul Park, and has consistently added to the range of commissary products offered: sandwiches, salads, and other prepared foods for today's customers and their families. It was also the first to install automatic teller machines—starting with the Highland Park store at Snelling and Ford Parkway.

With more than 60 stores in the Twin Cities area, there's an "SA" nearby at any time of the day or night. That's convenience. That's SuperAmerica.

The new Federal Building at Kellogg Boulevard and Robert Street replaced the original Federal Courts Building which became Landmark Center. Photo by Kay Shaw

The contemporary Farm Credit Bank building, was designed by Winsor Faricy Architects. Photo by Lea Babcock. Courtesy, Winsor Faricy Architects

and Science building went up at Tenth and Cedar, the site of the old state capitol, and four years later a building to house the Department of Employment Services was built at 39 North Robert. Northwestern Bell built a second addition in 1968. New buildings also were filling in the Capitol Approach area: the Veterans Service Building in 1954, the Department of Transportation and Centennial buildings in 1958, and the Administration Building in 1966.

But for Capital Centre a lull had set in. "It kind of ran out of gas," Nason recalled. "It was partially finished, but the CEOs had begun to lose interest. They were sending their public-relations people to the meetings instead of coming themselves. The enthusiasm and momentum died down." Amos Martin observes a pattern sadly familiar to communities all over the country—a decline in leadership, and projects having to wait as the old guard, growing steadily more senior, begin to withdraw almost before the new leaders are ready to step forward.

The Metropolitan Improvement Committee

was allowed to die, but the Chamber and the community's leaders persisted. They were helped considerably by an enlightened group of leaders from organized labor, including Robert E. Hess, at that time executive vice-president of the State Federation of Labor; Richard Radman, secretary-treasurer of the St. Paul Building

Right: *In contrast to the contemporary St. Paul Companies building is the 1860s Assumption Church in the distance. Photo by Shin Koyama. Courtesy, Ellerbe Associates, Inc.*

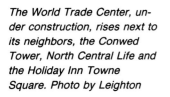

The World Trade Center, under construction, rises next to its neighbors, the Conwed Tower, North Central Life and the Holiday Inn Towne Square. Photo by Leighton

*Ellerbe Associates designed
The St. Paul Companies sleek
building. Photo by Shin
Koyama. Courtesy, Ellerbe
Associates, Inc.*

SHAW LUMBER

The wood comes from the United States and Canada, from Mexico, the Philippines, Europe, Africa, and other locales the world over. It comes in various lengths and thicknesses, and for various uses, from basic building materials to exotic wood trim for homes and offices. It comes to Shaw Lumber in St. Paul as it has for more than 100 years.

The large yard, plant site, and retail store on Como Avenue, just past the state capitol, turns out more than 16 million board feet of lumber per year—one of the last true "full-service lumberyards" in the Upper Midwest. It also stocks the tools, hardware, and other materials used by carpenters, specializing in their needs so completely that if a carpenter doesn't use it, the customer won't find it at Shaw.

The rough material that will someday become cabinetry, woodwork, and other architectural millwork has been the basic stock-in-trade of the Shaw family since the days when Minnesota, and especially the Twin Cities, was first being built. The Como Avenue address, home to Shaw Lumber since 1927, is a place with which most of the region's carpenters and many Twin Cities home owners and do-it-yourselfers are intimately familiar. In 1985 the firm opened a showroom for its custom architectural millwork in International Market Square (the former Minneapolis plant of Munsingwear).

The heart of the operation is a millwork plant that produces cabinetry, doors, custom wooden hinges, and other woodwork for modern homes and businesses. From Valley Fair to the World Trade Center and Town Square, Shaw's trained craftsmen have been involved in turning rough lumber into finished interior and exterior surfaces and structures. They use the hand tools that have traditionally been the carpenter's

Beautiful and exotic woods imported from all over the world are custom-crafted and showcased in various settings by Shaw Lumber at International Market Square in Minneapolis. The only complex of its kind in the world, it is exclusively for the display of architectural millwork.

mainstay and precision machines, including some that are computer-controlled, for cutting and shaping wood and glass.

In addition to working up new jobs, whether from a home owner's vague pencil sketches or a carpenter's detailed drawings, the steel knives used to cut out thousands of custom moldings are kept in inventory against the day when someone may wish to match a previous pattern. More than 20 hardwoods, from ash and alder to sassafras and wormy chestnut, also are kept in stock, both for new construction and to match existing woods in the reconstruction of classic millwork from years past.

The business began in the 1880s, when George Stearns Shaw took over a small lumber mill in Cloquet and built it into a thriving timber processor. In 1886 he backed his son, Willis R. Shaw, in a lumberyard at State and Concord streets in St. Paul. From the time of Willis Shaw's death in 1909 through 1925, management of the company rested with his widow, Margaret Bell, one of the city's first female executives. Meanwhile, a third generation en-

Willis R. Shaw (fifth from right) at 127 Concord Street in South St. Paul, the second location for the lumberyard.

tered the business in the early years of the new century: Willis' son, Louis F. Shaw, and son-in-law Z.H. Hutchinson.

After World War II the firm's operations were consolidated at the Como Avenue yard under the fourth generation of the family, George S. and John T. Withy, grandsons of Willis Shaw. Peter Miller, George Withy's son-in-law and president of the company since 1983, represents the fifth generation to be involved in the business.

The small lumberyard that started in St. Paul with just six employees more than 100 years ago today employs more than 80 workers and ships its custom millwork to job sites as far away as Florida and Southern California. But it's still the same basic business the Shaw family started when Minnesota was young.

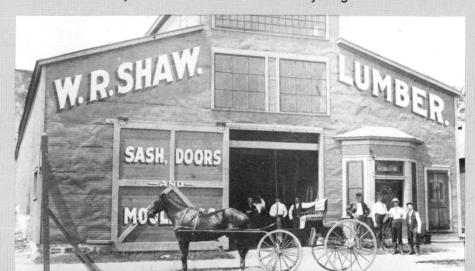

PEAT, MARWICK, MITCHELL & CO.

In 1957 Peat Marwick expanded its Twin Cities public accounting practice by opening an office in the First National Bank Building in St. Paul. At that time Peat Marwick demonstrated its confidence in the vitality and growth of St. Paul and its businesses. That confidence has been more than justified over the past 30 years. In cooperation with the Firm's Minneapolis office, which dates back to 1904, and the vigorous St. Paul practice, now based in the Conwed Tower, the Twin Cities practice ranks among the top 10 of Peat Marwick's 100 offices nationwide.

Founded in 1897, Peat Marwick is one of the oldest accounting firms in the world. It is a multinational partnership of more than 28,000 accounting professionals strategically located in 90 countries. The firm offers three distinct services—audit, tax, and management consulting—for Twin Cities businesses ranging from giant publicly held corporations to non-profit agencies and individual tax clients. In addition, the Private Business Advisory Services practice emphasizes privately held ventures, including big businesses of tomorrow just starting out today.

Peat Marwick's major business for more than 80 years has been accounting and auditing. The firm audits client financial statements and, also, assists clients in interpreting accounting rules, including pronouncements of the Securities and Exchange Commission. Other capabilities include public offerings and review of internal controls.

The firm's tax department aids clients in making short- and long-term tax and financial decisions. Tax professionals concentrate on state, federal, and international taxes for both individuals and domestic and multinational corporations. The national and international resources of the firm allow it to keep up with the latest developments in Congress, the Treasury Department, the courts, and state legislatures no matter where the local clients may have business interests.

Through its management consulting department, Peat Marwick provides a variety of specialized, management-related services designed to improve financial controls and general business perform-

From privately held to multinational corporations, Peat Marwick serves the St. Paul community.

ance. In the areas of strategy management, operations management, financial management, technology management, and human resources, specially trained professionals are available to respond to the unique needs of a broad range of disciplines and industries.

Complementing the basic practice of the Twin Cities office are industry specialists, including the national practice directors for agribusiness and high technology. In addition, the specialized industry expertise includes banking, education, government, health care, insurance, real estate, savings and loans, investment banking, and mutual funds.

In addition to the commitment to serving clients, more than 300 professionals in the firm's Twin Cities practice are involved in the communities in which they live. Peat Marwick people occupy leadership positions in a wide variety of industry, civic, philanthropic, and arts organizations in the Twin Cities. As has been the case for the past 80 years, Peat Marwick in the Twin Cities is committed to outstanding client service and improving the community in which its people live and work.

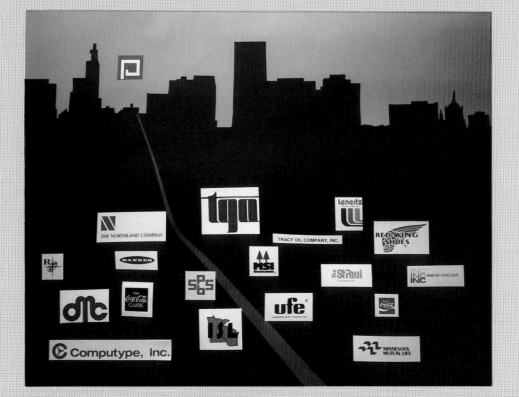

Trades Council, and Anthony DeZiel, business agent for the Trades and Labor Assembly. At one point an informal labor-business ad hoc task force was formed that worked together on the Civic Center, MIC, Operation 85, and other civic improvement projects. Van Hoef joined First National Bank's staff, then was loaned by the bank to the new enterprise that became Operation 85, so named because those involved had their eyes on 1985 as the completion date for downtown renewal. It was also a glamorized name for the Downtown Development Committee created by the Chamber of Commerce in the early 1970s to study city services and other amenities that would be needed to support the new surge of redevelopment everyone agreed lay ahead.

As part of a study called City Center 85, St. Paul architect Wayne Winsor developed a plan for a shopping center to compete with the Southdales and Rosedales. Women, he said, like shopping centers, so the downtown stores were moving out. Between 1959 and 1970 some 400 stores left the downtown as freeways were built and suburban shopping centers were created.

"I felt that we needed department stores, office buildings, entertainments, restaurants, that would bring people in and housing that would keep them here," Winsor recalled. He conceived a master plan for a covered mall about five blocks long to be called "Seventh Place." It was, in many respects, the forerunner of Town Square.

The Chamber loaned its planning director, Carl E. Ewert, to Operation 85. A committee was formed of thirty-five bankers, merchants, property owners, attorneys, and representatives of financial institutions, investment firms, and organizations under chairman John A. McHugh, president of Northwestern National Bank, to oversee the program. Names of some of the city's senior leaders sprinkle the list, but it is apparent that new leadership was beginning to take hold. On it were men like Ronald M. Hubbs

of The St. Paul Companies; Lewis Paper of Paper Calmenson; Dwight Opperman of West Publishing; Alex Tankenoff of Hillcrest Development; Charles Rafferty of the Trades and Labor Assembly; Robert E. Hess, now-Congressman Joseph E. Karth's administrative assistant; Weyerhaeuser Company executive John Musser; and Ben Agee of Northwestern Bell.

Operation 85 was designed partly as a way to move downtown redevelopment off dead center. These community leaders did not want to see St. Paul sidelined in federal and state planning, and they were concerned that the city would not make the most of its potential without substantial public improvements linked with private redevelopment.

For starters, Operation 85 faced the serious problem of what to do about "Super Hole," two downtown blocks also known as Block A and Block C that were the sites of some venerable city institutions—Bockstruck's Jewelry, St. Paul Book and Stationery, and the Ryan Hotel. Operation 85's mission also included a study of a downtown transportation system (the Downtown People-Mover that sounded so exciting in the 1970s) and the encouragement of a renewal effort in St. Paul's Lowertown district, some fourteen blocks of nineteenth-century warehouses and manufacturing plants that, virtually intact, surrounded old Smith Park.

In 1976 George Latimer was elected mayor. Events were about to coalesce, and just in time. Some corporations were thinking of leaving downtown. Minnesota Mutual had bought land in Woodbury. So had The St. Paul Companies for expansion. Dayton's was considering curtailing its downtown retailing in favor of Wooddale, a proposed shopping center also planned for Woodbury. However, a few more new buildings had been built downtown: Midwest Federal, next to the St. Paul Athletic Club, in 1971; Northern Federal, at Sixth and Wabasha, in 1973; American National Bank at Cedar and Sixth, in 1975. A year later, Northwestern Bell built another new tower, its third addition.

The Capitol Approach, once the site of decaying buildings, received a face-lift in the 1950s when much of the area was cleared. Today part of the interstate freeway skirts the Capitol Mall which has been developed, in part, according to Cass Gilbert's original design. Photo by Kay Shaw

Still, the city was not recovering sufficiently from its large-scale clearance program. During the 1950s, the Capitol Approach neighborhood, one of the oldest remaining sections of the city, had been cleared of its decaying boarding-houses and secondhand stores, and in the 1960s the freeway, Interstate 94, was carved through town just north of the Loop. Some 15,000 people were relocated in the course of these two projects. Furthermore, the state capital complex, a community of some 9,000 people, now was isolated from downtown. Added to this was the impact of clearing block after block to build the Civic Center, Capital Centre, and Riverview Industrial Park across the river.

"When we tore all those buildings down," Amos Martin said, "we moved out people who were the daily customers of those downtown merchants. We also lost the glove-menders, hat-blockers, tailors, and other small service shops that were located in those older low-rent buildings and that attracted people to the down-town."

However, the leadership factor that made earlier development efforts possible was surfacing again in men like Harry Heltzer of 3M, Carl Drake, Jr., of The St. Paul Companies, and John Nash of Northwestern National Bank, who began to work alongside some of the older leaders. The thread that held the new coalition together was Latimer, who took office just at the point where the city's development philosophy was changing from a purely public function

37

Performers entertain visitors and shoppers in restored open space at Bandana Square, formerly the Como Railroad Shops. Photo by Jim Gallop. Courtesy, Winsor Faricy Architects

to a partnership with the private sector.

Latimer was an unknown quantity for the business community, partly because of his background as a labor lawyer, so the Chamber of Commerce organized a series of luncheons to introduce him to its constituency. The city's top business leaders were invited to talk about how the business community and civic govern-ment could work together. The luncheons proved to be fruitful. The mayor learned of the prob-lems of dealing with City Hall. Webb Publishing, for example, was told it might take a year to put up a new building. When Webb said they couldn't wait, Latimer told his department he wanted the project cleared in six months. They did it in five. Latimer talked to the Port Authority, and Brown and Bigelow moved to Riverview In-dustrial Park instead of out of town. Minnesota Mutual's decision to once again build down-town, rather than on their Woodbury property, stemmed in part from a luncheon with the mayor.

Latimer had campaigned on a promise of streamlining local government, and these meet-ings convinced him of the wisdom of that de-cision. Government functions that had been administered through separate agencies— housing and redevelopment, planning and com-

ARTHUR ANDERSEN & CO.

The basic mission of an accounting firm is to provide services that relate in one way or another to a client's overall financial operations. Once that meant only general accounting and audit services. Today it means a great deal more. As business has become more specialized, more sophisticated, and more competitive the world over, the ultimate value of an accounting firm has come to involve areas beyond an audit. It is no coincidence that the world's largest accounting firm is also the nation's largest consulting firm: Arthur Andersen & Co.

Arthur Andersen's St. Paul office dates back to 1974, but the company began serving the city's businesses in 1940, when it first opened an office in Minneapolis. The Twin Cities practice ranks among Arthur Andersen's top 15 offices in a worldwide network of more than 200 offices in 49 countries. From interrelated offices in St. Paul and Minneapolis, more than 500 accounting and consulting professionals and support personnel serve businesses throughout the Ninth Federal Reserve District.

Arthur Andersen brings to St. Paul professionals dedicated to being true business advisors. They have a well-rounded business orientation and understand the needs and conditions of their client's particular business, and the industry in which it must compete. In addition to serving large, publicly held clients, the St. Paul practice offers special expertise in the needs of privately held businesses—not only their tax and financial management concerns, but also in strategic planning, organizing, and financing new business ventures, filing registration statements and "going public," and assisting growing companies in realizing their goals.

As the practice of accounting has advanced in this era of the computer, Arthur Andersen has developed worldwide expertise in

the planning, design, and implementation of effective computer-based information systems. That systems-design and installation-assistance expertise is a major strength of the firm. It has enabled the firm to assist clients improve their competitiveness, effectiveness, and productivity through such areas as computer-integrated manufacturing, Just-in-Time (JIT) manufacturing and inventory management techniques, the integration of computer hardware, and software from multiple sources and strategic management.

The heart of the business is still accounting and audit services. Arthur Andersen's "think straight-talk straight" culture traces back to the firm's founder, a college professor who placed a high priority on professional training and development of qualified accounting

John Thomas (left), a tax partner, and Tom Winkel, partner-in-charge of the St. Paul office of Arthur Andersen & Co—a worldwide organization providing professional services in accounting, audit, tax, and management information consulting.

personnel.

Through the firm's offices in the Twin Cities and worldwide, St. Paul businesses can call on experts in manufacturing, banking, health care, high technology, printing, oil and gas exploration and development, food and beverage processing and service, advertising, utilities, and more. That expertise goes to the bedrock of Arthur Andersen & Co.: practical, results-oriented innovation and a continuing commitment to client-focused excellence at every level of the practice of accounting.

Town Square Park, atop a downtown shopping mall, provides an environment for relaxation and special events. Courtesy, City of St. Paul, Planning and Economic Development Office

munity development—now were combined into a single agency, Planning and Economic Development.

The next major project was Town Square, a $100-million investment in downtown St. Paul, with three-quarters of that money coming from Oxford Development Company in Edmonton, Canada. The "Canadian Connection" has been present, although often invisible, in Minnesota's economic life since the 1840s when the Canadian fur trader Norman W. Kittson, the agent of the Hudson Bay Company, routed his Red River oxcarts through St. Paul, then settled there himself and became the partner of fellow Canadian James J. Hill. Van Hoef, who was leading Operation 85, made the first approach to Oxford. The Chamber of Commerce flew groups to Edmonton and Calgary to inspect Oxford's projects, and particularly their Calgary center, which is topped off by a park. Everyone concerned

decided that was what they wanted for St. Paul.

Oxford's decision to invest in downtown St. Paul was a courageous step that represented a major risk. To look at the empty blocks, to see some of the shabby old stores, to hear of companies that were on the verge of moving out was not exactly bracing. There were doubts that the project could be pulled off at all. Once again the public and private partnership swung into action.

"We fought for Town Square," the mayor remembered. "To be blunt about it, I was skeptical about the part the public sector could play in private development, but our role was to join with the Chamber in working with the developers."

One of the cornerstones for Town Square was another new downtown hotel, which became the Radisson Plaza, now the Holiday Inn Town Square. "It was a real initiation for me, working with developers of the muscle and aggressiveness of Curt Carlson of the Radisson Hotel Corporation and Don Love of Oxford," Latimer recalled. "I remember moving constantly from one room to another to see how we could bring them along."

The Radisson Plaza was a joint venture with the Radisson Hotel Corporation and the SPH (Saint Paul Hilton) Hotel Corporation, the old grouping of St. Paul money that twenty years earlier had built the Hilton. Another piece fell into place when the St. Paul Port Authority agreed to build a parking ramp. Block A, which had been cleared in 1967, finally would be filled. The last piece was the city's commitment to create "The Gardens," the 35,000-square-foot city park that rises above Town Square's mall.

Town Square opened in August 1980. Its major tenant is a new, 120,000-square-foot Donaldson's department store. The treelined mall Wayne Winsor dreamed of is enclosed within Town Square and filled with specialty shops and restaurants. The park has benches and greenery, natural light, and an artificial waterfall that creates the ambience of the old European town square that surrounded the town pump.

Towering over Town Square are the twenty-five-story Conwed Tower and the twenty-seven-story North Central Tower. The skyway system, the broad, busy walkways that are a modern version of city sidewalks, converges on Town Square and helps make it all work. Lined with shops, eating places, bakeries, candy stores, and travel agencies, the skyways again offer the services that once filled the old downtown buildings before the shopkeepers fled to the suburbs.

The creation of Town Square turned retailing around, as well as much else in the downtown. Minnesota Mutual was rethinking its move to Woodbury. The company's decision to build on that part of "Super Hole" known as Block C was a critical factor in giving the redevelopment movement a fresh start. This was, after all, Min-

The Conwed Tower is linked to St. Paul's unique skyway system. Photo by Kay Shaw

PORT AUTHORITY OF THE CITY OF ST. PAUL

One way to look at the St. Paul Port Authority is as a bank: In terms of assets, its base of some $647 million—up from just $60 million in 1971—would rank it among the four largest in the state. Another way to look at it is as a landlord: From that perspective, it is the state's largest, with more than eight million square feet of office and manufacturing space under its control.

But perhaps the best way to look at the Port Authority is to consider what St. Paul might look like without the presence of this unique and aggressive, quasi-public organization. To do that, take away 10 industrial parks with a total of more than 1,000 acres of land developed. Take away Energy Park. Take away financing for Galtier Plaza, Ordway Music Theater, Amhoist Tower, St. Paul Hotel, Conwed Tower, Sheraton Midway Hotel, the Brown & Bigelow plant, and many more commercial and industrial developments. Take away the results of that activity: more than $1.3 billion in investments in the city—and more than 30,000 new jobs since 1965.

When it was founded in 1929, the Port Authority's sole mission was to build industrial facilities along the Mississippi River in St. Paul. Not until the first stirrings of rebirth in the city in the late 1950s did a newer and broader mission—as a central real estate development organization for St. Paul—begin to evolve. In the early 1960s it put together the financing for the Riverview, Northport, Southport, and Red Rock industrial parks along the river. Over the next two decades Port Authority financing and management would become an increasingly common ingredient in development efforts large and small.

Under the leadership of Eugene A. Kraut, who joined the Port Authority in 1963 as an assistant to Frank Marzitelli and is now its executive vice president, the organi-

The Energy Park Business Center is a multitenant, 160,000-square-foot, light-industrial and office complex developed by the Port Authority of the City of St. Paul.

zation has helped St. Paul be more successful than any other northern city in the country at retaining and expanding its base of manufacturing jobs. And it has operated at a profit. The Port Authority makes money from interest and fees on the bonds it sells, from rents and related payments on the facilities it owns or operates, and from reinvestment of its revenues and profits.

By putting all lease payments from its various bond-financed projects into one "pooled" fund, the Port Authority lessens the risk of any one default and earns a higher rating on its bonds, which makes them easier to sell. Its tax-exempt bond issues carry an envi-

able "A" rating from Standard and Poor's, and have been used to underwrite the development of sleek office towers and small manufacturing plants, large-scale industrial parks and glittering theaters and hotels. The Port Authority can also sell non-pooled and taxable bonds, and has the authority to issue general obligation bonds, though it has not done so since the mid-1970s.

A study of its impact on the city from 1965 through 1983 revealed that in 1983 businesses financed by the Port Authority of the City of St. Paul, or located in its various industrial parks and office facilities, accounted for more than 30 cents out of each dollar in total sales generated by all firms in the city. Those same businesses paid 23 cents of every business real estate tax dollar collected, and provided close to 15 percent of all jobs in the city—more than 95 percent of all new jobs created in the past 20 years.

TOUCHE ROSS & CO.
ST. PAUL

The growth of the public accounting practice of Touche Ross St. Paul—in terms of clients, services, and staff—has paralleled the growth of the business community. As the city's resident businesses have grown in numbers, size, stature, and complexity, so has Touche Ross St. Paul.

The St. Paul office of Touche Ross opened in the Degree of Honor Building on September 1, 1962, a significant date in the firm's Twin Cities involvement, which dates back to 1913. The St. Paul office has grown steadily over the years, its expansion fostering moves to the Northwestern Bank Building, American National Bank Building, and, in 1985, to the current offices in the Amhoist Tower.

Today Touche Ross St. Paul is one of the largest public accounting firms in the city. The office's permanent staff of proven professionals offers a full range of traditional accounting, audit, tax, and management consulting services. In addition, Touche Ross St. Paul has a fully staffed actuarial and benefits consulting department.

Nationally, Touche Ross is a general partnership providing comprehensive accounting and audit, tax, actuarial, business, benefits consulting, and other services throughout the United States, its territories, and possessions. Its

services are provided to clients of virtually every kind and size in all major segments of the economy—business, industry, and government.

St. Paul is one of 82 Touche Ross locations in the United States, operating independently of but in association with the firm's Minneapolis office. In addition to its own resources, Touche Ross St. Paul can draw on the strengths of a National Office in midtown Manhattan, a Financial Services Center on Wall Street, and a Washington Service Center in the nation's capital. Touche Ross has a full-time professional and support staff of 8,400, including 821 partners.

In more recent years Touche Ross' practice has broadened into new areas where the emphasis is on expertise and strategic planning

Touche Ross applies new technology through a broad range of microcomputer programs used in the firm's auditing, business and tax planning, and consulting services. Photo by Mike Woodside

Touche Ross' "Battle Team" helped raise money for the Minnesota Special Olympics and the Courage Center sports program, while enhancing local corporate camaraderie.

rather than traditional verification of numbers in financial statements. As the needs of its business clientele have changed, Touche Ross St. Paul has initiated new services designed to meet specific needs: consulting on the most appropriate computer system, designing both group and flexible employee benefits packages and the communications to support them, and planning for acquisitions, reorganizations, and for contingencies such as business interruption.

An Enterprise Group has been established to serve the special needs of private and emerging businesses in the city. Other specialists, in St. Paul and stationed throughout Touche Ross' national network, are available to assist in personal financial management for business owners and executives, litigation support, feasibility studies, privatization concerns, business valuation, strategic planning, productivity and distribution management, and international tax law.

Through it all, Touche Ross has displayed a continuing commitment to the St. Paul area that manifests itself not only through excellence in client service, but also through the involvement of the firm and its individual members in professional, cultural, and civic endeavors. In St. Paul, as nationally, the Touche Ross tradition is to build on traditional accounting practice by anticipating client needs, and the needs of the larger business community.

Post office facilities occupied much of the first floor area of the Old Federal Courts Building, now Landmark Center. Pictured here is office space in what is now the open cortile. Courtesy, Minnesota Landmarks

nesota Mutual's second commitment to downtown. What influenced this decision? Coleman Bloomfield, Minnesota Mutual's president, expresses a deeply held conviction concerning the role of a company that has been part of the community for more than 100 years, and he may speak, also, for other companies whose roots are embedded in the city.

In determining a site for our home office, we were primarily looking for a home for our own people. We've been part of the downtown area for the entire lifetime of our company. We decided—and our people agreed—that to attract good people, to be accessible from all parts of the community, there were important advantages to being downtown. We're a national insurance and marketing company, but we do a lot of business with companies in the St. Paul area and we need to be visible. Our

people need to have the opportunity to mingle with others here. And the mayor, who is a great salesman, encouraged us to stay downtown. We had planned to expand on our old site but we decided that in the long term that couldn't satisfy our space needs, so we sold our 120,000 square feet on Cedar and Fourth and built 400,000 square feet here, with the capability of adding on still another 400,000 square feet.

An important catalyst for downtown renewal was the preservation of the Old Federal Courts Building, now Landmark Center. The campaign, begun in 1969 to save the massive old building, built in the 1890s as a post office, federal courthouse, and customs house, sought to transfer its title from Washington, D.C., to the City of St. Paul and to find a new use for it. The federal government had begun to abandon it in the late 1960s in favor of the new Federal Building at Robert Street and Kellogg Boulevard.

The preservation effort was led by Frank Marzitelli, then executive vice-president of the Port Authority and a founder of the St. Paul/Ramsey Arts and Science Council, and by Georgia Ray DeCoster, a member of the St. Paul City Planning Commission and chairman of the commission's Historic Sites Committee.

At the instigation of Mayor Tom Byrne, who was convinced that the public was strongly in favor of saving the building, Marzitelli and DeCoster in April 1969 put together the Mayor's Committee to Preserve the Old Federal Courts Building. This was a group of civic and business leaders, local philanthropists, public officials, architects, and representatives of the Minnesota and Ramsey County Historical Societies. Marzitelli served as chairman. The efforts of this group, and the organization that followed it, for more than a ten-year period represents the best that a special group of people can do for a community.

In 1970 the Mayor's Committee was incorporated as Minnesota Landmarks, and the cam-

Left: *Betty Musser strikes the first blow to the post office loading dock in groundbreaking ceremonies for the restoration of the Old Federal Courts Building. Photo by Joan Larson Kelly. Courtesy, Minnesota Landmarks*

Below: *Built at the turn of the century as the Federal Courts Building, Landmark Center was transferred by the federal government to the city of St. Paul and restored with funds donated by the private sector. Today it is owned by Ramsey County and is the home of many cultural organizations. Courtesy, Saint Paul Convention Bureau*

Following page: *This skylight radiantly illuminating the cortile of Landmark Center, was once painted over. Photo by Shin Koyama. Courtesy, Winsor Faircy Architects*

paign continued to develop new usages for the old building that would meet federal regulations for surplus-property disposal with no remuneration and also gain local support from both public and private sectors. Marzitelli was president of this nonprofit public corporation from 1970 to 1972 and DeCoster was executive director.

Malcolm Lein, at that time executive director of the Minnesota Museum of Art, led the movement of the St. Paul arts agencies, overcrowded in the St. Paul/Ramsey Arts and Science Center, to petition for space in the 200,000-square-foot Old Federal Courts Building. In the summer of 1972 the Minnesota Museum of Art, the Ramsey County Historical Society, and several other arts and education agencies were approved as new tenants for the building. At the same time, the City of St. Paul agreed to take title to the building and to provide for its maintenance and operation if the private sector would raise the money to restore and remodel it.

In October 1972 title to the building was transferred from the federal government to the City of St. Paul at a ceremony in Rice Park. Later, in 1975, the title was transferred again, from the city to Ramsey County. Elected officials of both St. Paul and Ramsey County repeatedly have taken action to further the preservation and reuse of this ninety-year-old building, a majestic Richardsonian-Romanesque structure that resembles a European city hall. The interior had been hacked up with wallboard, the lofty ceilings lowered with false ceilings covered with acoustical tile, the marble lobbies, courtrooms, and stained-glass skylights painted "government green." The building's granite exterior was darkened by grime and adorned by a ramshackle shed that was a post office loading dock.

In short, as architect Donald Leier, who worked on the interior restoration, has observed, everything that could be done to a nineteenth-century building in the name of twentieth-century "rehabbing" had been done. Then the exterior was cleaned, and the intricacy of its stone carv-

ing and the beauty of its pink granite stood revealed. Architect W. Cavin Brooks, who was working on some critically needed exterior renovation, believes that this helped encourage community support and dollars to flow toward the project.

The campaign to raise the $13.5 million that was needed to restore the building began in 1972 and was led with single-minded determination by Elizabeth W. Musser. Former president of the St. Paul/Ramsey Arts and Science Council's board of directors and a longtime supporter of the Minnesota Museum of Art, Musser, as chairman of the Minnesota Landmarks' Building Committee, presided over the fund-raising for the restoration program from 1972 to 1978, when the building reopened. She then headed the fund drive that completed the restoration in the early 1980s.

If the early investment in Landmark Center was an important part of the city's renaissance, so was the redevelopment of Lowertown, a dream of Norman Mears, St. Paul industrialist and president of Buckbee-Mears (now BMC), which was situated in Lowertown. Mears had seen Lowertown as a place where people could live and work, as they had more than a century earlier when the district was a residential neighborhood with nearby mercantile establishments and a number of great hotels, including the Merchants Hotel and the Ryan.

The city, the county, and the Chamber of Commerce had another concern—the need to rebuild the downtown housing that had been swept away in the throes of clearance. Two of the major thrusts of St. Paul's redevelopment have been to replace the 9,000 to 11,000 people who once lived downtown and to build the downtown market around them and the 42,000 who work in the downtown district—the largest employment center in the county. To draw others in, the program depended upon such attractions as the Ordway Music Theatre, the Science Museum of Minnesota, Chimera Theatre, Actors Theatre, Garrison Keillor's "Prairie Home

The Ordway Music Theatre in Rice Park offers concerts, operas, and special performances by prominent artists. It has been recognized nationwide for its advanced designs. Photo by Leighton

Companion'' Minnesota Public Radio show, the Ramsey County Historical Society, the Minnesota Museum of Art, the St. Paul Chamber Orchestra, and the Minnesota Historical Society's proposed new history center. The importance of the commercial center to the rest of the city cannot be underestimated. With less than one percent of the land, the downtown district pays 20 percent of the taxes, the highest percentage in the county.

Operation 85's efforts to help the Lowertown project were not particularly fruitful. On his own, Mears renovated an old building on the north side of Smith Park. Once headquarters for a wholesale drug company, Noyes Brothers and Cutler, then for one of the last remnants of the fur trade, the B.W. Harris Fur Company, the building became Park Square Court. Mears died in 1974 before the Lowertown redevelopment effort could gather steam, but he had launched a major city project, and Smith Park was renamed in his honor.

In the late 1970s Mayor Latimer approached the McKnight Foundation for a $10-million grant to help redevelop Lowertown. The commitment by the foundation, established by William L. McKnight of 3M, was the largest in its history and perhaps the largest made by any foundation for inner-city programs.

A nonprofit organization, the Lowertown Redevelopment Corporation was established and an eight-member board of directors formed to create a new urban village that would include housing, commercial and retail space, and light industry. The McKnight money was to be used to encourage low-interest loans to developers that, it was hoped, would generate millions more in investments in the district. The first major project, the $12-million Mears Park Place apartments across the street from Park Square Court, already was under way. Others followed. Control Data invested ten million dollars to convert two old buildings into a Business and Technology Center, and the Nalpak building was renovated for three million dollars.

Under the direction of Weiming Lu, the redevelopment corporation's executive director, and his board, chaired by Philip Nason and including Larry Buegler, chairman of Norwest Bank, St. Paul; James Reagan, chairman and chief executive officer of American National Bank; Norman Lorentzen, retired Burlington Northern Railroad executive; Roger H. Nielson of Master Framers; Robert E. Hess; Latimer; and attorney Emily Seesel, investors from inside and outside St. Paul have become interested in Lowertown.

Among them are Minneapolis developers Brian Nelson and Jim Masterman of Asset Development Services, Inc., who have restored a Lowertown showplace—the Union Depot—a place dear to the hearts of many of St. Paul's people, a stately if rather somber building of granite and stone completed in 1920. At one

Energy Park condominiums combine energy-efficient systems with designs reminiscent of railroad architecture. The monitor roofs light the interior spaces much the same as the monitor roofs once did atop the historic railroad buildings. Photo by Lea Babcock. Courtesy, Winsor Faricy Architects

Above: *The First Trust Center, once the largest office building in the Northwest, opened in 1916 as the Railroad and Bank building. The building originally housed the offices of the First National Bank and the headquarters of the Northern Pacific and Great Northern railroads. Although each enterprise had separate facilities, the railroads were linked by a common door in the office of the presidents. Photo by Kay Shaw*

Right: *At one time hundreds of trains passed through the Union Depot. Today, as Union Depot Place, it offers restaurants and office space. Photo by Leighton*

time 150 trains passed through the depot every day, but it is a sad irony of history that, even as the depot opened, the railroads of the nation had entered upon borrowed time. On May 2, 1971, the last passenger train pulled out of the depot, its doors were closed, and it crouched there on its slight rise up from the river, empty for more than a decade. This building had probably been the subject of more frustrated planning and more dashed hopes than any other in St. Paul. But Nelson and his associates saw that its uniqueness, its craftsmanship, and the sense of St. Paul history that surrounds it, were salable. Today Union Depot Place has three restaurants, two bars, a sidewalk cafe, and thousands of square feet of office space.

A block away is James J. Hill's seven-story red-brick General Office Building, built between 1887 and 1900. The building, with its decorative old fireplaces and marble embellishments, is being turned into apartments for moderate-income residents. Fascinating and little-known features are the cast-iron gate and cobblestone alleyway that lead to an inner courtyard where Hill once stabled his horse.

Hill's old office building is part of a new community that is being established in the warehouse district. Lowertown Lofts, across the street from the Union Depot, is one reason St. Paul won the sixth annual City Livability Award. This is a twenty-nine-unit housing cooperative for artists and writers in another old warehouse. It is expected to be a national model for such projects since artists, whose erratic income often makes it difficult for them to buy housing, will have some ownership in the project. It is a joint effort involving local foundations and developers, the city's Planning and Economic Development Department, and the St. Paul Art Collective. Undoubtedly it would have pleased Hill, the old empire builder, a noted collector and a patron of artists.

Historic Landmarks for Living, Inc., a Philadelphia firm Weiming Lu calls one of the nation's leaders in turning old buildings into residential space, is converting the ATR building and the Milton and Finch warehouses alongside Mears Park into market-rate rental units. Chicago's Palmer Group has acquired the massive Burlington Northern Building, once headquarters for the Great Northern and Northern Pacific railroads, and restored it as First Trust Center, which offers retail and office space. The historic Pioneer and Endicott buildings were acquired in 1981 by First National Bank of St. Paul, and their restoration has undone a number of earlier, less sympathetic remodelings. The Pioneer's open cage elevators still serve its soaring atrium, and the delicately beautiful stained-glass skylights, designed by the nationally famous architect Cass Gilbert, have been cleaned of the paint that covered them during one of the earlier "rehab" periods.

Just north of the Union Depot is a neat little narrow building, four stories high, that is giving another group of residents a foothold in a district that was once the wholesaling center of the Northwest. This is an eighty-five-year-old macaroni factory designed by Cass Gilbert. Now the American House Apartments, the building offers single rooms for rent to low-income people—housing that is fast disappearing from the downtowns of American cities.

On the other side of Mears Park is Galtier Plaza, a $128-million complex that includes some subsidized low-income apartments, although its two residential towers—one forty-five stories and the other thirty-two—are mostly for middle-to upper-income residents, with luxury condominiums added. Galtier Plaza, with its two-story glassed plaza that links Mears Park with Jackson Street, has been one of the city's most difficult projects, its complexities arising when Minneapolis developers Omni Venture and Boisclair Corporation took it over in 1981 and expanded it beyond its original concept. The variety of financing has involved nearly every type of subsidy available, although this is not untypical of big projects. Galtier Plaza houses one of the best of an inner city's ameni-

ties, a $6.2-million skyway YMCA, a prototype for downtown "Y's." Designed to serve people living and working downtown, the "Y" has a six-lane, twenty-five-meter swimming pool, saunas, a triple gymnasium, exercise equipment, handball and racquetball courts, and a running track.

Covered alleyways, like those found in European cities, are proposed for some sections of Lowertown. One will lead into the Farmers Market, the downtown warm-weather produce market that moves indoors, into adjacent Market-Place, during the winter months. This is a new Farmers Market, representing a happy solution to a problem created when protesting produce-growers were forced to move from the old market that had been at 10th and Jackson since 1902. That site was cleared to make way for the Embassy Suites Hotel.

Lowertown is the city's third National Historic District, its buildings studied as part of a two-year historic-sites survey of Ramsey County and St. Paul conducted by the Ramsey County Historical Society and the St. Paul Heritage Preservation Commission. The city has installed new sidewalks and curbs in some sections, and

bus stop shelters and nineteenth century-type street lamps throughout the district; it will also renovate Mears Park, the second such renovation to take place. Skyways eventually will provide a linkup with the river through Union Depot Place.

If Galtier Plaza and Minnesota Mutual are the bridges between Lowertown and the central business district, the Minnesota World Trade Center will link the central business district to the state capital complex, a link that was severed by the freeway. The decision to build the World Trade Center in St. Paul was pivotal for the city, coming as it did after strenuous competition with Minneapolis, Bloomington, and a latter-day entrant, Duluth. Richard Broeker, who was Mayor Latimer's chief of staff and the trade center's first executive director, sees the city's successful bid for the World Trade Center as growing out of some long-range planning that involved a "superb relationship among the key players"—Philip Nason, Amos Martin, the mayor, attorney James A. Stolpestad, Oxford Development Company, and the labor leaders who leaped into the breach with financial support when the center lost a crucial federal grant.

Facing page: *Mears Park (formerly Smith Park) was renamed for Norman Mears, president of Buckbee-Mears, whose dream of Lowertown's redevelopment has been realized. Photo by Leighton*

Left: *Recent redevelopment by Chicago's Palmer Group has restored the great hall of the First Trust Center to magnificent splendor. The hall area once housed the First National Bank. Photo by Leighton*

Together with the downtown financial institutions, labor kept the project alive. Oxford's properties in the Twin Cities have now been acquired by another Canadian firm, BCE Development Properties, Inc., of Vancouver, British Columbia.

The only inland world trade center in the country, it is expected to bring international trading back to St. Paul, a city that was a center for international trade when fur traders shipped buffalo robes and pemmican to the British army for use in the Crimean War, and James J. Hill's silk trains sped across the continent from Seattle to New York, their precious cargoes sealed and under armed guard. The World Trade Center should be, city leaders believe, an effective tool in moving the area's economy back into the

Above: Galtier Plaza's modern glass and brick materials are a sharp contrast to the 1890 McColl Building's rusticated red sandstone. Photo by Leighton

Facing page: The unique Galtier Plaza offers both moderate-income apartments, luxury condominiums, as well as an indoor skyway YMCA. Photo by George Heinrich. Courtesy, Lowertown Redevelopment Corporation

world marketplace, particularly as the future of the region's agriculture and high-tech industries may well lie in the international arena.

Broeker sees the World Trade Center as the beneficiary of the "home-grown economy" concept that grew out of St. Paul's first economic plan, developed in 1978. The plan examined, among other things, the use of public dollars to stimulate private development. Older cities, he points out, were export communities selling goods and services to the surrounding countryside. That revenue supported the cities. When the cycle reversed itself and cities began to ship out their capital and import their goods and services, poverty awaited them down the road. The remedy lay in increasing a city's export base by reinforcing local use of resources. This was the home-grown economy idea and it has been working quietly and effectively throughout the past five years in St. Paul as small businesses have been encouraged to grow, as a new brewery opened on University Avenue, as neighborhood commercial strips were spruced up, as a Control Data plant provided jobs in the heart of a low-income area, and as a new downtown marketplace was found where farmers could continue to sell their produce.

Thus, when Governor Rudy Perpich suggested a World Trade Center for Minnesota, St. Paul's leadership lost little time in identifying it as another tool for pumping new economic life into the community. The fundamental shift in the downtown as the twentieth century closes may well be in St. Paul's relationship to the global marketplace through the World Trade Center. Architect Richard T. Faricy, whose WZMH firm of Toronto is working on the World Trade Center, sees it as a unifying force for an area that still dulls the downtown's new luster. Another urban park north of the center, the focus of a nationwide competition organized by the National Endowment for the Arts for landscape architects and designers, will tie it to Minnesota Public Radio's headquarters across Eighth Street.

In the meantime, the city's neighborhoods beyond the downtown have been among the principal beneficiaries of the home-grown economy concept and of a conscious effort to strengthen neighborhood-oriented businesses and keep them there. St. Paul has a history of unusually active citizen participation in government, some of it stemming from the strong sense of identification many residents feel with their own neighborhoods. Much of this is a cultural bond with the immigrant groups that established enclaves within the city generations ago. District councils help their descendants deal with neighborhood problems, sometimes vociferously, at the neighborhood level.

The Neighborhood Partnership Program was established by the city's Planning and Economic Development Department at the urging of the neighborhood people themselves. Its purpose was to give them more opportunity to generate their own ideas for programs and to work with their business communities to bring them off. Highland Park residents drew up their own plans for public improvements, then got neighborhood businesses to agree to assessments for those improvements. Frogtown residents helped build a community center. In another project, the city furnished money for trees, provided that residents would truck them in, dig holes, and plant them. Between 1981 and 1984, sixteen neighborhoods received $1.5 million that leveraged $7.9 million in matching money for housing rehabilitation, crime-prevention programs, and other projects.

Faricy points to the impact of the city's renaissance on its older neighborhoods: for example, the enhancement of the North End and Como neighborhoods by AHW Corporation's converting the Northern Pacific Railroad's old Como Shops near Como Park into Energy Park and Bandana Square. This was another example of a private and public partnership—the vast legacy of nineteenth-century entrepreneur Amherst H. Wilder used by AHW, an arm of the Wilder Foundation, in cooperation with the St.

Paul Port Authority and the city itself.

Conceived in 1979, Energy Park was to be a model community drawing upon technology to create jobs and conserve energy in the face of skyrocketing oil prices. By the time it opened four years later, falling oil prices had diluted the energy business; still, industrial development was strong and the park now includes a mix of office space, high-tech industry, health-care services, a motel, housing, and retailing. The old Como shops themselves form another of St. Paul's National Historic Districts. One of the buildings has become Bandana Square, the community's retail component. Another has become the Children's Museum, created by a private non-profit organization to serve the Twin Cities region.

The next step in the city's renaissance is the redevelopment of its riverfront. The Mississippi, as it flows through downtown St. Paul, is the working river it always has been, studded with barges, pleasure boats, and Captain Bowell's excursion paddle-wheelers, and lined with railroad tracks. The challenge is to blend a commercial waterfront with a recreational and living waterfront.

This mix is not new to St. Paul. People have lived along the riverbank since the first cabin was built below the bluffs. Today's barges were preceded by steamboats and canoes; railroads, by Red River oxcarts. The river has been a recreational resource as well. The Minnesota Boat Club's crews began racing more than 100 years ago, and a menagerie once attracted Sunday picnickers to Harriet Island. In the 1920s children were taught to swim at a beach along the island. In short, most of the activities are still intact that have taken place through its history along this stretch of river. The goal is to maintain the vitality generated by the railroads, the barges, the grain trucks lined up alongside the terminals, and the manufacturing conducted within reach of this truly urban riverfront, and to combine it with pleasure boating, excursions, housing, and retailing.

Mayor Latimer has brought to the same table, through appointment to a Riverfront Planning Commission, men and women with a variety of

Bandana Square, a part of the Energy Park development, retains an original railroad theme. Formerly the Como Shops, these buildings served as railroad car repair shops from their construction in 1885 until the recent redevelopment. Courtesy, Saint Paul Area Chamber of Commerce

Right: "St. Paul's strength lies in her commerce," wrote Mark Twain in Life On the Mississippi in 1874. Today, St. Paul remains a large inland port with barges transporting various commodities from the region. Courtesy, Saint Paul Area Chamber of Commerce

Below: Mississippi River banks come alive with the variegated colors of autumn in St. Paul. The scenery along the riverbanks has been preserved ever since St. Paul park commissioners secured the land for parks at the urging of H.W.S. Cleveland, who, in 1888, expressed the hope that the riverbank be "preserved in its native grandeur and beauty." Photo by Kay Shaw

Above: *The* Jonathan Paddelford *makes its way toward
the Wabasha Street Bridge as
the city skyline reflects in the
waters of the Mississippi
River.*

agendas—neighborhood representatives, property owners, developers, bankers, attorneys,
heads of city departments, the Ramsey County
Historical Society, and the St. Paul Heritage
Preservation Commission—to work on plans
for a riverfront that already is one of the most
diverse in the country. Some 85 percent of the
land along the river is controlled by eight public
agencies. Acres of woodland, bluffs, and flood-
plain wetlands are included in a park system,
and most of the remaining land is in the hands
of a few owners. Such consolidation should
make change easy. Another strength is the
closeness of the river to the city. The downtown
district sits on top of bluffs that rise almost
from the water's edge.

A generation or more ago the city did try to
turn itself toward the river. With the support of
a municipal bond issue in 1928, the city tore
down the nineteenth-century buildings that lined
old Third Street, blocking the view, and replaced them with Kellogg Mall and a park that
sweeps along the curve in the bluff. The challenge now is to find ways to continue the turn-
about. Three primary areas are seen as lending
themselves to the retail, housing, recreational,
and people-oriented mixed uses the Riverfront
Commission and the planners have in mind.
These areas are the city's origins: the Lower
Landing, the steamboat landing at the foot of
Jackson Street; the Upper Landing, at the foot
of Chestnut Street; and Harriet Island, which
nudges the west bank across the river from
downtown.

ECONOMIC CORNERSTONES

Many American cities are unique. Of course there are common denominators. All cities have banks and urban transit systems, theaters and museums, and, most of them, zoos. But every one of them had its roots in a special set of geological, geographical, economic, sometimes personal circumstances that no other city duplicates—a sheltered harbor, the joining of two streams, the crossing of trails, or simply the place where the wheel fell off the wagon.

For St. Paul it was the presence of the Mississippi River and the fact that navigation above St. Paul was hazardous due to snags, shifting

"St. Paul is a wonderful town. It is put together in solid blocks of honest brick and stone, and has the air of intending to stay." Mark Twain, Life on the Mississippi, 1874. *Photo by Shin Koyama. Courtesy, Ellerbe Associates, Inc.*

Here, the Minnesota Historical Society tour staff reenacts life at Fort Snelling during the 1820s. Courtesy, St. Paul Convention Bureau

sandbars, and rocks—debris left behind by the Falls of St. Anthony as they retreated slowly upstream from near the mouth of the Minnesota River to its present location. The practical head of navigation on the upper Mississippi, the site that became St. Paul, was bracketed by clefts in eighty-foot-high bluffs that created levees or landing places.

Upstream from the site of St. Paul, during the 1820s, a group of French-Canadian fur traders (refugees from the Selkirk colony near present-day Winnipeg) had turned to a life of peaceful farming in the shadow of Fort Snelling, the frontier military post established in 1819-1820 at the junction of the Minnesota and Mississippi rivers to keep a watchful eye on the wilderness. Peace eluded these squatters on the military reservation, however, and when they eventually were evicted they moved down the Mississippi and settled around those landing places that give easy access to the river. One of them became the Lower Landing or the Jackson Street or Robert's Landing or, years later, Lambert's Landing.

Here, sitting on a small mound a few dozen feet up from the landing at Third and Jackson Streets, was the interesting establishment of Pierre "Pig's Eye" Parrant, a voyageur who had embarked upon a new career as a saloon-keeper. The wily Parrant was one of the first to recognize the commercial value of a landing close to the point where the river's current nudged upcoming boats toward the east bank. For some years the tiny settlement was known up and down the river as "Pig's Eye's Landing," a name mercifully changed when Father Lucien Galtier arrived, built a chapel on the bluff above the Lower Landing, dedicated it to St. Paul, and asked that the village also be known by that name.

A mile upriver was the Upper Landing, at the foot of Chestnut Street. Both Upper and Lower landings are still there. So to a great extent are the businesses and industries that after the Civil War grew up around them and made St. Paul the port and the commercial center for the entire region. Almost from the start, the cornerstone of the city's economy was the transportation industry and the services the industry and the community that thrived on it required—banking, insurance, warehousing, construction, agriculture, manufacturing, retailing, printing. And they still exist, although their operations have been drastically changed to meet the needs of the late twentieth century. Characteristic of nearly all of them is that they were founded to serve a frontier community, but they expanded outward into the state and the region. Many today are national and international in scope. More than that, they serve a complex, sophisticated society with equally complex, sophisticated functions that barely resemble the simple operations that served a simpler era.

St. Paul's transportation industry began with the Mississippi. The network of streams that flow into the great river provided the earliest means of penetrating the region by the earliest businessmen of all, the French and British fur traders and their Indian partners. For almost 150 years their canoes traveled the waterways, carrying furs downriver for shipment east and to Europe—the first of the region's world traders.

Keel boats and steamboats followed, hauling in pork, flour, tea, and sugar, which, pieced out with locally available honey, cranberries, and maple sugar, sustained St. Paul's early settlers during the icebound winter months. The number of steamboats docking at the Lower Landing rose steadily during the 1840s—forty-one in 1844; forty-six in 1847; sixty-three a year later; ninety-five in 1849, the year Minnesota became a territory; and 1,068 in 1858, the year Minnesota became a state. In a single day in May 1857, twenty-four boats were tied up at the Lower Landing. Upstream, steamboats serving the Minnesota River were arriving and departing from the Upper Landing. Within a decade shipping would be concentrated at the Lower Landing, and within yet another decade it would begin to decline altogether as the railroads took over the opening up of the hinterland.

The historic river commerce still exists today in St. Paul. Long rows of barges line the banks of the river—part of an industry that was virtually eclipsed by the railroads, then began to revive after World War I. By the late 1970s, river traffic was booming and robust. In 1980, according to the United States Army Corps of Engineers, total tonnage on the Mississippi had risen to 215.5 million. By 1983 it was 225 million. Most of it was grain, oil, and coal, shipped

St. Paul, the head of navigation on the Mississippi, experienced tremendous growth as a transfer point for immigrants and commercial goods. Steamboats which docked at the Lower Landing served as the primary mode of transportation until the coming of the railroad. Courtesy, Minnesota Historical Society (MHS)

Above: *In 1866 James J. Hill, at only twenty-eight years old, had already established himself in the freight transfer business at St. Paul's Lower Landing. His warehouse, circa 1867, is the center building with the large open door. Courtesy, MHS*

Above: *In the 1850s St. Paul's Lower Landing bustled with activity as steamboats, immigrants and commercial goods crowded its wharves. The steamboats captured the imagination of Mark Twain, who wrote: "She has two tall, fancy-topped chimneys, with a gilded device of some kind swung between them; a fanciful pilot-house, all glass and 'gingerbread,' perched on top of the 'texas' deck behind them. . ." Life On the Mississippi. Courtesy, MHS*

Left: *St. Paul owes its name to Father Lucien Galtier who built a chapel on the bluff above the Lower Landing in 1841, dedicated it to St. Paul, and asked that the settlement also be known by that name. Courtesy, MHS*

in barges owned by companies that produced those commodities.

Familiar sights each fall are grain trucks from western Minnesota and the Dakotas lined up for miles along the highways leading into St. Paul, their drivers waiting patiently for their cargoes to be unloaded onto barges. Tow boats push as many as twelve to fifteen barges at a time through the trickiest stretch of the Mississippi. Between St. Paul and St. Louis the river is narrow; it twists and turns through channels and islands, and it drops 500 feet through twenty-six locks. Modern technology in the form of radar and other navigational tools gives pilots an immense advantage over their nineteenth-century counterparts.

In recent years the steamboats' passenger traffic has reappeared in the form of Captain Bill Bowell's re-created paddle steamers, the *Jonathan Padelford,* and the *Josiah Snelling,*

From May to September the sternwheeler Jonathan Paddelford *provides up-river trips on the Mississippi. The boat docks on Harriet Island, directly across the river from downtown St. Paul. Courtesy, St. Paul Convention Bureau*

which offer river excursions from downtown St. Paul. Such organizations as the Science Museum of Minnesota and the Ramsey County Historical Society take groups on boat trips up and down the river; private pleasure craft tie up at Harriet Island and the Watergate marina opposite Fort Snelling; and the stately *Delta Queen* calls at St. Paul's Lower Landing.

The railroads that a century ago took passen-

The Jonathan Paddelford *plies the Mississippi River as paddlewheelers before it have for over a century. Photos by Kay Shaw*

Far left: *After nearly a century, railroads are still an integral part of the city's transportation network. The Soo/Milwaukee railroad is just one which serves the Twin City area. Photo by Leighton*

Left, above: *James C. Burbank, noted for his express business, also promoted the organization of a chamber of commerce, serving as its president from 1869 to 1871. Burbank also helped organize the St. Paul Fire and Marine Insurance Company, now The St. Paul Companies, subsequently becoming its president. Courtesy, MHS*

Left, below: *Born in Canada in 1814, Norman Kittson came to the Minnesota area in the 1830s. Known for his fur-trading enterprises, Kittson also distinguished himself in St. Paul as a land developer, territorial legislator and as mayor of St. Paul in 1858. Courtesy, MHS*

ger traffic and much of the freight-hauling away from the river are still an important industry for St. Paul, as they were when they made the city the transportation center of the Upper Midwest and the gateway to the Northwest. Anyone with the misperception that railroads are waning has only to sit in a traffic line at the Upper Landing's Chestnut Street crossing waiting for a long, slow freight to pass. It is true, however, that the freights don't pass as frequently as they once did.

It is almost impossible to exaggerate the railroads' impact on nineteenth-century St. Paul. It has been estimated that one out of four people in the country once worked for the railroads. This figure may also be a pretty fair estimate for St. Paul. The railroads, however, were the inheritors of an earlier system of overland transportation that first established the city's trade with the Red River country and the Northwest. Norman W. Kittson's Red River oxcarts hauled furs from Canada to St. Paul and carried back supplies. Stagecoaches and express wag-

ons of James C. Burbank's Northwestern Express Company carried both passengers and freight over some of the same trails used by the Red River drivers, expanded them, and built the first roads through the wilderness.

The harbinger of the end for the stagecoaches and express wagons arrived on September 9, 1861, when the *William Crooks,* the first railroad locomotive to reach St. Paul, was unloaded at the Lower Landing from the steamboat *Alhambra.* The following spring, track was laid from St. Paul to St. Anthony and on June 28, 1862, the first run was made. By the end of the century an enormous network of rails linked St. Paul with Chicago and the Pacific. James J. Hill had reorganized the St. Paul, Manitoba and Pacific into the Great Northern, and acquired operating control of the bankrupt Northern Pacific, and at least ten other lines were serving St. Paul. The nineteenth-century historian Henry A. Castle reported that eight million passengers passed through St. Paul's Union Depot in 1888, a peak year, and 150 trains arrived and de-

Above: *The* Delta Queen, *Mississippi* Queen *and other river excursion boats tie up at St. Paul's Lambert's Landing in Lowertown. More than 100 years ago visitors and immigrants alike arrived at this landing. Photo by Doris Buehrer. Courtesy, St. Paul Planning and Economic Development Office*

Top: *River and rail transport shared a common interest in St. Paul's Lower Landing, which for many years served as a transshipment point for commercial goods. Courtesy, MHS*

parted every day.

Today, airlines, buses, and automobiles have taken over the railroads' once-thriving passenger service (and that service's revenues), as has Amtrak, created by Congress to relieve the nation's other railroads of the burden of carrying passengers. Amtrak has transferred passenger service from the mighty depots in downtown St. Paul and Minneapolis to a new station in the Midway district. In 1984 a total of 165,000 passengers passed in and out of the Amtrak station. Barges, trucks, and the airlines have siphoned off some of the freight business, but the railroads still are a potent force in St. Paul's economy.

Amtrak runs on the tracks owned by the Burlington Northern (BN) and the Soo/Milwaukee, railroads now serving the St. Paul-Minneapolis metropolitan area. The two represent mergers of earlier lines. In 1970 the 25,000-mile Burlington Northern was created by merging the Great Northern, Northern Pacific, Chicago, Burlington and Quincy, and the Spokane, Portland and Seattle railroads. With its 2,511 miles of track, which is about 45 percent of the total rail mileage in Minnesota, BN is the major railroad presence in the state. Until 1983, when BN merged with the "Frisco" (the St. Louis-San Francisco Railway Company) and transferred its headquarters to Seattle and some of its other departments to Kansas City and Fort Worth, the Burlington Northern occupied the thirteen-story building James J. Hill built to house the Great Northern and Northern Pacific. BN still has some offices there.

The Chicago and North Western Railroad Transportation Company (the C&NW) operates about 15 percent of the trackage in Minnesota. Since 1983, when C&NW purchased 820 miles of the Chicago, Rock Island and Pacific Railroad, it has also operated about ninety miles of former Rock Island track in Minnesota. The Soo line (the Minneapolis, St. Paul and Sault Ste. Marie), which operates 998 miles of road in Minnesota, has acquired the Chicago, Milwaukee, St. Paul and Pacific (CMStP&P, also known as the Milwaukee Road) and, as the Soo/Milwaukee, operates the miles of former Milwaukee tracks in Minnesota.

Finally, the Minnesota Transfer Railway Company (MT), whose parent company consists of the other railroads, operates on ninety-nine

miles of track owned by those roads, plus another thirteen miles owned by MT itself. Situated in St. Paul, MT serves as a switching and terminal facility. Increasingly, today the railroads are cutting back on service to small towns and country elevators, abandoning one-by-one their short-rail segments despite protests from farmers, merchants, and suppliers in rural districts. Total miles of track in use in Minnesota in 1967 were 7,837; by 1984 that number had been reduced to 5,522.

The service the abandoned trackage represents has been absorbed for the most part, or was taken over by, the trucking industry, a rival but also a partner of the railroads in piggybacking, the intermodal facilities that have grown substantially in the past few years. This cooperative arrangement is the wave of the future for both industries, as truckers load their trailers onto flatbed railroad cars for long-distance hauling, then unload them at their destination and hook them up again to their trucks.

The trucking industry more closely resembles James C. Burbank's horse-drawn freight wagons than do the railroads. Wagons toiling along country roads could reach communities the rail-

A Minnesota Transfer Railway Company switch engine. Photo by Kay Shaw

roads bypassed. With the development of the internal-combustion engine in the 1880s, the practical aspects of combining wagon with gasoline-powered engines became apparent. In Minneapolis in 1910, writes Lucile Kane in *Twin Cities-A Pictorial History of Saint Paul and Minneapolis*, trucking pioneer Floyd Raymond cut away the rear part of a car and mounted a box on it. Manufacturers soon were making trucks of more practical design.

Today St. Paul's Midway district is a national center for the trucking industry, with trucks hauling the less-than-carload lots not handled by the railroads along miles of interstate freeways and trunk highways that link the Twin Cities area with the rest of the region and the nation. According to the Minnesota Motor Transport Association, about half the trucks registered in Minnesota are light pickups, panels, and delivery vans. Truck tractors and heavier straight trucks make up most of the rest.

Trucks haul almost two-thirds of the Minnesota-manufactured products that are shipped to intercity markets, as well as more than 84 percent of Minnesota-grown fresh fruits and vegetables that go to the principal markets around the country. Products needed for construction make up 15 percent, and wholesale and retail goods 10 percent. All livestock at the South St. Paul stockyards comes in by truck. At one time it came in by train—carload after carload.

In 1977 almost 40,000 trucks were registered in Ramsey County, with an estimated value of more than $82.5 million. But with deregulation three years later, the number of Interstate Commerce Commission (ICC) trucking firms throughout the country jumped from 17,000 to 30,000, creating a highly competitive climate that led to rate-slashing. Overall, concerning tonnage of freight moved, the railroads, which now haul only in carload lots, are still dominant, according to the Minnesota Motor Transport Association; however, in terms of dollar-value, trucks are ahead, because they are more efficient at moving manufactured goods.

Some of the nation's largest national regular-route common carriers serve the Twin Cities, and some of the largest local and regional carriers have their headquarters in Minneapolis and St. Paul. A number of them are nationally recognized for their expertise in moving sensitive industrial equipment, electronic and robotic equipment, and household goods.

The interstate freeways, so crucial to the trucking firms, are just as important to those other segments of the transportation industry—passenger buses and private automobiles. The interstate highway system had its beginnings as far back as 1944, when the National Interregional Highways Committee, looking toward the years beyond the eventual end of World War II, proposed an interstate system that would link cities of more than 300,000. Implemented chiefly after the 1956 adoption of the Interstate Defense System, the interstates today link St. Paul and the metropolitan region with every other major urban area in the country.

The system has been a boon to tourism within the region and to that part of passenger travel that the airlines do not serve. The Minnesota Motor Transport Association reports that in the early 1980s more than three million vehicles were registered in Minnesota. Available for their use were more than 12,000 miles of state highways, including almost a thousand miles of interstates—but not including thousands of miles of county and township roads. Among the vehicles that travel those highways are close to 4,000 school buses and about the same number of charter passenger buses. Another 1,400 or so transit buses operate mostly within the Twin Cities.

St. Paul's city buses are the descendants of the first horsecars that in 1872 rumbled along a primitive two-mile track laid on dirt streets that ran from Seven Corners in Upper Town to Lafayette and Westminster in Lowertown. Thomas Lowry, founder of the Minneapolis Street Railway Company, and a number of other Twin Cities businessmen acquired the St. Paul Street

The interstate freeway system links St. Paul and Minneapolis and the metropolitan area with all major urban areas in the country. Photo by Kay Shaw

ASK FATHER HE'LL REMEMBER.

FIRST HORSE CAR
OPERATED IN TWIN CITIES
JULY 15 1872
SEATING CAPACITY-14.

Railway Company in 1884 and formed the Twin City Rapid Transit Company. Five years later Lowry began to electrify the system in both Minneapolis and St. Paul. For the next fifty years the trolleys' gleaming rails linked St. Paul with Hastings, Stillwater, Mahtomedi, White Bear Lake, and North St. Paul, as well as with Minneapolis, where passengers then could travel to the western suburbs of Wayzata and Excelsior.

Just after midnight on October 31, 1953, the last of St. Paul's familiar yellow streetcars rocked along into the carbarns after its final run. Buses replaced streetcars, and the Metropolitan Transit Commission (MTC) eventually replaced

Above: *St. Paul's first horsecar, dating from the 1870s and on display circa 1921, carried passengers along a primitive two-mile track that ran from Seven Corners in Upper Town to Lafayette and Westminster in Lowertown. Courtesy, MHS*

Right: *The electric streetcar line, completed in 1890, linked downtown St. Paul with the area's newest residential suburbs—Macalester Park and Groveland Park. Courtesy, MHS*

Right: *Streetcars transported passengers to and from St. Paul through the Selby Avenue tunnel, passing through what is now the Summit Hill neighborhood. Although streetcar service was abandoned in 1953, the closed overgrown tunnel remains today a reminder of a bygone era. Courtesy, MHS*

The Metropolitan Transit Commission operates specially designed buses such as the "art" bus, pictured here at the Farmers Market. Photo by Leighton

the Twin City Rapid Transit Company. MTC now serves the seven-county, 900-square-mile metropolitan area. MTC has more than a thousand operating vehicles in a fleet that serves 125 bus routes. The fleet includes eighty-two articulated buses and almost 1,000 standard forty-foot coaches. Thirty-eight Project Mobility buses, equipped with wheelchair lifts, carry some 40,000 handicapped people on 15,700 trips a month.

MTC buses carry more than six million riders a month. The system is complex, but computers help keep it going. MTC was one of the first urban transit commissions in the United States to use computers in its scheduling section. The approximately 1,400 men and women who drive for MTC bear little resemblance to the drivers who once stood in all types of weather on the open platforms of Tom Lowry's horsecars guiding the horses, watching for passengers, collecting the five-cent fare, and making change.

The most potent force in capturing passenger traffic and, to an increasing extent, cargo and container freight, is the airlines. They have added more than two billion dollars a year to the metropolitan area's economy and provided jobs for more than 16,000 people directly and another 17,000 indirectly through related industries. About 95 percent of those jobs are with commercial airlines based at the Minneapolis-St. Paul International Airport—mostly with Northwest, which has its headquarters in the Twin Cities and has just merged with Republic Airlines.

All the airlines that serve the Twin Cities have made the St. Paul-Minneapolis area an international point of entry and departure for overseas and Canada. In 1984 almost 5,000 international flights carrying half-a-million passengers arrived at or left the Minneapolis-St. Paul International Airport. Dedicated in 1962, the airport spreads over 3,000 acres south of the two cities. It ranks thirty-first in the world in the number of passengers and twentieth in total operations (takeoffs and landings). With its secondary airports, the metropolitan airport system is the third busiest in the country, according to the Metropolitan Airport Commission. Minneapolis-

NORTHWEST AIRLINES, INC.

In 1986, with the completion of the merger with Twin Cities-based Republic Airlines—a company whose history is also deeply rooted in the area—and the completion of its new administrative complex on 158 acres across the Minnesota River from the Minneapolis/St. Paul International Airport in Eagan, Northwest Airlines enters an exciting new era.

The third-largest U.S.-based airline, and the nation's second-oldest air carrier with a continuous identification, has called St. Paul home for more than 50 years. In that time Northwest has grown from a small, regional mail carrier to a leader in international air travel, the only U.S. carrier serving multiple destinations in North America, Asia, and Europe. Its newly combined fleet of more than 300 aircraft covers a route system that encompasses two-thirds of the globe—nearly 140 cities in 17 countries on three continents— and serves more than 30 million passengers annually.

No one could have predicted such phenomenal growth when Northwest Airways began carrying the mail between St. Paul's Speedway Field and Chicago in 1926. Backed by businessmen in the Twin Cities and Detroit, the airline expanded to passenger service in 1927—and carried 106 people before suspending operations for the winter.

By 1934, when the airline was reincorporated under Minnesota law, Northwest Airways was serving cities from Minnesota and Michigan westward through the Dakotas and Montana to Washington. Its initial growth set a pattern of expansion that foreshadowed the leap across the Pacific to serve Asia in the 1940s.

But before that could happen, World War II intervened. For Northwest's operations in St. Paul—at that time located on University Avenue in the Midway—it meant a change of activity. Drawing on the airline's expertise in flying harsh-weather routes in the northern part of the continent, the government called on Northwest to set up and operate a military cargo route to Alaska, Canada, and the Aleutians. Northwest pilots flew more than 21 million miles in Army C-46s and C-47s, and with a better performance factor than many airlines operating domestically at the time.

Meanwhile, Holman Field in St. Paul became the site of one of the two bomber modification plants Northwest operated during the war, with as many as 6,000 workers—some of whom worked outside during the bitter cold of Minnesota's winters—preparing B-25s and B-26s for both desert and cold weather operations. Northwest also contributed to research into plane icing, communications static, and high-altitude flying that ultimately benefited commercial air travel as well.

When the Korean War broke out in 1950, Northwest's expertise was again enlisted in operating the now-famous Korean Airlift along the "Great Circle" route across the Pacific. Without disrupting any of its commercial flights, Northwest flew nearly 1,400 round trips between the West Coast and Korea, 13 million miles in all, carrying 40,000 military passengers and 12 million pounds of cargo before its part of the airlift was completed.

Northwest had envisioned a "Northwest Passage" to the Orient in the early 1930s, and that vision became reality in 1946 when the airline was certified to begin flying to the Far East via the shorter Great Circle route. (Because of the earth's equatorial bulge, the distance from New York City to Hong

The full-size Northwest 747 landing at Taipei, Taiwan. The magnificent Grand Hotel is in the background.

The firm's new administrative complex on 158 acres across the Minnesota River from the Minneapolis/St. Paul International Airport in Eagan.

Kong is nearly 2,000 miles shorter along the Great Circle than across the mid-Pacific.) In July 1947 Northwest began offering scheduled service to Tokyo, Seoul, Shanghai, and Manila. A year later it became the first airline to link Hawaii with the Pacific Northwest.

Today Northwest's route system stretches from Singapore in Asia to Stockholm in Europe, with domestic service to every major destination in the United States. More than 34,000 employees, from pilots and flight attendants to mechanics and ticket agents, many of them based at Northwest's home at Minneapolis/St. Paul International Airport, serve passengers and air freight customers throughout the system. (The airline's major reservations, maintenance, and engineering complex at the airport, which was opened in 1961, is actually part of the city of St. Paul.)

In addition to being widely recognized as the leading U.S. airline across the Pacific, Northwest takes great pride in being the industry leader in noise-abatement policies and procedures designed to reduce the impact of modern air travel on residential areas near major airports. Many of the policies pioneered by Northwest have subsequently been adopted industrywide.

In addition, Northwest's newer generation of jets, including the Boeing 747-400 soon to come into service, are significantly quieter than previous airliners, yet offer greater passenger comfort and cargo capacity. The 747-400, for example, was designed to North-

west's specifications for transpacific travel. As the standard of comparison for efficiency and passenger comfort in the 1990s, Northwest's newest airliners will carry up to 450 passengers and a full cargo load to destinations as much as 8,000 miles away.

Northwest is also acknowledged within the airline industry as the leader in aviation meteorology. It has pioneered techniques, methods, and policies designed to further enhance the safety and comfort of air travel.

The new direction of air travel under deregulation is the genesis of Northwest's move to a more vertically integrated route structure and operating profile. The merger with Republic Airlines creates an opportunity for the two complementary systems to capitalize on

their unique strengths and redeploy their aircraft for maximum efficiency and flexibility. Northwest Airlink agreements allow small regional carriers, including Minnesota-based Mesaba Airlines, to coordinate their flight schedules with Northwest's to help business travelers make connections more efficiently. The 1985 acquisition of Mainline Travel, Inc. (MLT), as a wholly owned subsidiary, gives Northwest a significant position in the tour wholesaling market through more than 4,000 independent retail travel agencies.

Today's Northwest combines the best of both Northwest and Republic, and looks ahead confidently to air travel in the twenty-first century—travel that may well be conducted at hypersonic speeds.

Northwest's 757

Right: *The "Gold Concourse," the newest addition to the Minneapolis-St. Paul International airport, demonstrates the continued growth of the airline industry. Photo by Leighton*

Bottom: *A replica of Charles Lindbergh's* Spirit of St. Louis *suspends on display at the international airport. Lindbergh achieved fame when he successfully completed the first non-stop transatlantic flight from New York to Paris in 1927. Photo by Leighton*

St. Paul International began as Wold-Chamberlain Field, named for two Minneapolis aviators who were killed in World War I. It dates back to 1920 when the field was established on the site of the Twin City Motor Speedway which had opened in 1915 with a race involving Eddie Rickenbacker.

Crucial to the future of air service in the Twin Cities was airmail service. The airmail contract that finally went into effect in 1926 was the motivating factor in the organization of Northwest Airlines, which was founded in St. Paul and incorporated on August 1, 1926, as Northwest Airways. Colonel Lewis H. Britten, vice-president of the St. Paul Association (a forerunner of the

Saint Paul Area Chamber of Commerce), and a group of St. Paul and Detroit investors provided the capital for the new company.

At the same time, the City of St. Paul was establishing its own airport. The city had bought 230 acres of land on the river flats across the Mississippi from downtown and there, in 1926, it opened the St. Paul Downtown Airport, later named Holman Field for Charles W. "Speed" Holman, a colorful figure during the early years of aviation. Holman flew Northwest Airways' first mail plane and served as Northwest's operations manager until 1931, when he was killed during the Omaha air races.

Northwest's headquarters remained at Holman Field for some years before moving to Wold-Chamberlain. It became both hazardous and uneconomical to have two airport stops—Holman and Wold-Chamberlain—so close together, so the stop at Holman was discontinued. However, during World War II Northwest maintained a modification center at Holman. There more than 5,000 men and women installed guns and other special equipment on military planes that were flown in from all over the country, many of them ferried by women pilots. The equipment included gunsights developed by Norman B. Mears of St. Paul. Holman Field was for a time the home of Minnesota's Air National Guard, while at Wold-Chamberlain an important Naval air station was established during the war years.

Holman Field—still the St. Paul Downtown Airport—is the main reliever airport for Minneapolis-St. Paul International Airport. Now used primarily by private aircraft, including corporate jets, Holman Field is one of several smaller airports whose private and business planes brought some 187,000 visitors into the metropolitan area in one year, according to the Metropolitan Council's figures.

Essential to the transportation industry are the warehouses that, since the 1850s, have stored goods hauled into St. Paul for distribution to city dwellers or shipment elsewhere. It began, as did so much else, with the fur trade when bales of furs brought in by oxcart were stored to await shipment downriver, and supplies and equipment needed on the frontier were held to await pickup by the oxcart drivers. Before long the city's enterprising settlers began to manufacture their own goods, not just for local consumption but also for export to an ever-widening regional market. These required warehousing of inventories.

C.P. Bratnober, who founded Central Warehouse in 1902, was among the first in St. Paul to provide storage and public warehousing, as was H.G. McNeely, Sr., who founded the St. Paul Terminal Warehouse Company in the early 1900s to handle building and hardware materials, agricultural chemicals, and household furnishings, among other items. And E.L. Murphy, an enterprising politician who recognized the need for moving freight that was piling up at the Lower Landing and railroad yards, launched Murphy Transfer and Storage in 1903 with his son.

St. Paul Terminal Warehouse has become Space Center, Inc., with several million square feet of space available in the Twin Cities and millions more in such cities as Chicago, Kansas City, Houston, and Dallas. In Missouri a wide variety of government food and other products are stored underground in abandoned mines where Space Center, still owned by the McNeely family, operates hundreds of thousands of square feet.

Murphy's business mushroomed from the operation of a single horse and wagon into five Murphy companies, managed by the first E.L. Murphy's grandson. One is Murphy Warehouse, which stores food and tobacco products, chemicals, and some appliances in 1.4 million square feet of storage space. And Central Warehouse, still controlled by the Bratnober family, extends over twenty-seven acres and operates its own railroad.

The demand for warehouse space is growing, fueled by the high-growth companies of the past decade. A tool and supply company, which sells to electrical contractors, needed a few thousand square feet seven years ago. Now it requires 45,000. Space Center, for example, offers a choice of leasing space: either the client runs the warehousing operation, or Space Center handles the inventory as a public warehouse service, filling the needs of a wide spectrum of clients—many of them in the high-tech production of computers, their components, and software.

While many companies need warehousing space, their need for office and assembly space is often just as critical, particularly for those firms that have been expanding rapidly. As times have changed, space uses have changed, too. Warehouse firms have become space merchants and the use of the buildings themselves has changed. What was a warehouse becomes an office building, even an office park, such as Lafayette Park, now being developed by Space Center next to the Lowertown district.

If transportation was the earliest cornerstone of St. Paul's economy, banking was a close second, as barter, one of the first forms of compensation for goods and services, had its

MAUN, GREEN, HAYES, SIMON, JOHANNESON AND BREHL

Law firms reflect the character and personality of the people who build and guide them. In the case of Maun, Green, Hayes, Simon, Johanneson and Brehl, that character and personality takes the form of an active role in civic affairs in addition to the practice of law.

A general practice law firm, Maun-Green offers specialized expertise in the areas of taxation, real estate, estate planning, trusts and probate, antitrust, corporate organization and finance, business planning, mergers and acquisitions, public utility law, administrative law, and litigation. Through the years it has been one of the city's most active and successful firms, with more than 22 attorneys located in an office in downtown St. Paul and seven in an office that opened in Bloomington in the mid-1970s.

Both the firm's practice and its civic involvement bear the initial imprint of Joseph A. Maun, who began practicing law in St. Paul in 1935 where he eventually became a principal in the St. Paul firms of Bundlie, Kelly and Maun, and Maun, Hazel and Busch, forerunners of the current practice. The present firm was founded in 1961, including among its initial partners Joseph A. Maun, Merlyn C. Green, Jerome B. Simon, and Lawrence J. Hayes, all of whom remain active with the firm.

Maun was president of the Saint Paul Area Chamber of Commerce and a prime mover in its reorganization and revitalization. He also has served on the Metropolitan Council, the Metropolitan Airports Commission, and the Metropolitan Planning Commission—three organizations working to coordinate planning and services for the benefit of the entire Twin Cities area.

Other partners similarly have served the public and private sector extensively on a wide variety of boards, including those governing charities, colleges and secondary

Partners (left to right) Bill Green, Jim Brehl, John Johanneson, Larry Hayes, Joe Maun, and Jerry Simon.

Founder Joseph A. Maun (second from right) with younger members of the firm (left to right) Tom Puff, Gar Mulrooney, Phil Colton, Mike Monahan, Mary Knoblauch, and Charlie Bans.

schools, and governmental entities. The firm is committed to continuing this tradition of community service.

Maun-Green has gained a reputation for expertise in business-oriented legal practice: taxes, real estate financing and development, complex business litigation, product liability and insurance defense work, public utility law, and representation of buyers and sellers in business acquisitions and mergers. Major clients have included 3M Company; Chas. Pfizer & Co.; Northwestern Bell Telephone Company; The Northland Company and its subsidiaries, including United Properties and Northland Financial; Donovan Companies, Inc.; Murphy Motor Freight Lines, Inc.; Home Insurance Company; The First National Bank of Saint Paul; Commercial State Bank; Shelard BancShares; and The Theodore Hamm Brewing Company. The firm has been distinguished by its frequent involvement in complex and public-interest business transactions and litigation.

As the practice of law has become more specialized, Maun, Green, Hayes, Simon, Johanneson and Brehl has continued to stress personalized service to its clients by focusing on the areas of law most responsive to its clients' needs. To serve the more complex needs of larger businesses, the firm has added staff and specialized expertise—yet the strength of its practice continues to be responsive and cost-effective service to the owners of family-held and growing businesses. It has also ventured into emerging areas of legal practice: employment law, government regulatory activity, and developing issues relating to computers and trade secrets.

Now in its second quarter-century, Maun, Green, Hayes, Simon, Johanneson and Brehl continues to serve the legal and civic interests of St. Paul's businesses and their owners, employees, and customers.

AMERICAN NATIONAL BANK

When the management of American National Bank developed a business plan for operations in the 1980s, it found it could crystallize that plan in six words: "St. Paul's what we're all about." Since its founding in 1903, the bank has focused its attention on the special needs and concerns of the city.

And that specialized focus has paid dividends for both the bank and the city it serves. From initial deposits of just $232,000, American National has grown to become the largest bank owned and operated in the city of St. Paul and the largest independently owned bank in the Upper Midwest, with total assets of more than $600 million and nearly 400 employees in its downtown headquarters and new Highland Village branch on South Cleveland Avenue.

That growth has been accomplished in large part due to the bank's emphasis on serving consumer, retail, and business customers, especially businesses that are owned and operated by St. Paul people. American National has been a major source of funding for downtown development and Lowertown construction financing as well as residential and business loans throughout the St. Paul metropolitan area. It also has helped countless professional businesses—medical practices, law firms, dental offices, CPAs, and others—get started and grow, and has developed thousands of loyal customers among the area's senior citizens.

The original national charter was granted to what had been the American Exchange Bank in the spring of 1903. At the same time the Union Bank was absorbed into the new American National. German immigrant Otto Bremer and his brother, Adolph, were instrumental in establishing the new bank. Otto had come to St. Paul in 1886 and began his banking career with the National German American Bank, which served

The downtown home of American National Bank is one of the most distinctive sights on the St. Paul skyline.

the city's German immigrant community.

Bremer, who served five terms as St. Paul's city treasurer beginning in 1900, served on the board of directors of American National from its founding until his death in 1951, and the Bremer family remains an important part of the bank's ownership to this day. (American National should not be confused with the Bremer Banks, which operate under a foundation established by the late Otto Bremer.)

In 1974 American National determined to link its future visibly with that of downtown St. Paul, moving into 10 floors of the newly constructed American National Bank Building at Fifth and Minnesota streets. Current chairman of the board and chief executive officer James W. Reagan has taken an active role in civic affairs as well as the business of the bank. Joseph R. Kingman III is president and chief operating officer.

American National Bank's special focus on the needs of St. Paul area businesses and residents has made it a powerful resource for a growing community, and one that promises to continue to provide personal and quality service specifically tailored to the needs of the city and its people in the years to come.

American Bank above, and
First Minnesota Bank right,
are just two of the many
banks which carry on the
city's banking legacy. Above
photo by Leighton; right photo
by Kay Shaw

limitations when frontier businessmen had to deal with Eastern banking institutions. St. Paul's first banker may well have been Charles W.W. Borup. Born in Denmark into a distinguished family, he arrived in St. Paul in 1848 from La Pointe, Wisconsin, where he had been chief agent for John Jacob Astor's American Fur Company. In June of 1853 Borup and his brother-in-law, Charles H. Oakes, formed the Bank of Borup and Oakes. Although Borup died in 1859, the firm remained in business until 1866.

In 1854 a young fur-trading entrepreneur from Vermont settled in St. Paul without much cash but with a great deal of faith in the frontier and the future of its banking business. With less than $40,000 in capital, Parker Paine opened his bank. Some years later, two Southerners, James and Horace Thompson, joined him. In 1863 a national charter was issued to First National Bank of St. Paul, capitalized at $250,000.

Today St. Paul and its suburbs are served by some thirty banking institutions, plus the branches of St. Paul's three major banks and their bank systems—First National Bank, a member of First Bank Systems; Norwest Bank (formerly Northwestern National Bank), a member of Norwest Corporation; and American National Bank, a member of American Bancorporation. First Bank, Norwest, and American represent the banking interests, often through mergers, of some of nineteenth-century St. Paul's most powerful financial forces. First National Bank grew out of a merger with two other

St. Paul banks. The National German American Bank dates back to 1856, when two young men from Germany, Ferdinand Willius and Henry Meyer, arrived in St. Paul and announced the opening of their banking business. Gustav Willius and Frederick Meyer joined them the next year. Over the years, stockholders included lumberman Frederick Weyerhaeuser, and jurists Charles E. Flandrau and John B. Sanborn. In 1872 a group of merchants, chiefly wholesalers led by Maurice Auerbach and including Amherst H. Wilder, Joseph L. Forepaugh, and Bruno Beaupre, organized the Merchants Bank.

In 1912 the National German American Bank and Merchants Bank merged, a move that seemed prudent since James J. Hill had decided to go into the banking business. In October 1912 Hill bought St. Paul's Second National Bank, founded in 1853 as the MacKubin Edgerton Bank. Three months later Hill bought First National's capital stock for $3.35 million and merged the two institutions. Understandably, the bank was known as "the railroad bank." In 1929 Merchants and First National merged, a

step that was precipitated by the interest of Northwestern National Bank of Minneapolis in acquiring a strong St. Paul bank. Northwest Bancorporation, formed in 1929, had initiated talks with Louis W. Hill, Sr., about First National, but nothing came of them at that time. St. Paul's business leaders apparently did not want control of their largest bank transferred to Minneapolis.

Northwestern did come to St. Paul soon afterwards. In 1930 Northwest Bancorporation acquired the Empire National Bank. Empire was a successor to the nineteenth-century National Exchange Bank that in 1926 had been rescued from failing and recapitalized, mainly with money from Merchants National Bank. The list of the men and the institutions that preserved that bank reads like a "Who's Who" of St. Paul's business leadership: Louis W. Hill, Sr., Otto Bremer, William Hamm, Minnesota Mining, St. Paul Fire and Marine, Griggs Cooper, and The Golden Rule. In 1959 the bank's name was changed to the Northwestern National Bank of St. Paul—now Norwest.

American National Bank and Trust Company

Nineteenth-century railroad magnate James J. Hill (above) greatly contributed to the rise of St. Paul's banking industry. His mansion (left) is today a National Historic Site, open to the public for tours. Above portrait courtesy, Cirker's Dictionary of American Portraits; left photo by Rosemary Palmer

grew out of the banking concerns of the Otto Bremer family and the Jacob Schmidt Brewery. American also traces its origins to the old National Exchange Bank, located before the turn of the century at Seventh and Jackson streets in Lowertown. In 1896 a fire burned out the bank, forcing a move to temporary quarters two blocks away. Two years later the name of the bank, by this time situated at Sixth and Minnesota, was changed to American Exchange Bank. In 1908 it became American National Bank of St. Paul. Today American is the sixth-largest commercial bank in the Ninth Federal Reserve District. Its new twenty-six-story building, completed in 1974 at Fifth and Minnesota, anchors a segment of the city's skyway system.

First National, Norwest, and American rank in the top 100 of Minnesota's 738 commercial banks, which in 1984 had assets of $48.4 billion, according to the July 1985 issue of *Corporate Report Minnesota.* Together, First Bank System and Norwest Corporation, the Upper Midwest's two dominant banking systems, owned fifty-one banks in the top 100—First Bank System owns twenty-five and Norwest Corporation owns twenty-six.

St. Paul's swashbuckling entrepreneurs would scarcely recognize banking today, nor would they most likely function with much comfort under the regulations that grew out of the disasters of the Great Depression. The challenges ushered in with deregulation in 1980 are of more pressing concern to bankers than any other subject, according to E. Gerald Corrigan, former president of the Federal Reserve Bank of Minneapolis.

And challenges there are. Insurance companies and brokerages have moved into traditional banking activities; banks have moved into the insurance business; retail firms, into the loan and brokerage business; savings and loans, into both insurance and banking; manufacturers have moved into banking; and new financial instruments have proliferated. The banks are not alone in feeling the impact of changes that have been developing since the 1970s. The "thrifts," the savings and loans, and the insurance companies began to offer higher interest rates and broader services when demand grew for services banks had difficulty providing.

St. Paul's savings and loans also descend from such venerable institutions as Borup and Oakes and other early banks that in the middle of the nineteenth century were in the business of loaning money besides dealing in mortgages, real estate, domestic exchange, and money-changing. The savings aspect of the business arrived later when the institutions began to help working men and women save to build or buy a home.

First Minnesota Savings Bank represents a merger of Minnesota Federal Savings and Loan, one of the largest savings and loan associations in the country and the only major Minnesota S&L with its headquarters in St. Paul, and First Federal Savings and Loan of Minneapolis. Minnesota Federal was founded in St. Paul in 1922. First Minnesota will build its new headquarters in downtown St. Paul at Fifth and Minnesota, the block Minnesota Federal has occupied for some years.

What is now the state's largest S&L, Twin City Federal, organized in Minneapolis in 1923, then opened a St. Paul office. Midwest Federal of Minneapolis has a St. Paul office and Green Tree Acceptance Corporation, a Midwest Federal subsidiary, is in St. Paul. The three savings and loan associations in the metropolitan area, with assets totaling almost ten billion dollars, serve the statewide community through close to 100 out-of-state and branch offices. S&Ls are still a major source of capital for home mortgages, but they have also moved into consumer lending and checking accounts.

It is scarcely surprising, then, that the companies that made St. Paul one of the insurance centers of the country have also changed dramatically over the years since the 1850s, when the need to protect buildings and cargo was basic to a community dependent upon riverboats,

MIDWEST FEDERAL SAVINGS AND LOAN ASSOCIATION

The oldest thrift location in the city of St. Paul is the one opened in the Commerce Building on East Fourth Street in 1917 by Midwest Federal, which in those days was known as The Minneapolis Savings and Loan Association. These days Midwest Federal has more than three billion dollars in assets and offices statewide, including eight in St. Paul and its surrounding suburbs. Although the financial services industry has changed tremendously in recent years, Midwest's distinctive green oak tree symbol still shines brightly atop the Commerce Building, a familiar sight on the St. Paul skyline for more than 30 years.

The business began, appropriately enough, with a $500 home loan in the summer of 1891, shortly after a state charter was received. Home loans remain a cornerstone of the business to this day (since its founding, Midwest Federal has financed more than one billion dollars in home mortgages in the metropolitan area), part of a comprehensive package that also includes savings and checking accounts, insurance products, commercial mortgages, business loans, and IRA and Keogh retirement accounts.

Since 1963, when a federal charter was granted to allow for branching, new openings and mergers have added additional offices in both the Twin Cities and outstate Minnesota. Three St. Paul-based savings and loan associations have been part of that growth: Ben Franklin Federal merged its four offices into Midwest Federal in 1965, St. Paul Federal Savings & Loan brought its five offices into the family in 1972, and First Federal of St. Paul merged into Midwest Federal in 1974.

In recent years the firm has gained national recognition for the progressive and innovative ways in which it has restructured its operations to meet the changing needs and conditions of today's fi-

Harold W. Greenwood, Jr., chairman of the board, president, and chief executive officer of Midwest Federal, is a member of the Federal Reserve Board's Thrift Advisory Council and past president of the National Council of Savings Institutions.

nancial consumer. Under the leadership of Harold W. Greenwood, Jr., who was elected president in 1965 at the age of 33, Midwest Federal has organized savings activities and the sale of insurance products in its own offices through its insurance subsidiary, while conducting mortgage banking and lending operations through outside subsidiary service corporations.

A former subsidiary is St. Paul-based Green Tree Acceptance, Inc., the nation's leading lender to the manufactured housing industry, and one of St. Paul's newest

success stories. Launched by Midwest Federal in 1975, the company went public in 1983 and is now traded on the New York Stock Exchange; Midwest Federal currently retains approximately 20-percent ownership.

In 1978 the firm acquired United Mortgage Corporation, its current mortgage banking subsidiary. United Mortgage is involved in both conventional and FHA/VA home loans, serving the Twin Cities through its own network of eight offices. The Great Oak Agency, Inc., Midwest Federal's insurance subsidiary, provides annuities and a variety of products oriented to retirement savings needs. MWF Mortgage Corporation, formed in 1985, generates interim financing and permanent loans for commercial real estate.

Through all the growth and change, Midwest Federal Savings and Loan Association has remained a warm, good neighbor to nearly a half-million customers. More than 100,000 are members of the Midwesterners Club, the region's largest savers club, which provides hospitable clubrooms in St. Paul and Minneapolis. It's just one more example of the strength and stability that has made Midwest Federal one of the largest savings and loan associations in the country.

Midwest Federal's distinctive oak tree is a familiar sight on the St. Paul skyline.

THE ST. PAUL COMPANIES, INC.

St. Paul Fire and Marine Insurance Company began in 1853 in a Minnesota Territory river town. A group of businessmen realized that major insurance companies on the East Coast couldn't provide the necessary insurance protection for the pioneer community of St. Paul. From that beginning over 130 years ago, the company has grown to become a major property-liability insurance firm with assets of nearly seven billion dollars and annual revenues approaching three billion dollars. The company that began on the banks of the Mississippi River in St. Paul today serves a growing base of individuals and businesses worldwide.

Today the name is officially The St. Paul Companies, Inc., as a result of restructuring in 1968 to make the company a general business corporation while maintaining the original charter of Minnesota's oldest business corporation.

The St. Paul Companies is a one-

Robert J. Haugh, chairman and chief executive officer, The St. Paul Companies.

The St. Paul Companies' Juvenile Crime Prevention Curriculum teaches students about the negative effects that property crimes, such as arson, shoplifting, and vandalism, have on their neighborhoods. Here Rita McGuire, from the firm's home office, talks to a Juvenile Crime Prevention class at Roosevelt High School in Minneapolis.

stop-shop for any individual, commercial, or professional property-liability insurance or reinsurance protection. St. Paul Fire and Marine, the major subsidiary, is the 14th-largest property-liability insurance company in the United States. The firm is the largest insurer of medical malpractice in the United States and ranks sixth among writers of fidelity and surety bonds. From basic fire insurance to highly sophisticated insurance and reinsurance needs, The St.

Paul Companies has the products, services, and distribution system available to meet its customers' needs.

During its first century The St. Paul Companies built its reputation as a dependable and innovative insurance underwriter. Formed four years after Minnesota became a territory and five years before it became a state, The St. Paul Companies developed into a strong and successful firm that survived and prospered despite such calamities as the Chicago Fire of 1871 and the San Francisco Earthquake and Fire of 1906.

While property-liability insurance continued to be the mainstay of The St. Paul's business, the company began to diversify in the late 1950s. First, the company moved into other types of insurance—life and health, and title, for example. Later, non-insurance financial services companies were added. Although the management company was formed in 1968, St. Paul Fire and Marine remained by far the dominant subsidiary.

In the late 1970s The St. Paul Companies' board of directors began to reevaluate its financial services' focus. The firm had moved in that direction before most other major insurers. The board determined that The St. Paul Companies' core business—property-liability insurance—was its driving force and should remain so.

Thus, during the 1980s, the company expanded its business through focusing attention on doing what it does best—property-liability insurance products and services. Financial services and non-property-liability insurance subsidiaries were sold. New companies were added—specialty lines, reinsurance, and wholesale brokerage. With more than $2.2 billion in written premiums, the property-liability insurance underwriting group now includes St. Paul Fire and Marine Insurance Company plus Atwater-McMillian,

a surplus lines and specialty risks management company; Seaboard Surety, a bond underwriter; and St. Paul Reinsurance Management Corporation.

In addition, Reinsurance Facilities Corporation, one of the top 10 U.S.-based reinsurance intermediaries, serves as a national and international reinsurance broker for The St. Paul Companies. And The Swett & Crawford Group gives The St. Paul Companies the largest network of wholesale insurance brokers in the United States. Besides wholesale brokers, The St. Paul Companies is also represented by 7,000 independent insurance agents.

On the international scene, The St. Paul Companies is tied to the world insurance market through its investment in Minet Holdings PLC, London, one of the largest international insurance organizations. The company also has an interest in St. Katherine Insurance Company PLC, a London-based insurer and reinsurer.

The St. Paul Companies has long been a prominent force and concerned corporate citizen in the city from which it took its name. Nearly 2,500 of its approximately 10,000 employees are based in St. Paul—two-thirds of them in the firm's handsome downtown headquarters complex on Washington Street (next to the Landmark Center and across the street from the St. Paul Civic Center); others work in nearby downtown buildings.

The headquarters location represents the firm's continuing commitment to the city in which it began its pioneer days. Between 1958 and 1961 the home office facility was completely rebuilt on the Washington and Fifth streets site. Since then, an additional building—completely financed from private funds and completed in 1981—has been added to the complex. The attractively landscaped plaza that faces the Civic

The St. Paul Companies' present home office building was expanded in 1981. The corporate headquarters has been at its present location at Fifth and Washington streets since 1909.

Center offers a visually striking entrance to downtown St. Paul for visitors and workers entering from the west.

Since the late 1940s a series of strong and innovative leaders has kept The St. Paul Companies at the forefront of its industry and active in the local community. Two of its chairmen received the "Great Living Saint Paulite" award for lifetimes of service to the community, A.B. Jackson in 1977 and Ronald M. Hubbs in 1986. Their successors, Carl B. Drake, Jr., and current chairman Robert J. Haugh, have continued that leadership tradition. And employees at every level of the firm have added their own effective contributions of time and expertise. The St. Paul Companies wears the name of its home city proudly and well.

oxcarts, freight wagons, and hastily built warehouses. St. Paul Fire and Marine was founded in 1853 to insure goods against the fires that periodically leveled entire blocks in the frontier town and "to provide protection against the perils of marine and inland navigation," a somewhat restrained description of such risks as steam-generating boilers, gas-lighted saloons, and hazardous sandbars.

The oldest business corporation in Minnesota, the company was organized on March 5, 1853. Its list of incorporators rings with the great names in Minnesota history: Alexander Ramsey, first territorial and second state governor; Henry M. Rice, first senator; Socrates Nelson, who helped draft Minnesota's petition for statehood; Isaac Atwater, George Farrington, John Irvine, David Loomis, all territorial legislators; William Pitt Murray, president of the state constitutional convention; businessman William Ames; Charles W.W. Borup, John Farrington, Charles Fillmore (brother of President Fillmore),

C.H. Bigelow (at desk), president of the St. Paul Fire and Marine Insurance Co., discusses business in this 1894 photograph with Amherst Wilder (left) and Peter Berkey (right), both corporate officers of the insurance company. Courtesy, MHS

Auguste Larpenteur, William LeDuc, and Levi Sloan. Colonel Alexander Wilkin, the company's first president, was the highest ranking officer from Minnesota to be killed during the Civil War.

St. Paul Fire and Marine issued insurance that covered some monumental disasters. It paid out $140,000 in claims from the Great Chicago Fire of 1871, $1,267,000 after the San Francisco earthquake and fire of 1906 (a sum almost equal to the company's entire net worth at that time), and claims for 260 vessels damaged or sunk during World War I. The company was the only insurer of London property against damage from Germany's zeppelin air raids.

Now a general business corporation, its name was changed in 1968 to The St. Paul Companies, Inc., retaining the name St. Paul Fire and Marine for its major property and casualty insurance company. The second-largest employer in downtown St. Paul, and with operations that are international in scope, The St. Paul Companies has pioneered in writing insurance for commercial aviation, banks, hospitals, and data processing, and it is noted for insuring the unique: a boatload of elephants, gibbons, monkeys, myna birds, lemurs, pythons, and a bear from Thailand to San Francisco; a man who planned to ride an ostrich; and an elephant riding a raft. All of these unusual insurees would have astounded the men who founded the company more than 130 years ago and took in $380.40 in premiums in their first year.

Minnesota Mutual Life Insurance Company had its start in 1880 in the office of St. Paul Fire and Marine's president, Charles H. Bigelow. Eight St. Paul businessmen had gathered to organize an insurance company that would be mutually owned by its members, as opposed to a stock company owned by shareholders. Today Minnesota Mutual is the fifteenth-largest life insurance company in the country, with 120 general agencies and twenty-three regional offices serving almost six million people.

One of the fastest growing of St. Paul's insurance companies has been The North Central

Company, which began life in 1921 as the Modern Life Company. Among its founders were J.A.A. Burnquist, former Minnesota attorney general and governor, and Julius Schmahl, former state treasurer and widely known as a Minnesota history buff. Today North Central does business throughout the country from its headquarters in North Central Tower, one of Town Square's twin office towers.

Stemming from the rural cooperative movement, another St. Paul company, Mutual Service Insurance, ranks in the top 14 percent of all life insurance companies in the nation. Mutual Service grew out of the need for farmers to join together to help each other. "Co-op" creameries, grain elevators, stockyards, and life insurance companies were part of this. In 1949 Mutual Service emerged as the result of five small companies pooling their staffs and resources. The company now serves members in twenty-five states.

In its earliest form, the purpose of insurance was to protect property. The idea of insuring the lives of wage earners, a concept that implied recognition that workers also were of value, did not take hold until after the Civil War. Even then most life insurance was bought by business and professional men. Women, the majority of whom were not wage earners, usually were not covered and probably could not have afforded coverage even if available. Many companies did not begin insuring women until about the time of World War I, a move that might have been precipitated by the flood of women into offices and factories after the outbreak of the war.

In 1910, however, a unique insurance organization had been established that was entirely for women. The Degree of Honor Protective Association was formed at a time when the average coverage on a woman's life, reflective of her economic status, was $500, and she was not permitted to buy more than $1,000. Originated in St. Paul by two women, Edna Dugan and Frances Buell Olson, who became the as-

sociation's first national president, Degree of Honor was more than an insurance company. The organization formed lodges in city neighborhoods where social ties could be nurtured through meetings and special community projects. (Today it would be called "networking.") Men were admitted in 1924, and a junior department was set up for children.

If Degree of Honor has moved beyond its original concept, so have St. Paul's other insurance companies as the profession itself has been dramatically reshaped by events of the past decade. Insurance companies have become financial services organizations offering multiple opportunities for investment. Besides insurance, The St. Paul Companies is in investment banking. Minnesota Mutual, which developed its first pension plan (for University of Minnesota faculty members) in 1930, offers variable annuities and sells mutual funds and money market accounts.

The insurance industry is caught up in a movement that the Minnesota Insurance Information Center calls "financial wellness," a counterpart to the health and wellness programs that have attracted the American public, and with many of the same characteristics. Just as people are taking over responsibility for their health, they are also taking over control of their financial well-being. A growing number, and particularly younger workers, no longer are relying solely on the government through Social Security or the employer or union through a pension plan to provide for their future. Through tax benefits the government has encouraged Individual Retirement Accounts (IRAs), tax-sheltered annuities (TSAs), Keogh plans for the self-employed, and so on, that make it possible for working men and women to develop their own savings, investment, and retirement plans to supplement Social Security and other pensions. The variety of financial instruments available today is so complex as to be intimidating for many. To help people sort it all out, financial planners have come forward to play a role in a

FARM CREDIT SERVICES

St. Paul is the headquarters of Farm Credit Services, the area's leading lender of agricultural credit. Established 70 years ago, Farm Credit Services, St. Paul (FCS) is today a $9-billion lending institution offering credit and financial services to more than 100,000 farmers and nearly 700 agricultural cooperatives across a four-state district.

Farm Credit Services is part of the national Farm Credit System, a farmer-owned, farmer-directed cooperative created to provide farmers and their cooperatives with a permanent and dependable source of agricultural credit.

Established in 1916 by an act of

Farm Credit Services provides credit and related financial services to farmers and cooperatives across Minnesota, Wisconsin, North Dakota, and Michigan.

Congress, the Farm Credit System is comprised of 12 districts. FCS is the nation's Seventh Farm Credit District, serving farmers and cooperatives in Minnesota, Wisconsin, North Dakota, and Michigan.

FCS offers midwestern farmers a full range of credit, including short, intermediate, and long-term loans. In addition, FCS offers insurance, tax-planning, record-keeping, and other financial services, fulfilling a philosophy of complete, convenient, and competitive service.

Twenty-three local FCS Service Centers—six of which are in Minnesota—are located throughout the district to best serve farmers and their needs. Each FCS Service Center is staffed by highly trained professionals and support personnel. An equally skilled staff can be found in each of FCS' eight Cooperative Credit offices, which provide credit and other financial

services to area cooperatives.

District policies and long-term strategic direction are set by FCS' seven-member board of farmer-directors, who meet regularly in St. Paul. The district's management and administrative functions also are performed at the St. Paul headquarters office, which currently is staffed by about 450 employees.

The Farm Credit System, on behalf of FCS and the 11 other Farm Credit districts, generates its funds through the sale of Farm Credit bonds and notes. The capital is used to help finance agriculture, a $700-billion industry employing 23 million people. Farm Credit Services, St. Paul, like the entire Farm Credit System, is committed to agriculture. Throughout its history, FCS' mission has remained constant: to serve the financial needs of farmers and rural America.

family's financial life not much different from that of a family doctor who examines, diagnoses, and prescribes.

If changes in the investment world have been breathtaking, for the casualty business the past ten years have been difficult, to say the very least. Rates were relatively uniform in the 1930s, but new state and federal laws, inflation, high interest rates, and court decisions created turmoil in the insurance market. Rates shot up, values of insured property escalated, and some insurance companies are either not renewing policies or not accepting new business.

If transportation, banking, warehousing, and insurance are among the foundations of St. Paul's economy, so is construction, one of the earliest of all the city's industries. The cabin erected in 1839 by Edward Phelan and John Hay below the present Kellogg Boulevard bluff near Eagle Street was St. Paul's first dwelling, but not for long. From 1850 to 1858 immigration into St. Paul was so heavy and hotels and boardinghouses so crowded that people slept in the streets. The city's early settlers built reasonably

Lighting, designed by Ellerbe Architects, illuminates the St. Paul Cathedral which rises above St. Paul. Photo by Shin Koyama. Courtesy, Ellerbe Associates, Inc.

serviceable and sturdy wood, limestone, and brick structures. However, not until German and Scandinavian carpenters, stone masons, woodcarvers, and other artisans began to pour into the state in the 1870s and 1880s did St. Paul begin to see fine construction and architectural work, some of which still stands in the downtown district and the older neighborhoods.

By the 1880s the building boom was on. Cass Gilbert, who would later design the Woolworth building in New York, the United States Supreme Court building in Washington, and the Minnesota State Capitol, and plan the University of Minnesota's mall, opened his office in down-

HARRIS MECHANICAL CONTRACTING COMPANY

For nearly 70 years Harris Mechanical Contracting Company has been an integral part of the building of St. Paul. A full-service mechanical contractor with capabilities in sheet metal, plumbing, heating, cooling, industrial piping, maintenance, fire protection, and service, Harris is a firm with a family heritage deeply rooted in the city that has always been its home.

Over the past few decades Harris has played an important role in the shaping and reshaping of the St. Paul skyline. Among notable projects in which the company has participated are the construction of the Amhoist Tower, the remodeling of Burlington Northern's headquarters and the St. Paul Athletic Club, the renovation of the historic St. Paul Hotel, and the development of Galtier

The board of directors of Harris Mechanical Contracting Company. From left (seated): Robert F. Hosch, president; Ronald Bierbaum; and Jerry C. Sandin. From left (standing): Gerald S. Mullenbach, Anthony E. Kammerer, William Marshall, and Dean T. Osland.

Plaza and Town Square.

Harris also has been involved in filling a wide range of new and expanded business construction needs for major corporations active in the city: American National Bank, Minnesota Mutual Life Insurance, Sperry, the Stroh Brewery, Western Life Insurance, West Publishing, and many projects at 3M. Its red-and-white trucks have become a familiar sight at the University of Minnesota, where Harris has been part of the work on the Animal Science Building, the Animal Holding Facility, and the Biological Science Center.

Other major contracts include Humboldt and Highland Park high schools, the Vocational Technical Institute, remodeling of the Pioneer Endicott and FOK office buildings, several Wilder Foundation projects, the state offices of the Department of Natural Resources, Block 7A, and the Lyngblomsted and Regency apartments.

Beyond the city's borders, Harris has been involved in a number of major projects: in Minneapolis, the headquarters of Lutheran Brotherhood Insurance Company and Abbott Northwestern, Fairview, and the University of Minnesota hospitals; in outstate Minnesota, IBM's facility in Rochester and the Hormel Meat Processing Plant in Austin.

Harris offers the skill and know-how necessary to install today's complex mechanical systems within strict financial controls and an experienced team of management and supervisory talent that allows it to handle even the largest and most specialized undertakings.

The company's "family" management is now in its third generation: founder Charles Harris was succeeded by his son and son-in-law; they in turn kept the firm in the unofficial family when they sold the business to several long-time employees in 1983.

The small business founded in St. Paul in 1918 has now grown to employ 300 people. With a branch office in Denver, Harris Mechanical Contracting Company now operates throughout the western United States, but the Twin Cities remain both home and center of most contracting activity.

NORWEST BANK ST. PAUL, N.A.

Banks traditionally bring a strong sense of community involvement to their daily business activities. Perhaps no bank in the city better exemplifies that tradition than Norwest Bank St. Paul, N.A., the state's sixth-largest bank and one of the largest institutions in the Norwest family throughout the Upper Midwest. From the Winter Carnival to summer's Taste of Minnesota, the growth of the downtown skyway system to the needs of growing businesses and families around the metro area, Norwest has been an involved and active participant in the life of the city.

When Norwest St. Paul, then known as the Northwestern National Bank of St. Paul, moved into its new offices at 55 East Fifth Street in 1969, it marked the opening of the first new building specifically designed for the city's innovative response to Minnesota weather: the skyway system. That the bank's new headquarters and office tower was in the heart of the city's financial district—on a site vacant since the fire that had consumed the old Frederic Hotel years before—was an important vote of confidence in the efforts to revive downtown St. Paul.

It was also a reaffirmation of Norwest's heritage as a downtown bank, a heritage that stretched back to its founding as the National Exchange Bank in St. Paul, the recapitalized successor to the National Exchange Bank of St. Paul, in 1926. The new institu-

tion's bloodlines also included the Scandinavian American Bank and the Peoples Bank. In 1929 the name was changed to the Empire National Bank. Although it was acquired by Northwest Bancorporation a year later, the Empire National name was used until 1959. In 1983, when Northwest Bancorporation became Norwest Corporation, the institution's official name became Norwest Bank St. Paul, National Association.

Today, in keeping with the far-sighted design of its main facility, Norwest St. Paul greets most of its customers in its large, open lobby on the skyway level. Special events join with a full range of banking services and other retail merchants along the skyway to make the Norwest Center an important downtown commercial address.

In its 60 years of service to the city, the bank has become known for its high level of civic involvement. When Dutch elm disease devastated many city neighborhoods in the late 1970s, Norwest St. Paul launched an ambitious "reforesting" project that distributed more than 36,000 free trees on Arbor Day. Since 1980 Norwest St. Paul employees have designed and built their own float—and always an award-winning float at

To meet the needs of its growing number of downtown customers, Norwest St. Paul's Skyway Banking Center was enlarged and refurbished.

that—for the Winter Carnival. Management and staff at all levels, specifically chairman Larry D. Buegler and president Richard A. Klingen, have been instrumental in the development of everything from the World Trade Center to the Taste of Minnesota Festival and the management of the 1985 United Way campaign.

At the same time, Norwest St. Paul has become one of the most successful institutions in the Norwest family, which now includes 77 commercial banks with more than 200 locations in seven states, ranking Norwest as the 21st-largest bank holding company in the nation. With assets of more than $500 million, and service locations in Maplewood and Arden Hills in addition to downtown, Norwest Bank St. Paul, N.A., is committed to playing an active and supportive role in St. Paul's future growth.

Norwest employees take their community spirit to the street each January with their own Winter Carnival float.

THEME AWARD

91

Above and left: *The capitol building, designed by Cass Gilbert, is characterized by its white Georgia marble dome which overlooks the entire city. Above photo by Kay Shaw; left photo by Herb Ferguson*

Following page: *Inside, the capitol is constructed of limestone, sandstone, granite, and more than twenty varieties of marble. Photo by Herb Ferguson*

handle small electric powerline jobs, became one of the largest electrical construction contractors in North America, moved into natural gas, and during World War II made hand grenades and built hemp mills and wooden submarine-chasers.

Ray Hoffman, who was selling Welsbach mantles for gaslights, looked ahead to the safety and convenience of electricity and founded the oldest electrical contracting company in St. Paul and one of the largest in the Midwest. Hoffman Electric has lighted highways 94 and 35E and the Metropolitan Waste Treatment Center in St. Paul. Joseph Shiely, Sr., a railroad timekeeper and roadmaster, went into the sand-and-gravel business with $1,000, fourteen horses, and seven wagons. The company he founded established St. Paul's first ready-mixed-concrete plant; built and operated eight plants for the Great Northern Railway, supplying ballast for the system and aggregates for the eight-mile Cascade Tunnel; and supplied 100 million cubic yards of fill for the huge Fort Peck dam, built in Montana in 1933. Now the Shiely Company concentrates on producing ready-mixed concrete and crushed stone for construction projects and it operates the "Irish Navy," a fleet of barges that carries aggregates from plants on Grey Cloud Island to other sites along the river.

There are others, many of them with roots deep in the nineteenth century—McGough Construction Company, which built the Ordway Music Theatre; George J. Grant Construction, which built James J. Hill's brooding stone mansion on Summit Avenue, then worked on its restoration 100 years later; Kraus-Anderson, which built Dayton's downtown St. Paul store and transformed Joseph L. Forepaugh's Victorian mansion in Irvine Park into an elegant restaurant; Butler Construction Company, which built the state capitol and the Federal Building on Robert.

These are among the companies that have turned the plans and dreams of St. Paul's leadership into the reality of billions of dollars'

town St. Paul. The Foleys—Timothy, Thomas, John, and Michael—who learned lumbering in Canada, went into the construction business. Their company, Foley Brothers, would build the St. Paul Cathedral, the present Union Depot, the Ramsey County Courthouse, and the Minneapolis-St. Paul International Airport terminal. George Donovan, who had been installing rural telephone lines, put together a company to

MINNESOTA MUTUAL LIFE INSURANCE COMPANY

In 1953 the Minnesota Mutual Life Insurance Company broke ground for a new headquarters building. A downtown St. Paul business since its founding in a one-room office at Third and Jackson in 1880, Minnesota Mutual took a step that would foreshadow the coming rebirth of development in the city: It decided to stay downtown. Its new headquarters at 345 Cedar (today the home of the *St. Paul Pioneer Press and Dispatch*), put an end to 25 years of minimal development in the central city, at the same time giving St. Paul its first fully air-conditioned building.

But that home office, moved into in 1955 as part of the firm's 75th-anniversary celebration, would very quickly prove inadequate. It wasn't that the location wasn't right, or the city not hospitable enough. Rather, Minnesota Mutual had embarked on a period of sustained growth that continues to this day. From slightly more than one billion dollars of insurance in force in 1953, Minnesota's largest life insurance company surpassed the $64-billion mark in 1985, in the process serving more than 10 million people nationwide.

By the late 1970s, then, the company once again faced the need for expanded headquarters offices, and with it an important

Excitement prevailed as employees marched to the ground-breaking ceremonies for the second headquarters building at 345 Cedar Street in St. Paul.

Russell R. Dorr, who founded the insurance firm in a one-room office at Third and Jackson in 1880.

decision about its future location. Once again, the answer was emphatically downtown St. Paul. The Minnesota Mutual Life Center at Sixth and Robert—just a few blocks from the first one-room base of operations—was designed as the firm's home for its second century. It opened in 1982: a striking, 21-story, $40-million addition to downtown St. Paul, totally financed by Minnesota Mutual, that links Lowertown with Town Square and the financial district.

More than 1,400 people are employed in the headquarters complex, another 125 at the satellite Lafayette Service Center, located across the river about two miles away on Florida Street. They are at the heart of an organization that also includes some 70 group sales representatives in 26 major metropolitan areas, more than 1,000 independent insurance agents who represent Minnesota Mutual insurance and investment products, and a subsidiary, MIMLIC (Minnesota Mutual Life Insurance Company) Asset Management Company, which offers investment management services.

Minnesota Mutual's insurance products fall into three broad categories: insurance for individuals, group insurance, and pension plans. Since 1984 Minnesota Mutual also has operated in affiliation with Minneapolis-based Minnesota

Mutual Fire and Casualty Company.

Insurance has changed immeasurably in the century since Russell R. Dorr and eight St. Paul businessmen first met to make plans for the Bankers Association of Minnesota. Originally the company operated on an assessment basis—charging yearly dues and assessing its members whenever a death claim needed to be paid.

By the turn of the century, however, fixed-premium insurance policies had begun to replace assessments. In 1901 an act of the Minnesota Legislature authorized the change to a mutual company that would be owned by its policy-owners, and Minnesota Mutual was adopted by the trustees as the firm's new name.

By 1917 the business had entered the group policy field, covering the 132 employees of McGill, Warner and Company of St. Paul, and had also begun insuring women who had their own source of income. In 1930 it designed its first pension plan, developed for faculty members at the University of Minnesota. Insurance in force reached the billion-dollar mark by 1953, and three years later Minnesota Mutual purchased its first computer—so great an object of curiosity that it was housed behind a glass wall so employees and visitors could see it in operation.

In more recent years innovation has been a prime ingredient in the company's growth. In the late 1950s Minnesota Mutual began providing group mortgage life insurance. Today more than 3,000 financial institutions offer the firm's coverage, and Minnesota Mutual is the largest mortgage life insurer in the country. In the 1960s Minnesota Mutual pioneered the use of direct mail to make it easier for home owners to apply for insurance coverage. In the 1970s the company introduced Joint Life insurance policies for families with two home owners. The 1980s have brought the addi-

The striking 21-story Minnesota Mutual Life Center at Sixth and Robert, just a few blocks from its roots, was occupied by the firm in 1982.

tion of four mutual funds and more varied insurance and retirement-oriented investment products.

It was Minnesota Mutual that introduced the insurance industry's first Adjustable Life policy in 1971, nearly 10 years before flexible life insurance became a mainstay of personal insurance coverage. Through the use of computers, this form of coverage can be readily changed to meet changing personal needs.

Over the years Minnesota Mutual's people, executives and employees alike, have played an important role in the life of St. Paul. Harold J. Cummings, who guided the company for nearly 30 years, earned the nickname "Mr. St. Paul" for his many civic contributions. Walter Rupert and Franklin Briese played their parts in the rebirth of the city, and current chairman of the board and president Coleman Bloomfield, who joined the firm as an assistant actuary in 1952, has been active in the Minnesota Business Partnership and the Ordway Theatre.

The firm also has been an active supporter of the concept of art in the work environment. Employee representatives from each floor in the headquarters tower were involved in selecting the various forms of painting and sculpture in their work areas. Most of the works were commissioned for specific spaces in the building, often using artists native to or familiar with the Twin Cities. Because the building is designed around a central core, with a minimum of interior walls and places to hang traditional art forms, many of the works chosen are suspended from the ceiling or placed on work station partitions.

In 1985, based on the participation of more than 150 employees

from all parts and levels of the firm, Minnesota Mutual Life Insurance Company adopted a Corporate Plan of Action, "The Vision Is Ours," designed to serve as a working guideline for its future. It lays out ambitious and impressive goals, and proposes the strategies to achieve them. Equally important, this "vision statement," developed through the active involvement of Minnesota Mutual's employees, speaks to the values and fundamental character of the company that has grown to be numbered in the top one percent of all U.S. life insurance firms, but without outgrowing the principles of that homegrown business begun in a small office in downtown St. Paul more than 100 years ago.

TOLTZ, KING, DUVALL, ANDERSON AND ASSOCIATES, INC.

TKDA's renovation of the Pioneer-Endicott Building included removing each piece of two 240-foot skylights that had been painted over, cleaning them individually, and reinstalling them in their original positions.

Toltz, King, Duvall, Anderson and Associates, Inc. (TKDA), is a multidisciplinary engineering and architectural design firm established in 1910. The firm offers the public and private sectors a broad range of services in planning, design, and construction administration. Since its beginning the St. Paul-based company has continued to grow and expand on its reputation as a designer of high-quality, built-to-last facilities.

TKDA offers complete consulting services to its clients. The firm's range of services include all phases of a project from the initial planning through the design and construction. Throughout the design process, value engineering and life cycle cost analysis play a major role in determining what clients will receive for the total construction cost. To meet project schedule, cost, and quality objectives, TKDA also offers state-of-the-art technology with a Computer Aided Design and Drafting (CADD) System, which enables the

company to produce very accurate drawings of complex structures and systems on full-size, detailed, dimensional engineering drawings.

In St. Paul, TKDA has played a key role in many local projects through the years. Among the familiar city landmarks designed by the firm are the Como Park Conservatory, the Hamms Building, the Griggs-Midway Building, and the Robert Street Bridge.

In more recent years TKDA has served the City of St. Paul as consultant engineer on numerous projects and has added to the growth and restoration of the city. The Port Authority commissioned TKDA to design the Central Heating and Cooling Plant for the St. Paul Energy Park. The facility utilizes heat pumps to extract energy from groundwater to provide heat and cooling for more than three million feet of building area. Playing a part in preserving historic downtown St. Paul, TKDA managed the renovation of the Pioneer-Endicott Building. It is the unique design of facilities such as these that has demonstrated the company's ability and has resulted in many state and national design awards.

Commercial and industrial clients

based in the Upper Midwest have added to the firm's repertoire of experience. Companies such as 3M, IBM, NSP, General Mills, Honeywell, Nash Finch, Kraft, and SuperAmerica have and still do retain TKDA to provide design services for warehouses, manufacturing space, laboratories, research centers, offices, and food-processing facilities.

The firm has long been noted for its civil engineering accomplishments with special expertise in public works facilities including airports, bridges, highways, and municipal water and wastewater systems.

Because TKDA is wholly owned by its professional employees, the firm brings a high level of personal involvement to its work. Its diverse staff includes architects; planners; civil, mechanical, electrical, environmental, and agricultural engineers; landscape architects; construction administrators; and surveyors. Backed by more than three-quarters of a century of experience throughout the region, Toltz, King, Duvall, Anderson and Associates, Inc., has grown from a small engineering practice into St. Paul's largest consulting engineering firm.

For St. Paul's high-tech-oriented Energy Park, TKDA's Central Energy Plant design provides hot water to heat commercial, industry, and residential buildings in winter, and chilled water to cool them in summer.

FIRST BANK SYSTEM

Over the past three decades the people and businesses of First Bank System have been intimately involved in the continuing rebirth of St. Paul. From the personal concern for the community exemplified by Philip Nason, a former president of First Bank Saint Paul, to the diverse financial services provided to the city and its residents by the firm's many subsidiaries and affiliated banks, First Bank System has been and remains a premier financial services organization and an important resource to the city of St. Paul.

A highly successful network of more than 75 banks and trust companies in seven states, First Bank System is among the top 15 bank holding companies in the United States: a company with national scope, yet with an abiding concern for meeting the needs of the individual communities it serves. It operates nearly 150 banking offices in Minnesota, North and South Dakota, Montana, Washington, and Wisconsin; a trust company in Florida; and a number of domestic and international subsidiaries and facilities. Its full range of financial services includes not only commercial banking and trust operations, but also

After 10 years of darkness, the landmark 50-foot 1st sign on top of First Bank Saint Paul—first lighted in 1931—was relighted in 1983.

agricultural finance, international banking, insurance brokerage, mortgage banking, leasing, data processing, venture capital, merchant banking, and discount brokerage.

In addition to the offices of First Bank Saint Paul, the firm's presence in the city includes the offices of First Trust, FBS Information Services, FBS Mortgage Corporation Residential, FBS Services, Inc., and the banking offices of First Bank Grand, First Bank East, First Bank Security, and First Bank White Bear Lake. More than 2,800 of First Bank System's 9,600 employees are based in the St. Paul area.

The most familiar evidence of First Bank System's presence in the city is First Bank Saint Paul's downtown building. With total assets approaching six billion dollars, First Bank Saint Paul is the city's largest commercial bank and the second-largest bank in First Bank System—a strong financial resource to people and businesses throughout the region.

Since its founding in 1853, the institution has been a major participant in the city's growth. In recent years that commitment has included support of Lowertown redevelopment and riverfront activity, transit systems, youth development, and child care. Financing for the renovation of the World Theater, home of "A Prairie Home Companion";

First Trust is housed in James J. Hill's newly refurbished Railroad Building that has been renamed First Trust Center.

the beautiful Ordway Music Theatre; and the new Lowertown studios of Twin Cities Public Television was provided by the bank.

In addition, the downtown offices of First Trust (a 1986 consolidation of First Trust Company, Inc., in St. Paul and the trust operations of First Bank Minneapolis) represent one of the 20 largest trust operations in the country. FBS Services, Inc., has also consolidated formerly separate Minneapolis and St. Paul check-processing operations in St. Paul, representing First Bank System's continually growing presence in the city.

Since 1979 the FBS Foundation and the First Banks have contributed more than $30 million to the communities they serve, backed by the enthusiastic personal involvement of employees and executives alike. As a business, and as a good corporate citizen, coming in first is a hallmark of First Bank System.

Above: *F. Scott Fitzgerald lived in this house, at 599 Summit Avenue, in the summer of 1919, while revising the manuscript of* This Side of Paradise. *Fitzgerald was born in St. Paul and lived in a variety of homes. This house is now a historic site. Photo by Kay Shaw*

Right: *Designed by Cass Gilbert and James Knox Taylor, this elegant Queen Anne style residence illustrates the graceful styles of architecture situated along the winding tree-lined streets of Macalester Park. Photo by Kay Shaw*

Left: *New construction in St. Paul's historic Irvine Park captures architectural imagery reminiscent of earlier styles. The park, which is surrounded by many restored homes—some predating the Civil War—lies just minutes west of the central business district. Photo by Kay Shaw*

Below: *These restored Victorian apartments are examples of the historic restoration taking place throughout the city. Courtesy, St. Paul Convention Bureau*

Architect Thomas Ellerbe, Sr., was behind several of St. Paul's developments. Courtesy, Ellerbe Associates, Inc.

worth of redevelopment all over St. Paul's metropolitan area. The construction boom in the city's downtown is evident in the housing figures alone. Between 1980 and 1984 construction of apartments and condominiums had increased from 1,768 to 2,453 units, indicating the progress that is being made in re-creating a downtown residential community. Downtown restaurants and bars grew from fifty-three in 1979 to seventy-five in 1984; auditorium and theater seats increased from 30,408 to 33,853, figures that do not include the Ordway Music Theatre or the newly restored World Theater; hotel rooms went from 787 to 1,384. Since 1979, 1.4 million square feet of leasable floor space have been added as the result of renovation or new construction.

Between 1981 and 1984 almost 470 single-family units were built throughout the city, and 2,098 were rehabilitated with eight million dollars in low-interest and deferred loans. A little more than three million dollars was used to rehabilitate 817 rental units.

Although architects of national renown, such as Ben Thompson and Skidmore, Owings & Merrill, have designed several of the city's significant structures, many projects have been designed and guided by St. Paul architects, a number of whom are fellows in the American Institute of Architects, an honor that recognizes professional achievement. Among them are W. Brooks Cavin, Clark Wold, Bernard Jacob, Louis Lundgren, George Rafferty, Richard T. Faricy, Lloyd Bergquist, and Tom Ellerbe, Sr., dean of the St. Paul architects.

The construction industry is closely linked to real estate, another cornerstone of St. Paul's economy. The first of Minnesota's great real estate booms was the result of the critical lack of housing in the 1850s, coupled with the wild speculation in land that gripped many frontier towns. Henry McKenty was one of the more successful of St. Paul's speculators during that period. He bought several thousand acres of land in Washington County for $1.25 an acre and sold them the next year for five dollars an acre. For many land speculators on the cash-poor frontier, the need for working capital was acute. At one point McKenty was offering 42 percent interest a year.

By the 1880s St. Paul's real estate community in a very real sense was a driving force behind the growth of the city. This was the period when real estate boards were being established in cities throughout the country in an effort to regularize the activities of the McKentys of that era. Joining with the major forces in their communities, this new breed of real estate men helped attract investors to their projects, persuaded local governments to upgrade streets, and convinced streetcar companies and commuter railroads to extend their lines.

Real estate promoters were behind much of the expansion of St. Paul beyond its downtown core: William R. Marshall and St. Anthony Park; Colonel John Merriam and Merriam Park; Thomas Cochrane, joining with Archbishop John Ireland and Macalester College's trustees to create Macalester Park. To link Macalester, the St. Paul Seminary, and St. Thomas College to the downtown, they helped Tom Lowry build the city's first electric streetcar line along Grand Avenue. By 1900 the city's structure with its distinctive neighborhoods and their commercial and business districts was established, and much of that fabric remains.

For today's realtors, their profession may be

THE GILLETTE COMPANY

The St. Paul Manufacturing Center of The Gillette Company is one of the most productive and successful operations of that well-known, international consumer products firm. The manufacturing plant and distribution center is also, in its own way, a St. Paul landmark—more than 850,000 square feet of work space occupying the equivalent of almost four city blocks at East Fifth Street and Broadway on the eastern edge of the downtown.

More than 700 employees run the production lines and supporting operations that produce such familiar products as White Rain hair spray, Dry Idea antiperspirants, Silkience shampoo and conditioner, Foamy shaving cream, Adorn hair spray, Liquid Paper correction fluids, and Toni home permanent kits.

The story begins with Toni, the home permanent wave launched in 1944 by R.N.W. "Neison" Harris, a St. Paul cosmetics salesman. In 1941 Harris was selling supplies to beauty shops when the "cold wave" method of curling hair was introduced. Prior waving methods involved the use of heat. (Cleopatra, according to Toni lore, rolled her hair around twigs, plastered her head with mud from the Nile River delta, then lay in the sun until the mud had baked and a hairdresser could chip it away to reveal the curls that so captivated Mark Antony.) Harris recognized that the new method was simple enough to be used at home—and a national phenomenon was born.

His brother Irving soon joined him in the new company, whose name was derived from the word "toney," a popular term for quality in the 1940s. To keep pace with demand, the small St. Paul plant ran around the clock, with workers mixing the solutions in large stone crocks and corking the filled bottles by hand. The business grew rapidly, from regional to national, national to international markets, and one of America's

More than 700 employees run the production lines and support operations that manufacture the familiar Gillette products.

classic advertising campaigns was launched with the enduring themeline: "Which twin has the Toni?" In 1948 the Harrises sold the firm to what was then the Gillette Safety Razor Company—for $20 million.

Gillette today is a $2.4-billion international leader in the manufacture and sale of personal care products, with nearly 60 manufacturing facilities in 27 countries. The corporation has continued to invest in its St. Paul operations, from initial construction to continuing upgrades and modernization of equipment.

The 660,000-square-foot manufacturing center, originally constructed in 1969, is the largest single, privately financed construction project ever developed in the city of St. Paul. In addition to the mixing and filling operations for shampoos, conditioners, skin creams, home permanents, hair sprays, deodorants, correction fluids, and other products, the St. Paul plant also molds and manufactures the plastic containers used for many of the products. The 180,000-square-foot warehousing and distribution center in

Occupying almost four city blocks on the eastern edge of the downtown area in the St. Paul Manufacturing Center, The Gillette Company plant produces a wide range of personal care products.

the complex assures that the nearly 100 different Gillette products made in St. Paul move efficiently to distributors and store shelves throughout the region.

For its part, the St. Paul center—many of whose employees are represented by the Oil Chemical & Atomic Workers and International Association of Machinists unions—can take justifiable pride in remaining one of the most efficient and productive of The Gillette Company's operations worldwide.

more complex, but presumably it is not quite so adventurous. The St. Paul Board of Realtors lists 1,850 members doing business through 258 companies. But the strongest force on St. Paul's real estate scene is the Port Authority of the City of St. Paul, a quasi-governmental body created by the state legislature in 1929 at the request of the St. Paul City Council. The purpose of the authority was to develop the river bottomlands and river commerce at a time when commerce had declined almost to the point of nonexistence. St. Paul's first industrial park was Red Rock Industrial Park, several miles downriver from downtown St. Paul. In 1957 the Port Authority was granted permission by the state legislature to develop industrial parks throughout the city itself. A series of projects followed, among them Riverview Industrial Park across the river from the downtown and the Southport-Anapolis project on the river south of Holman Field.

Some of these projects meant massive relocations of families who were living on land that was considered marginal because of repeated flooding by the Mississippi. For the Riverview project, more than 2,700 people were relocated. The Port Authority spent $5.7 million to acquire the land and nine million dollars to dredge some three million cubic yards of fill from the river and install sewers, water mains, railroad trackage, and other improvements. The United States Corps of Engineers and the city built a flood wall that ran from Smith Avenue downstream to the airport.

The Port Authority's impact on St. Paul's real estate development has been particularly astonishing in the past decade, when it has been responsible for more than a billion dollars worth of new construction. At least three-quarters of the new building projects around the city have been accomplished with Port Authority help, according to Eugene Kraut, the Port Authority's vice-president and general manager. The list is impressive: the Radisson parking ramp at Town Square, the Saint Paul Hotel, the Amhoist Tower,

Galtier Plaza, the Embassy Suites Hotel, the Ordway Music Theatre and Energy Park. As of 1985 its assets had more than doubled to 500 million dollars.

A 1984 study of Port Authority projects, conducted by the Midwest Research Institute, indicated that between 1980 and 1983 Port Authority activity had created almost 12,000 jobs and produced a billion dollars in increased business activity. An additional 203 million dollars was generated by Port Authority investments in new plants. Around 14 percent of the jobs in St. Paul stemmed from Port Authority property, a 5 percent increase over 1980. Nearly all (97 percent) of the job growth the city experienced in the almost twenty years since 1967 came from authority projects, the study revealed.

The ripple effect of expanding business activity can be seen in a variety of areas. For instance, retail sales in downtown St. Paul were up 7 percent between 1977 and 1982, according to United States census data reported by the Metropolitan Council. After ten years of stagnation, downtown sales topped 97 million dollars in 1982, the last year for which figures are available. In all of St. Paul, sales reached more than $1.3 billion. Retail sales figures for Ramsey County were $2.6 billion, up 52.8 percent over 1977.

Midway Shopping Center led other retail centers in St. Paul and Ramsey County, with more than 222 million dollars in sales in 1982. Next was Rosedale, with 205 million dollars. Rosedale, however, was up 131 million dollars over 1977, while Midway had increased by 100 million dollars. They are among eleven major retail centers in the greater St. Paul area, not including downtown St. Paul. Others are Har Mar, Highland, Hillcrest, Maplewood, Midway East, Phalen, Signal Hills, Southview-South Robert, and Sun Ray. St. Paul has other important retail and commercial centers, including Grand Avenue and Highland Village, as well as commercial strips along East and West Seventh streets (Fort Road).

THE PEDRO COMPANIES

At age 17 he made shoes in Calabria, Italy. By the time of his death in 1975 at the age of 84, Carl Pedro, Sr., had made a place in St. Paul history. The leather repair business he founded in the city in 1914, six years after his arrival in the United States, had grown to occupy most of a city block at 10th and Robert streets in downtown St. Paul. The PEDRO Companies today are a diversified combination of retailing, manufacturing, and distributing operations involving luggage, business cases, industrial cases, sports cases, and accessories.

Pedro customers enjoy savings, selection and style—plus the personalized red carpet treatment Pedro's is known for.

Tenth and Robert has been home since 1966, when Carl Pedro, Sr.'s, growing business expanded into the former Dayton's warehouse. The growth in the business was mirrored in the involvement of his family: All four children of Carl and Mary became active in Carl Pedro & Sons, Inc. The children continued the business after their father's death, reincorporating in 1983 the eight different divisions of the family business under one name: The PEDRO Companies.

The 7,500-square-foot retail store and factory outlet on the Robert Street side of the company complex is undoubtedly the most familiar part of the business. PEDRO Luggage of St. Paul serves a five-state region with the firm's own factory-direct line of luggage, business and industrial cases, and

sports cases. In addition, the retail store stocks many nationally and internationally known lines of name-brand luggage and a unique collection of handbags, wallets, and leather accessories, including some by famous designers.

Behind the store are the quarters of PEDRO Manufacturing,

Colorful flags from around the world welcome visitors to Pedro's international collection of fine leather goods, travelware, and business cases.

where modern technology and Old World craftsmanship are combined to create cases developed to individual specifications. Every PEDRO case is cut, glued, sanded, covered, sewn, or molded in the company's 100,000-square-foot manufacturing and warehousing complex, in some cases using equipment designed by Alfred Pedro, one of Carl Sr.'s sons. PEDRO Manufacturing is one of the very few luggage factories in the country that maintains its own in-house workshop and vacuum forming department to assure quality control from start to finish.

Several specialty manufacturing operations have developed over the years. PEDRO Industrial, which began as a multipurpose and catalog case supplier, has grown to include custom cases and carts for tools, printed circuit boards, and electronic instruments. Sea'n Air Business & Travel Cases

originated as an advertising specialty division; its business and travel cases are now sold through retail outlets and used as premiums, incentives, and gifts for business and industrial customers. Gun-Ho Sports Cases are designed for the special needs of hunters and sports shooters who

desire top-quality transport cases for their firearms and archery equipment.

PEDRO Luggage Repair and Replacement Specialists began in 1938 as an airline bag repair service. Today it is nationally known as a leader in professional bag repairs. PEDRO, The Casemaker, is the firm's national mail-order division catering to the needs of the professional. And PMC Advertising operates as a full-service, in-house agency for the corporation.

Through all the growth and diversification, The PEDRO Companies have held on to Carl Pedro, Sr.'s, lifelong commitment to superior workmanship and personal customer service.

Right: *The Farwell, Ozmun and Kirk building, pictured here circa 1906, was located adjacent to the railroad lines and the Lower Landing, pictured in the foreground. Courtesy, MHS*

Below, left: *For almost twenty years prior to his arrival in St. Paul, Daniel Ingersoll operated mercantile businesses in the eastern United States. But in 1855 he moved west, settling in St. Paul where he opened a business that was the forerunner of Field-Schlick, once a well-known department store. Courtesy, MHS*

Below right: *D.D. Merrill managed this store for fifty years since it opened in a log cabin in 1851. Courtesy, MHS*

It's somewhat of a far cry from the day in 1859 when two men named Cheritree and Farwell arrived in St. Paul from Boston and opened a small hardware store on Third Street, near the site today of the St. Paul Public Library. In 1868 their store became Farwell Brothers, the main source of hardware for settlers arriving in Minnesota. The Farwells prospered. In 1887 the company was incorporated as Farwell, Ozmun and Kirk. Today F.O.K. is a subsidiary of American Hoist and Derrick.

Daniel Ingersoll arrived in St. Paul in 1855 to open a dry goods store at Third and Wabasha. In his kerosene-lighted store Ingersoll sold cloth, thread, and shoes that came in small, medium, and large and were identical for both left and right feet. As partners came and went, the store's name changed to Ingersoll and Mahler, Ingersoll and Field, Field and Mahler, and, finally, in 1898, to Field-Schlick, a men's and women's clothing store that remained in business for more than eighty years.

D.D. Merrill sold notions, books, twine, and wrapping paper from a log cabin store he opened in 1851 across today's Kellogg Boulevard from the downtown Radisson Hotel. Merrill, who managed the store for almost fifty years, expanded his business into alloyed zinc pens (which he invented), then to school desks ($2.90 each), folding chairs (65 cents), and desks (nine dollars). His little store became St. Paul Book and Stationery.

These were some of the pioneer predecessors of the close to 15,000 employers in St. Paul's downtown district who by the 1980s were providing jobs for the more than 42,000 men and women who work there, according to the 1984 Downtown Survey Report of the city's Department of Planning and Economic Development. More than half work in a twenty-four-block area bounded by Eighth Street, Jackson, Kellogg Boulevard, and St. Peter, where Ingersoll and Merrill and Farwell also set up their shops. Of those men and women employed downtown, almost 10,000 work for city, county, state, and federal government; another 10,000 for service organizations, such as hotels, hospitals, law firms, museums, bars, restaurants; and almost 9,000 for financial, insurance, and real estate firms. Seven thousand are in manufacturing, 3,000 in retailing; another 3,000 in transportation; 200 in wholesaling, and 34 in construction and agriculture.

In the downtown district, the finance, insurance, and real estate sector, the survey points out, has an interesting record—a decline in the number of employees but more than an 18 percent increase in the number of jobs available, nearly three-fourths of them in the banking industry. These are figures that undoubtedly would have pleased Charles W.W. Borup, Parker Paine, and the Willius brothers.

Throughout Ramsey County more than 9,000 men and women work in construction; almost 11,000 in transportation, communications, and public utilities, not including the railroads; more than 58,000 in wholesaling and retailing; 16,000-plus in finance, insurance, and real estate; and nearly 39,000 in government.

Shoppers today frequent the convenient Midway Center. Photo by Kay Shaw

ST. PAUL: A MODERN RENAISSANCE

Autumn sunlight casts striking silhouettes and shadows in Como Park. Photo by Kay Shaw

Springtime in Mears Park. Photo by Leighton

Above: *Visitors and downtown employees enjoy leisurely lunches in St. Paul's Rice Park. Courtesy, St. Paul Convention Bureau*

Left: *Sunrise dances through ice crystals flaring a brilliant sun dog above a wintry skyline. Photo by Rosemary Palmer*

THE NEWCOMERS

For Minnesota, the computer age dawned in St. Paul a year after the end of World War II, marking a shift away from manufacturing heavy industrial and agricultural products to high-technology electronic products. Together, computer manufacturing and medical technology have placed Minnesota and the Twin Cities in the forefront of today's technological, economic, and social revolution.

In September 1985 *Corporate Report Minnesota* magazine ranked, according to the size of their 1984 revenues, Minnesota's "top 100" high-technology companies—those who had their corporate headquarters

Though 3M has been in St. Paul since 1910, it has grown from a small company manufacturing Scotch tape to one of the state's top 100 high-tech companies. Pictured is the Health Care Research Lab Cafeteria. Photo by Shin Koyama. Courtesy, Ellerbe Associates, Inc.

Right: *Sperry's Shepard Road plant is just one of many Sperry facilities located in the Twin City area. Photo by Kay Shaw*

Below: *Elmer A. Sperry, inventor of the gyroscope, founded a company in 1910 that merged with Remington Rand in 1955. Courtesy, Cirker's* Dictionary of American Portraits

in the state and who manufactured or assembled computer hardware, software, and precision electronic equipment, or worked with implantable medical devices, microbiology, and membrane technology. Seventeen of the top 100 were in St. Paul and its suburbs.

Three of Minnesota's, and the nation's, giants among these manufacturers of high-tech products are multinational firms with St. Paul roots: Minnesota Mining and Manufacturing (3M), Control Data, and Sperry. Two of these three—Control Data and Sperry—share a common past.

Although Sperry's story traces back to 1873 through a series of mergers—most notably with Remington Rand—it is linked, as is Control Data, to the invention of the world's first elec-

tronic computer in 1946, a significant year. The computer industry that has so revolutionized the workplace and helped to transform America into a service-oriented nation is to some extent the beneficiary of World War II espionage, as well as war-born needs for sophisticated processing of such information as how to calculate artillery trajectories.

A group of mathematicians and engineers who had been working for the United States Navy on super-secret intelligence assignments banded together as the war ended to form Engineering Research Associates (ERA). With financing from outside investors, ERA's researchers began work in the fall of 1946 in a building on Prior and Minnehaha in St. Paul's Midway district. Their worksite had been a foundry, warehouse, and wartime glider plant. The skylights in its high ceilings were opened and closed by an antiquated system of pulleys. When it rained, ERA's engineers were drenched before they managed to close the skylights.

Despite the less-than-ideal working conditions, ERA developed a computer system called "Atlas." Within two years ERA had delivered two electronic computers to the Navy and the Georgia Institute of Technology. These were not the first, however. In Philadelphia, J. Presper

MULTI-ARC

Multi-Arc is an excellent example of successful new businesses emerging in the high-tech era. Since its modest beginnings as a St. Paul venture capital start-up in 1980, Multi-Arc has quickly established itself as the world leader in surface enhancement technology. As a principal division of Andal Corp., a growing and diversified American Stock Exchange company located in New York, Multi-Arc serves a large number of industries with metallurgical coatings. These thin-films enhance the hardness, extend the wear, improve the appearance, and increase the corrosion resistance of substrate metals and other materials.

In the patented Ion Bond® process used by Multi-Arc, multiple cathodic arcs evaporate solid titanium into a vapor that reacts within a vacuum chamber to coat a substrate with an extremely hard, long-wearing titanium nitride film. The process is called physical vapor deposition, or PVD, and can also be used to apply a wide variety of other coatings to products.

Cutting tools, such as the dies used in the automotive industry, which are coated in this manner last from three to 10 times longer than tools without the protective coating, yet the improved wear and longer life is obtained at a fraction of the replacement cost of uncoated tools. As a result, PVD coatings are proving cost effective for a growing array of products, from drill bits and military hardware to wristwatches and household faucets.

In addition, Multi-Arc specializes in other coating technologies known as CVD or CVI—chemical vapor deposition and chemical vapor infiltration. CVD/CVI uses a combination of high temperatures and low pressures to form protective coatings for a variety of surfaces or porous substrates, including metals, ceramics, and advanced composite materials. CVI deposited coatings are especially

Multi-Arc's two-meter PVD coating system, which is capable of coating items up to 80 inches in length, 20 inches in diameter, and weighing up to 2,200 pounds.

important for new generation materials, such as those used in aircraft engine parts that operate at very high temperatures.

The St. Paul headquarters of Multi-Arc, consisting of a research center, manufacturing facility, and coating center, is now the hub of a growing network of coating operations and research ventures worldwide. Multi-Arc operates regional coating centers in the United States and Canada, where customers send materials for coating treatment. Multi-Arc also builds and

sells PVD and CVD/CVI coating systems directly to major customers worldwide in the automotive, aerospace, defense, and materials industries. These complete in-house systems enable customers to coat and recoat materials at their own plant sites. To service R & D and small-scale industrial applications, Multi-Arc manufactures smaller configurations of its coating systems.

Extensive research in thin-film coatings is carried on at the St. Paul laboratory as well as through innovative joint ventures with two major international partners:

Siemens/Interatom of West Germany and Sumitomo Metal and Mining of Japan. In addition, a joint-venture effort of Siemens and Multi-Arc operates coating centers

Composite of wear parts, cutting and forming tools, molds, and decorative items coated by the patented Multi-Arc Ion Bond® PVD system.

in West Germany, the United Kingdom, France, and Spain, while licensed coating centers are operated in Japan (by Sumitomo) and India.

Multi-Arc is now well positioned to not only manufacture coating systems, but also to increase its technological lead and market share in the rapidly expanding field of surface enhancement.

Eckert and John Mauchly had designed ENIAC (Electronic Numerical Integrator and Calculator), a huge electronic computer that was the first of its kind in the world. It had been built for the United States Navy to solve ballistics problems.

In 1950 Remington Rand purchased the Eckert-Mauchly Computer Corporation. Two years later ERA's investors, hampered by a lack of working capital, sold the company to Remington Rand, and its computer models became part of the UNIVAC series. By 1955 Remington Rand had merged with Sperry, founded in 1910 by Elmer A. Sperry, inventor of the gyroscope and other pioneering navigation instruments.

In 1986 Sperry was acquired by the Detroit-based computer-maker, Burroughs Corporation. The $4.8-billion acquisition by Burroughs is expected to propel the combined Burroughs-Sperry operation to the second spot in worldwide computer revenues, after IBM. Like Sperry, the new company will focus on commercial computers and defense systems. The Twin Cities are the headquarters for Burroughs' seventeen-state North Central region.

While Sperry's corporate headquarters reside in Pennsylvania, its business units are positioned around the country. One such unit, Defense Products Group, is headquartered in the St. Paul suburb of Eagan with a large manufacturing facility in St. Paul. Large-scale computers and their components are manufactured by Information Systems Product and Technology in Roseville, Brooklyn Center, Eagan, and out-state Jackson. A regional reclamation center and an air-traffic operation are located in Mendota Heights. Sperry is Minnesota's fourth-largest industrial employer. With most of Sperry's employees living and working in St. Paul and the surrounding area, the Twin Cities have the largest concentration of Sperry employees in the world.

When ERA was sold in 1952, Remington Rand agreed to let its small band of research associates remain in St. Paul. Among them was William C. Norris, a former Nebraska farm boy

who had been a sales engineer for Westinghouse. Assigned to Naval Intelligence after the bombing of Pearl Harbor, Norris helped found ERA when the war ended. He and his colleagues stayed on with Sperry-Rand, Norris as vice-president and general manager of computer operations. It was a restless association. In 1957 Norris and several of his key engineers left to form Control Data Corporation (CDC). It was a pattern that would repeat itself in the next decades as other computer pioneers, some of them members of the old ERA group, continued to split off and form and re-form, as they developed their own companies in the Twin Cities area, sometimes with the help of their peers in the profession. One of them was Seymour R.

A solar collector skylight atop the atrium and custom-designed computer software that regulates the energy system are just a few of the high-tech features of Control Data's Energy Technology Center located in St. Paul's new Energy Park development. Courtesy, Control Data

Cray, who founded Cray Research, based in Mendota, in 1972.

CDC rented an old warehouse in downtown Minneapolis and began a growth-by-acquisition policy. Again, circumstances were right. The computer industry's early years were characterized by small, privately owned companies established by a designer/inventor or a small group of talented engineers, mathematicians, or salesmen and financed by private investors dazzled by the possibilities of the new technology. To some extent and on a larger scale this pattern can still be seen today. The computer industry may be the last bastion of the visionary who becomes his own entrepreneur, a pattern common during the nineteenth and early twenti-

eth centuries when a corporation's identity was its leader.

Control Data's early contracts were with the Navy. Its strategy was to concentrate on giant computers—its first system, the fully transistorized CDC 1604 was announced in 1958—and it has continued to do so from its Bloomington headquarters, built in 1962.

Under Norris's leadership, Control Data took a number of interesting excursions into other arenas, based on his deeply held belief that the purpose of business was to address society's unmet needs. CDC thus pioneered employee-assistance programs, flex time, and business "incubation" centers where small-business owners could find office space and services to help them get started. To make jobs more accessible to minority workers, CDC built plants in two inner-city locations, on Selby Avenue in St. Paul and in north Minneapolis.

CDC's major business continues to be the production of some of the most powerful computer systems in the world. Due to Control Data, to ETA Systems—a new Control Data affiliate located in St. Paul's Energy Park—and to Cray Research, Minnesota is likely to become the supercomputer center of America. With their high-performance machines, Control Data and Cray Research dominate the supercomputer industry in the United States, and Cray is the leader with its newer, faster machines.

Energy Technology Assistance, or ETA, was founded by a group of former Control Data executives who helped develop CDC's supercomputer, the Cyber 205. The Twin Cities' super-

SPERRY BURROUGHS

Forty years ago Engineering Research Associates (ERA) introduced the computer age to the Twin Cities. The new company, made up of former Navy mathematicians and engineers, moved into an old glider factory in St. Paul in 1946. There they pioneered many of the world's first significant computer-related inventions. At a time when most computers worked only in theory, ERA engineered, built, and delivered the most reliable machines in the industry.

Today, in a new technological age, Sperry in Minnesota is continuing ERA's commitment to quality, reliability, performance, and innovation. Sperry acquired ERA in its 1955 merger with Remington Rand and consolidated it into the first UNIVAC division. Sperry has since become one of Minnesota's largest employers, merging with Burroughs in 1986 to form the world's second-largest computer company.

The company's commitment to quality begins with its people. Nearly a third of those based in

Technology and the human touch combine in the production of high-quality information systems products.

consistently meets the needs of customers. This philosophy is an integral part of Sperry's major business units operating in Minnesota: commercial, defense, and other computer-related activities.

The commercial information systems operations design, manufacture, market, and support the company's broad array of large-scale computer systems. Sperry computers help people in science, business, and industry to solve needs around the world. The Sperry 1100 computer series is used by Chinese seismologists to predict earthquakes and by the government of France to coordinate its donor kidney program.

at the heart of the system.

Sperry's Minnesota operations also serve the Federal Aviation Administration by providing automated air traffic functions at major facilities throughout the United States.

The company's dedication to solving today's problems is balanced with its concern for the future. That is why the firm supports extensive research and development. At Sperry's Knowledge Systems Center, researchers are probing the useful applications of Artificial Intelligence (AI), a technology that seeks to develop "reasoning" computers to serve as valuable decision-making assistants to humans.

But the company's attention to needs goes beyond technological solutions. It also includes responsible citizenship. Through the Sperry Partnership program, the firm actively supports community-based initiatives by coordinating employee volunteer efforts leveraging corporate resources to meet community needs. The tradition of community involvement focuses on four major areas: education, human services, arts and culture, civic and community. Sperry has placed special emphasis on science and mathematics education programs and encourages employee participation on nonprofit boards and community advisory councils.

Sperry, a pioneer developer of large-scale computer systems, is now a full-product-line systems supplier.

Minnesota have been with the firm for 15 years or more. The largest single concentration of Sperry's worldwide employees work in the Twin Cities.

Sperry's people have built their reputation on practical yet innovative technology—technology that

Sperry computers have been used by the United States Census Bureau since 1950, when the census was computerized.

The defense products operations design, manufacture, and market reliable ruggedized digital computers, systems, and components for use in almost every environment. Whenever there is a computational need on land or water, in space or in a submarine, a Sperry defense computer is often

computers are in use in industries around the country, as well as in the nation's colleges and universities. Research Equipment, Inc., the agency that operates supercomputers for the University of Minnesota researchers, uses two from Cray and one from Control Data.

3M was founded in 1902, due to a mistake, as a company history observes. America's industries needed abrasives. When a group of enthusiastic businessmen in Two Harbors, north of Duluth, seized upon the discovery of what they took to be corundum, one of the hardest minerals in the world, they thought their fortunes were made. For years the company that would eventually be built upon a foundation of sandpaper stumbled down the wrong path, unaware that what they had discovered was not corundum at all but an inferior mineral that was worthless as a commercial abrasive. That 3M stayed afloat at all during its first critical years was due chiefly to the efforts of a number of optimistic St. Paul businessmen. One of them was Edgar B. Ober, freight agent for the Chicago, St. Paul, Minneapolis, and Omaha Railroad, who invested $5,000 in 3M's first stock offering and would serve as its president for twenty-one years, the first eleven of them without pay.

Ober's methods for raising capital were sometimes informal. Harold Bend had founded a successful St. Paul sugar brokerage, the Bend-Sleepack Company, in 1895 when he was twenty-five years old. Sometime before World War I he had amassed $5,000 with which he intended to buy a car. Pursuing his mission, he fell into conversation with his good friend Ober, who at that precise moment was wondering how he would meet 3M's next payroll. Ober persuaded Bend to forget about the car and loan 3M the money. However, when the note came due, the company was unable to redeem it and Bend accepted stock instead. His stock subsequently split 192 times. At his death in the 1960s, Bend was one of the last of 3M's early stockholders.

Far more important than occasional fortuitous loans, however, was the seemingly endless flow of cash poured into the floundering company by Lucius Pond Ordway, who became president of Crane and Ordway, a St. Paul plumbing supply

3M rose in prominence as a result, in part, of its production of tape products. This 1931 manufacturing scene illustrates the production of cellulose tape. Courtesy, MHS

CONTROL DATA CORPORATION

In the years immediately following World War II, a tight-knit group of former enemy-code breakers from U.S. Navy intelligence started a private firm called ERA. Working out of a glider factory on Minnehaha Avenue in St. Paul's Midway district, this group turned its collective talents to developing new devices that were to be the forerunners of modern digital computers. Their fledgling company was acquired by Sperry in the early 1950s, but within a short time William C. Norris and his compatriots spun themselves off to form another venture: Control Data Corporation.

Today Control Data is a worldwide computer and financial services company dedicated to providing business solutions through the innovative use of technology. From its international headquarters in Bloomington, and through its operations in 47 countries the world over, the firm concentrates its activities in two primary areas: computer-related products and computer-enhanced services. A high percentage of Control Data's employees are concentrated in the Twin Cities, working in a number of varied and productive facilities—many of which are located in St. Paul and its surrounding suburbs.

Control Data was incorporated in 1957, at which point it numbered just four employees who worked out of a building in Minneapolis that also was used to store paper for the presses of the *Minneapolis Star and Tribune*. A year later the company announced its

The CDC CYBER 180 computer systems offer a broad range of performance and are used primarily by customers in engineering, educational, and scientific environments.

first major computer system, the fully transistorized CDC® 1604. Some of the newsprint had to be moved out to make room for an assembly area.

The developing base of technical talent in the Twin Cities was instrumental in the firm's early growth. In turn, Control Data has had a profound impact on Minnesota's high-technology industry as well as that of the entire computer industry. The rich pool of technical experts assembled by Control Data has been responsible for many spin-off companies that have prospered and created thousands of jobs in this area. Among these companies are Cray Research, ETA Systems, Network Systems, and Data 100, which later was acquired by Northern Telecom.

As Control Data continued to expand, its need for additional facilities in the Twin Cities area grew. To meet this need, new facilities were constructed, including the Selby Bindery Operation and the World Distribution Center in St. Paul.

The Selby Bindery Operation near Selby-Dale provides part-time work with flexible hours to its workers, most of whom come from the inner-city neighborhoods nearby. The Bindery allows mothers of school-age children to work in the morning until school is out, then provides valuable job opportunities for high school students in the afternoon. It was the first new business to be built in the Selby-Dale area in many years, evidence of a Control Data philosophy of putting jobs where they are most needed.

Control Data's World Distribution Center, also located in the inner city near Dale and Interstate 94, is an impressive 250,000-square-foot facility employing an extensive solar energy system for heating and cooling. Many minority contractors participated in the construction of this high-technology building.

In a renovated building in downtown St. Paul, Control Data established the first nationwide network of Business and Technology Centers. These centers provide facili-

Control Data's Selby Bindery Operation answers the need for job opportunities with flexible hours for residents of St. Paul's inner-city community.

PLATO computer-based education provides a window to knowledge with which students can interact and proceed at their own pace.

ties and services for new, small, and emerging businesses.

Additionally, Control Data worked closely with the City of St. Paul and the Port Authority to establish the Energy Technology Center (ETC) in the new Energy Park development near the State Fairgrounds.

Energy Park is also home to ETA Systems, an independent company established by Control Data in 1983. ETA's mission is to market the CDC CYBER 205 super computer, and to develop and manufacture its successor, the ETA-10—the next generation of supercomputers, and the world's most powerful computer system.

Under the direction of chairman, president, and chief executive officer Robert M. Price, Control Data has rededicated itself to becoming the most technologically advanced supplier of cost-effective, high-quality computer products and services. The company expects its future growth to come from focusing its energies on a combination of five promising and often interrelated markets.

In Scientific/Engineering Systems and Services, the emphasis is on manufacturing, environmental, utility, petroleum, higher edu-

cation, and government markets. Control Data was founded to manufacture computers for scientists and engineers, and these systems remain the cornerstone of its business. Each system, from the entry-level CDC CYBER 810 to the 60-times-more-powerful CDC CYBER 990, is compatible allowing customers to grow within the Control Data family of computer products as their computing needs change and expand.

Typical uses of this division's products include university research and student instruction, weather forecasting, engineering design, energy management, and petroleum exploration and production worldwide. Control Data also develops and produces specialized computing equipment and services for use in aerospace and defense applications.

Through its Data Storage Products group, the company is the world's largest supplier of high-performance, high-capacity data storage devices to original-equipment manufacturers (OEMs). In addition, more than 1,500 computer manufacturers and systems integrators have used Control Data peripheral equipment in their systems. From advanced thin-film recording heads and optical recording products to more conventional forms of computer memory storage, the company is translating new technology into products for use in a world that is increasingly computer oriented.

Using the ever-growing power of the computer, Control Data's Business Services provide transaction processing and information

solutions to broadcasting, financial, and legal marketplaces as well as to *Fortune* 1000 and midsize companies.

Human Resources Information Services addresses medical markets; government agencies at the federal, state, and local level; and public schools.

In these areas, the network of Control Data Institutes prepares students for careers in the office and in the computer industry. In addition, Control Data's pioneering PLATO computer-based education and training, first introduced in 1976, is meeting learning challenges from kindergarten to college, from manufacturing plants to executive suites. PLATO technology is also incorporated as a value-added component in many of the firm's major businesses.

Finally, Commercial Credit, a wholly owned subsidiary, directs its marketing strategy to both the consumer and businesses: the consumer through its finance and insurance activities; businesses through vehicle leasing and management, and business credit insurance.

Control Data Corporation grew from its modest roots in St. Paul's Midway district to become a leader in the computer field. Yet it continues to be unique for its emphasis not just on building computers, but on using their power to solve the important problems of business, industry, and government.

Control Data markets one of the broadest lines of data storage devices for use with its own computer systems as well as with systems of other computer manufacturers.

3M

In the 1950s the 3M was just entering its first international markets and beginning a long and sustained growth curve that has made it Minnesota's largest employer and one of the world's largest and most successful corporations. Back then a search was conducted for a site that could be developed for a research laboratory and still leave room for more development in the years to come. "My middle initial is 'L,' and this means land," said William L. McKnight, then the president of 3M. "Buy plenty of land."

The site selected was a farm on

Corporate scientist Art Fry, inventor of Post-it brand notes, in his laboratory at 3M Center.

the east side of St. Paul, a mile long and a half-mile wide. The first building to occupy it, a central research laboratory with 200 employees, seemed a lonely outpost from the firm's headquarters in the downtown area, just off the East Seventh streetcar tracks. However, McKnight's middle initial was to prove well deserved. Today that former farm on the outskirts of town is better known as 3M Center, home to more than 10,000 of the company's 85,000 employees in 49 countries around the globe.

Born on the north shore of Lake

Superior in 1902 as Minnesota Mining and Manufacturing, 3M has grown into a diverse, worldwide corporation with a broad range of innovative, high-quality products and services. It is said that each day close to half of the world's population benefits in some way from one or more of 3M's 45 major product lines, from sandpaper and Scotch™ tapes and Post-it™ notes to road signs, lithographic plates, and health care and safety products.

The firm's business is built on more than 85 distinct technologies. They include precision coating and bonding, fluorochemicals, nonwoven fabrics, imaging, magnetic and optical information storage, and more. 3M scientists, engineers, and product developers, organized into four broad product sectors, expand and combine these technologies to meet the needs of customers the world over.

The Industrial and Consumer Sector includes businesses serving the specialty chemical, office supply, and building maintenance markets. Among its products are Post-it™ note pads; packaging for

Scientists at 3M's Space Research and Applications Laboratory are working with a computer (white box, center) they developed to operate the company's space experiments. When space shuttle flights are resumed 3M will have another experiment they hope to have on one of the first flights.

An aerial view of 3M Center, the company's world headquarters in Maplewood.

food, drugs, and cosmetics; reflective film; and hook-and-loop fasteners. Products in the Electronic and Information Technologies Sector include electronic connectors, computer diskettes, videotape, and optical recording systems.

In the Life Sciences Sector are health care, and traffic and personal safety products, including pharmaceuticals, medical equipment and supplies, reflective markings for road signs and pavement, and personal protection products for occupational health and safety needs. The Graphic Technologies Sector serves markets from outdoor advertising and electronic imaging to printing and photography.

While each business sector operates autonomously, it has constant access to the full spectrum of 3M's technologies and expertise. To meet its stated goal of achieving 25 percent of sales each year from new products that did not exist five years prior, 3M fosters an environment that prizes innovation and growth.

At the same time the firm places a high value on its involvement in the hundreds of communities in which it operates worldwide. From the activities of 3M volunteers to the grants of the 3M Foundation and gifts-in-kind through its many offices and plants, 3M works to enhance the quality of life through the full range of products and services it creates.

house, and was already a millionaire. Ordway was a man who cared deeply about St. Paul and about helping new firms establish themselves there.

In 1910 he and Ober moved 3M to St. Paul, the better to keep an eye on it. Already working for the company were the two men who would enormously influence its future—William L. McKnight, hired in 1907 as an assistant bookkeeper, and Archibald G. Bush, who succeeded him in 1909 when McKnight was promoted to cost accountant. The rest, as they say, is history. McKnight and Bush would guide 3M through the forty years that saw the introduction of Scotch tape, Wetordry sandpaper, roofing granules, industrial adhesives, Scotchlite reflective tapes, gift-wrap ribbons, magnetic recording tape, and the dawning of the brave new post-World War II world of electronic telecommunications.

3M's entrance into the field of sound recording on tape, the foundation of today's complex electronic communications, was due in part to the work of German scientists who during the 1930s had invented the Magnetophone, an instrument for recording sound on magnetic plastic tape. In 1944 3M's researchers also were investigating the possibilities of magnetic tape as a substitute for the wire recordings used by the American military for training and intelligence work. After the war ended, United States scientists uncovered the work of their German counterparts and brought samples to America. Studying the German tapes, 3M became the first company in the United States to produce high-quality magnetic sound-recording tape.

Today 3M, known as one of the most-admired companies in the United States, heads *Corporate Report's* list of Minnesota's top 100 high-tech companies. The company's products and spinoffs of products range all the way from laser-imaged graphic arts film to computer tapes to diskettes and data cartridges, to the eminently practical disposable-diaper tapes and the gummed Post-It pads.

3M, together with Minneapolis' Honeywell, and Control Data, employ more than 235,000 people. Not all of them, of course, live and work in St. Paul and Minneapolis, or even in Minnesota. Considering the diversity of these three major companies, it is scarcely surprising that not all their employees work in their high-tech divisions. Still, these figures, combined with those of the other top 100 corporations in Minnesota, are a gauge of the economic health of the state and the Twin Cities, as *Corporate Report* has pointed out.

More recognizable, perhaps, to the general public than the exotic computer world is the technology that is revolutionizing the medical and health-care fields. 3M is noted for its work in medical technology. Several other major medical-technology firms with corporate headquarters in the St. Paul area have earned international renown as part of the Twin Cities' highly praised "medical alley."

These are fast-growing firms. Founded in 1976, St. Jude Medical of suburban Little Canada is already famous for its heart valve and other implantable cardiovascular products. New to the field is Cardio-Pace, formed in 1981 as a spinoff from St. Jude and manufacturer of a low-cost version of that company's pacemaker, a product St. Jude developed, then sold to Cardio-Pace's organizers. Medical Graphics, based in Shoreview, makes computerized medical testing systems. And Genetics Laboratories in Roseville has been a pioneer in the manufacturing of synthetic materials used to treat burns and other injuries and for cardiovascular use. AVI developed an intravenous system, then was sold in 1985 to 3M for its medical-surgical division. SenTech Medical Corporation in Arden Hills manufactures what the company calls a lightweight portable computer that allows doctors to run sophisticated blood tests and analyses in their offices, rather than sending out samples to laboratories.

Few aspects of the health-care industry remain untouched by the technology of the past

3M's walkway between the Health Care Research Lab and the Electronic Research building symbolizes the bridge the company makes between medical technology and electronic manufacturing. Photo by Shin Koyama. Courtesy, Ellerbe Associates, Inc.

few years, including St. Paul's hospitals. It was inevitable that hospitals, physicians, and health care would follow immigrants to Minnesota. St. Paul's first hospital, St. Joseph's, still stands at Ninth and Exchange streets, its original site in downtown St. Paul, although its earlier buildings—with the exception of the chapel—have been replaced by modern structures. St. Joseph's Hospital, now merged with St. Mary's—the Sisters of St. Joseph of Carondelet hospital in Minneapolis—provides radiation therapy and is second only to the Mayo Clinic in Rochester, Minnesota, in the amount of therapy provided.

The hospital was founded as the result of a

MEDTRONIC, INC.

About a quarter-century ago the human heart was still one of the great medical mysteries, its workings—and its failure to work—perhaps the most perplexing challenge then facing medical researchers.

Today the heart is the beneficiary of wide-ranging biomedical engineering advances that once were considered unattainable, many of them tracing to one single, dedicated company in suburban Fridley: Medtronic, Inc. Since the introduction of the first successful implantable heart pacemaker in 1960, Medtronic has been and continues to be the world's leading manufacturer of implantable biomedical devices. Over the years Medtronic has created a variety of pacemakers that have been used by more than one million people worldwide.

The increasingly global reach of this Twin Cities-based company is in marked contrast to its peaceful headquarters complex, where 1,900 of the firm's 4,800 employees worldwide are concentrated. It is also a long way from the Twin Cities garage where Earl Bakken, a graduate student in electrical engineering at the University of Minnesota, and Palmer Hermundslie, his brother-in-law, began repairing and building medical devices in 1949.

Some seven years later the firm began moving toward the biomedical specialty that would ultimately make it the world leader in heart-pacing technology. Pioneering open-heart surgeons at the University of Minnesota were troubled by the cumbersome nature of the external pacemakers of the day. So large that they had to be carried on wheeled carts and plugged into wall outlets, they were impractical for long-term use.

In 1957 Medtronic engineers and University Hospital researchers developed a way to attach a wire electrode directly to the heart. It was Bakken who designed a

Medtronic's corporate center in Fridley.

As the world's leading manufacturer of implantable biomedical devices, Medtronic has created a variety of pacemakers that have been used by more than one million people worldwide.

portable, transistorized, battery-powered pacemaker that could be worn by the patient. But the device was still external, requiring an electrode through the skin, and the patient was subject to infections. The next major advance had to be inward.

In 1960 Medtronic negotiated a license to produce the implantable device developed by a New York surgeon and an electrical engineer. In the process, it pioneered a new industry. Today, with about $400 million in sales, Medtronic has renewed its leadership role through the 1986 introduction of the Activitrax™ pacemaker, the first single-chamber pacemaker designed to respond to the body's own demands.

In contrast to previous pacemakers that maintained a single pacing rate, the Activitrax has the capability to recognize and respond to changes in the body's activity level, increasing the heart rate to compensate for increased activity, then returning to a lower rate when the body's demands lessen. The company also is actively involved in the manufacture of heart valves, and devices for neurological and muscular stimulation.

The success of Medtronic, Inc., is a continuing fulfillment of the first objective set for the company by Bakken more than 25 years ago, and continued under the leadership of Winston R. Wallin, chairman, president, and chief executive officer: to contribute to human welfare by the application of biomedical engineering in the research, design, manufacture, and sale of instruments or appliances that alleviate pain, restore health, and extend life.

SISTERS OF ST. JOSEPH OF CARONDELET

In 1851 four Sisters of St. Joseph of Carondelet traveled up the Mississippi River to St. Paul. The teaching sisters had come at the invitation of Bishop Joseph Cretin to help spread God's message through education, but their plans changed abruptly when a cholera epidemic struck the frontier town in 1853. Their small log chapel was transformed into a makeshift hospital and became Minnesota's first hospital. Their educational mission took on a health care counterpart that was to remain a strong part of St. Paul's heritage.

Today, education and health care remain the dual mission of the Sisters of St. Joseph of Carondelet. Their educational activities in the St. Paul Province—one of four provinces in the United States— include grade schools, high schools, and the College of St. Catherine, founded in 1905. Their health care activities are centered around St. Joseph's Hospital in St. Paul and St. Mary's Hospital & Rehabilitation Center in Minneapolis, divisions of Carondelet Community Hospitals. Both hospitals are part of Carondelet LifeCare Corporation and the national Health Care Corporation of the Sisters of St. Joseph of Carondelet.

St. Joseph's is the modern successor to the original log cabin near the Mississippi River. Located on the northern edge of the downtown area, the hospital provides the full range of inpatient and outpatient treatment, from the joys of birth at the Maternity Center to the hospice's caring environment for death with dignity and compassion. St. Joseph's is also noted for the programs of The Cancer Center, which offer a comprehensive spectrum of diagnostic and therapeutic services to address the physical, psychological, social, and spiritual implications of the disease.

St. Joseph's Seton Center provides support for low-income, single mothers during pregnancy and birth. The Recovery Center is dedicated to helping individuals and families suffering from psychological problems and chemical dependency. The hospital's hospice program is one of few such programs in the state to be Medicare certified; it has an emphasis on home care as well as inpatient treatment.

Education has always been a strong theme for the Sisters of St. Joseph of Carondelet. Members of the order study worldwide, and that tradition is expressed in the curriculum of the College of St. Catherine, the largest Catholic college for women in the United States. Students from nearly every state and some 30 foreign countries mingle and learn on a picturesque, 110-acre campus, whose stately buildings mix with woodland and rolling lawns, yet is within minutes of downtown St. Paul.

Named by *U.S. News and World Report* as one of the nation's top academic institutions in 1984 and 1985, the College of St. Catherine provides its 2,500 students with more than 30 undergraduate majors

Two College of St. Catherine students study in front of I.A. O'Shaughnessy Auditorium, anchor of the Mother Antonia McHugh Performing Arts Center on the campus. The auditorium, which opened in 1970, hosts dance, music, and theater productions by a wide variety of local, regional, national, and international performing artists each year.

Located in the heart of St. Paul, St. Joseph's Hospital is a full-service medical facility sponsored by the Sisters of St. Joseph of Carondelet. Here Sister Marian Louwagie, who provides pastoral support and counseling at the hospital, visits with a multiple sclerosis patient.

and 30 minors in fields ranging from accounting and communications to music and art. The institution also operates St. Mary's Campus in Minneapolis and is a member of the Associated Colleges of the Twin Cities, a consortium of five private colleges within a five-mile radius, allowing its students to choose from among 30 additional majors available through the five-college network.

More than a century after their arrival in St. Paul, the Sisters of St. Joseph of Carondelet continue to fulfill their twin missions of education and health care.

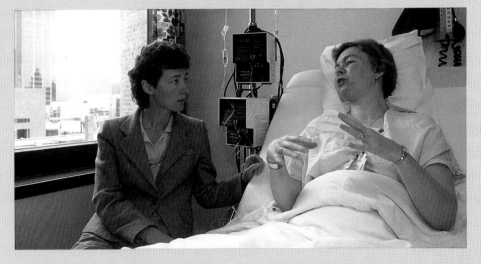

cholera epidemic that descended upon the little settlement in 1853. A handful of nuns, vanguard of the Sisters of St. Joseph of Carondelet, an order which would later have an enormous impact on St. Paul's institutions, nursed victims of the disease and by 1854 had opened their hospital.

Cholera had been appearing with dreadful regularity in the village since 1849, when the steamboat *Cora* was docked with two lumberjacks aboard who died shortly afterward of the disease. So terrified were the settlers that steamboats known to be carrying victims were forbidden to land, and a boat captain had no qualms about abandoning a dying man somewhere along a deserted stretch of river. Although perhaps the most dramatic, cholera was scarcely the only health hazard the pioneers faced. Scarlet fever, diphtheria, typhoid fever, tuberculosis all were prevalent. Every household had its recipes for home remedies—plaster of balsam for burns, pond-lily tea or gunpowder dissolved in water as a gargle, birchbark to flavor medicines, whiskey for lockjaw.

Ironically, during the 1800s Minnesota was striving hard to promote itself as a health resort. Hotels were built at White Bear Lake and Lake Elmo to lure invalids arriving from the East. The truth was difficult to face, but physicians eventually reached the cautious conclusion that Minnesota was neither more nor less healthful than other regions of the country. They already knew it was a difficult place to practice. They braved hordes of mosquitoes, crossed swollen rivers, and waded through snowbanks. Dr. William C. Renfro, an early St. Paul physician, froze to death. Dr. John J. Dewey, who arrived in 1847 and opened the first drugstore, prospered in an era when doctors compounded their own pharmaceuticals.

As of the mid-1980s, hundreds of physicians are practicing in St. Paul and Ramsey County. There are almost fifty nursing homes and boarding-care facilities and eleven hospitals, many of which, like St. Joseph's, have their roots in the nineteenth century. United Hospital, Inc., in St. Paul's Seven Corners neighborhood, is a consolidation of several hospitals under one banner. United was established in 1972 with the joining of St. Luke's and Miller hospitals under a single administration. In 1976 United, in cooperation with Children's Hospital, built a $72-million medical center on the site at Smith and Walnut streets that St. Luke's hospital had

St. Joseph's Hospital, founded in 1853, still stands on its original site at Ninth and Exchange Streets. Part of this site was donated to the hospital by Henry M. Rice, a prominent St. Paul civic leader and philanthropist for whom Rice Park is named. Photo by Kay Shaw

occupied for most of its history. Founded in 1855 by Christ Church, St. Paul's pioneer Episcopal parish, St. Luke's originally was an orphanage and home for the sick. The portions of St. Luke's that were built before 1960 were torn down and the new hospital built onto its remaining rectangular wing and its three circular wings.

With its consolidation into United Hospital, the Charles T. Miller Hospital, a massive seven-story brick structure that for almost seventy years had overlooked the downtown district from the College Avenue hill, was abandoned in 1980. Miller Hospital had been established in 1920 by the estate of Martha Miller to fulfill her late husband's wishes that medical care be provided for the poor. Miller Hospital at first had fifty beds for the free care of the needy, then added ninety-four lower-than-cost beds. The hospital also offered seventy-two private beds. Not only was it noted for its care of the indigent, but Miller also became a leading heart

hospital and attracted some of the city's wealthiest patients, who brought along their own linens, crystal, wines, and servants and sent out to the Minnesota Club for catered meals. The vacant hospital complex has been torn down and the site will hold the new history center to be built by the Minnesota Historical Society.

St. Paul's Children's Hospital, which opened in 1924 in a white clapboard house at Smith and Walnut, shares the United Hospital complex, although it remains a separate hospital with its own board and medical staff. Founded by Dr. Walter R. Ramsey, the hospital was the first facility devoted to the care of children in the northern part of the country between Chicago and the West Coast. The United and Children's Hospital complex was completed in 1980 with six million dollars from United Hospitals and sixty-six million dollars from the sale of Port Authority bonds.

St. Paul's city-county hospital, St. Paul-Ramsey Medical Center, is a descendant of Ancker Hospital, named for its administrator of forty years, Dr. Arthur B. Ancker. Its beginnings date back to 1869 and to a ten-room house on Richmond Avenue, off West Seventh Street, that the city purchased for $20,000 from pioneer physician Dr. Jacob H. Stewart. Incorporated in 1872, it was considered the finest in the area. Stewart and Dr. Charles Wheaton ran the hospital until 1883 when the Ramsey

---

The Twin City Rapid Transit Company constructed Wildwood Park on the east side of White Bear Lake to encourage patronage of the streetcar system. Area residents bene- *fited from this development, enjoying a variety of leisure-time activities including amusement rides, boating, and picnicking. Courtesy, MHS*

Above: *United Hospital's Bi-plane cine machine provides a two-dimensional view of the heart and arteries, aiding diagnosis of heart abnormalities and heart disease. Courtesy, United Hospital*

Left: *Two major research areas at United Hospital are the world-renowned research and teaching program in cardiovascular disease led by Jesse E. Edwards, M.D., and the cancer research program conducted through United's Clara and Bruce Burnham Harris Cancer Research Laboratory. Courtesy, United Hospital*

CHILDREN'S HOSPITAL OF ST. PAUL

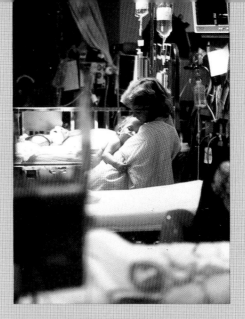

Children's Hospital of St. Paul began serving the needs of infants, children, adolescents, and their families in 1924. But with the opening of its new, 116-bed facility on a combined campus with United Hospital, just off Fort Road west of the downtown, Children's has emerged as a true pediatric specialty center designed to provide comprehensive health care to the young residents of St. Paul and the surrounding region.

The hospital's more than 480 physicians, representing 23 distinct medical specialties and numerous subspecialties, have pioneered many techniques and procedures for the treatment of critically ill children. A dedicated staff of more than 500 nurses, health care professionals, and support personnel works in both inpatient and outpatient settings to provide high-quality, yet cost-effective, care.

The partnership with United allows Children's to draw on the campus' combined medical resources while maintaining a specialized commitment to its young patients, their families, and their community. Children's is also an associate member of HealthOne Corporation, allowing it to retain its own autonomy while participating in a regional network of health care services that includes United Hospital.

The first Children's Hospital was a converted house at the corner of Walnut and Pleasant streets, not far from the current campus. Its 16 beds were replaced by a true hospital facility that opened in 1928 at 311 Pleasant Avenue and served for 50 years. But as health care has changed and improved its ability to respond to the special needs of the young and very young, a new facility was needed—one

that could benefit from the best of modern technology and treatment, yet provide an environment designed to comfort and reassure its patients and their families.

The new Children's Hospital building, which opened in 1979, reflects those priorities. Its cheerful, vibrant patient rooms, play areas, and treatment facilities were created to provide emotional as well as physical care, its staff trained to meet children's developmental and recreational needs in addition to their medical conditions. Relaxed visiting policies encourage family activity throughout the day, and parents can spend the night with their children and participate in their nonmedical care if they wish.

At the same time Children's newborn intensive care unit, designed to respond to the needs of premature and critically ill infants, is the largest and oldest of its kind in the state. Its companion pediatric intensive care unit serves as a regional center for critically ill infants, children, and adolescents with respiratory, neurological, metabolic, and cardiovascular problems. The hospital shares a common emergency entrance with United but provides its own pediatric emergency room and staff. It also sends special teams into the surrounding region to transport critically ill and injured children to

Personal attention from caring staff members supplements high-tech medical care in the intensive care units at Children's Hospital of St. Paul.

the hospital. Outpatient care is provided through a large general clinic and more than 30 specialty clinics.

Children's has a long tradition of teaching and research. As a teaching hospital, it is affiliated with the University of Minnesota Medical School and also provides training for the full range of health care professionals, as well as education offerings for the community. Research activities include special projects in cytomegalovirus, immunology, and infant breathing problems.

When the first patient was admitted to the new hospital in 1979, he told his parents, "I like this place!" He was speaking for the thousands of young patients who have since come to know Children's Hospital of St. Paul as a place built for their special needs.

Children learn through play, and playing with medical equipment in hospital playrooms helps them to understand what they experience at Children's Hospital.

UNITED HOSPITAL

Formed in 1972 by the consolidation of the former Charles T. Miller and St. Luke's hospitals, United Hospital today is the largest private hospital in St. Paul and a leading medical center of the region. United accounts for one out of every five St. Paul hospital admissions. Employing 2,200 and drawing on the expertise of a 700-member medical staff, United is one of downtown St. Paul's largest employers.

The institution is located two blocks west of the St. Paul Civic Center on a medical campus opened in 1980. The hospital building is shared with Children's Hospital of St. Paul, with which it has a cooperative working agreement.

The facility is well named. It was created by uniting two former downtown hospitals (St. Luke's and Miller) into a stronger, more comprehensive health care system that in later years added Riverview Memorial Hospital on St. Paul's west side, River Falls Area Hospital in Wisconsin, and several neighborhood urgent care centers and medical specialty centers.

St. Luke's Hospital began as the Church Hospital and Orphan's Home of St. Paul in 1855. In 1881 the institution moved to Pleasant Avenue, the present-day location of United Hospital, where it gave excellent medical service for nearly 100 years.

Miller Hospital opened its doors on nearby Summit Avenue in 1920. It was named for Charles T. Miller, a successful businessman whose estate (and that of his wife, Martha), helped fund the new hospital.

United Hospital today has emerged as the private hospital of choice for specialty care and referrals. During the past decade more open-heart surgeries have been done at United than at all other St. Paul hospitals combined. The Heart Center provides one of the region's most advanced diagnostic, treatment, and rehabilitation facilities. The United Hospital Eye Institute builds on the leadership role of Miller Hospital in the treatment of eye disorders.

Other specialties include cancer care and psychiatric services, rehabilitation, neurology, helicopter-supported emergency care, the treatment of diabetes, and general surgery. Comprehensive medical service to those unable to pay the full cost of their medical care is offered through the MOD Clinic.

More babies are born at the

Perinatal Center (a shared service of United and Children's) than at any other St. Paul Hospital. The Perinatal Center specializes in care of high-risk maternity patients and critically ill newborns. The Family Birth Center offers the experience of giving birth in a homelike setting. The Genetic Counseling Center and the Twin Cities Fertility Center offer resources unduplicated in the city for couples contemplating having a baby.

United features the most advanced technology, including microsurgery and laser surgery facilities, and the newest generation of computerized monitoring equipment for patients needing intensive care.

In 1983 United, with Metropolitan Medical Center in Minneapolis, formed HealthOne, the first multi-hospital system to link St. Paul and Minneapolis. HealthOne provides a wealth of resources such as ambulance and home health services to the communities of each hospital.

United Hospital is most proud of its reputation for giving personal and high-quality care, cost-effective management of resources, and for its responsiveness to community needs.

New parents enjoy their first precious minutes together with their just-born baby. More babies are born each year in the homelike Perinatal Center at United and Children's hospitals than at any other St. Paul hospital.

ST. PAUL-RAMSEY MEDICAL CENTER

The nearly 300,000 residents of the region surrounding St. Paul-Ramsey Medical Center may not notice the changes. Yet it was for them that the area's largest regional medical complex was reorganized following an act of the Minnesota legislature in 1986. The goal of the reorganization was to be more responsive to community needs by allowing the medical center to be more competitive.

The modern 18-acre campus on Jackson Street just north of I-94 and downtown is actually a combination of institutions and services designed to serve the comprehensive health care needs of the city, Ramsey County, and a region that extends from the Dakotas to Wisconsin. St. Paul-Ramsey Medical Center itself is the trauma center for the East Metro area, the primary hospital in the area for the stabilization and treatment of the victims of severe accidents or illnesses. It is also the East Metro center for medical education.

In addition, the St. Paul-Ramsey campus includes Gillette Children's Hospital, a regional hospital specializing in the treatment of disabling illnesses in children, and Ramsey Clinic, a multispecialty group practice of 160 physicians who staff the medical center and Gillette.

St. Paul's rebirth and renewed economic vitality are mirrored in the recent history of one of its oldest and most successful health care organizations. The Jackson Street campus was constructed in 1965 to provide a new, modern, state-of-the-art medical center, a home for the treatment, research, and educational activities that had their origins more than a century ago in a 10-room stone mansion on Richmond Street.

Founded in 1869 and incorporated three years later as City and County Hospital, the health care center grew to become better known as Ancker Hospital, the name it formally adopted in 1923

at the death of Arthur B. Ancker, M.D., its superintendent and administrator for nearly 40 years. In 1965 it became St. Paul-Ramsey Hospital with the move to the new campus. To better describe its range of services and emerging regional care mission, the name St. Paul-Ramsey Medical Center was adopted in 1977.

Under Ancker's leadership, the hospital first became known as a leader in the treatment of communicable diseases, notably tuberculosis, that were major health problems in the early 1900s. Later, as the city's population of poor and elderly grew, it was Ancker Hospital that shouldered the responsibility for their health care, pledging to serve all people with all kinds of needs, regardless of their financial well-being.

In more recent years the growth of a mobile urban life-style brought with it the need for sophisticated emergency care to treat traumatic injuries from accidents. St. Paul-Ramsey provided that care, and evolved a prototype intensive care unit to continue treatment for the injured and the critically ill. In addition, it created regional burn and poison centers and a unique emergency operating room, Room 10, modeled on the experiences gained by MASH units in the Korean War.

The regional Burn Center, created in 1963, serves the entire

St. Paul-Ramsey Medical Center and Ramsey Clinic share a modern 18-acre medical campus just north of downtown St. Paul. While visiting their physicians at Ramsey Clinic, patients have access to all medical specialties, any necessary tests or procedures, and prescribed pharmaceutical products in one convenient location.

Upper Midwest for acute care, convalescent care, and rehabilitation of burn patients. The Minnesota Regional Poison Center is staffed by certified toxicologists to provide treatment for poisonings, drug abuse, and toxic industrial substances.

In addition, St. Paul-Ramsey provides the regional medical resource control, allowing physicians to direct emergency life support units and paramedics in the East Metro area. And it maintains a perinatal intensive care center for high-risk obstetrical patients and newborns in Minnesota and Wisconsin. The medical center and Ramsey Clinic are the area's leaders in the care of seniors, providing a variety of medical and support services for that age group. Its women's center concentrates on the special health care needs of women. And in conjunction with Gillette Children's Hospital, St. Paul-Ramsey provides a pediatric teaching and referral center.

St. Paul-Ramsey has remained at the forefront of changes in health care because of its focus

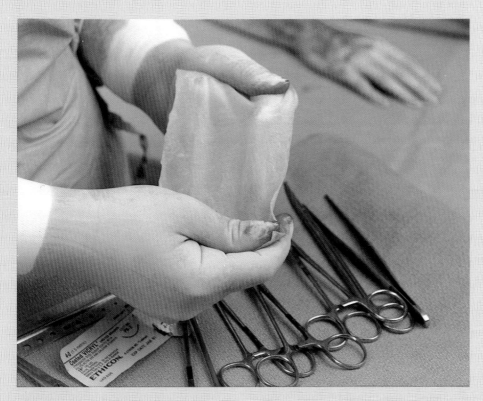

medical technology.

In addition to education, the medical center has earned a well-deserved reputation in the field of medical research, a tradition that goes back to the 1920s, when the Foley catheter—developed at Ancker Hospital by Frederic E.B. Foley, M.D.—made its debut. Today that tradition continues with research involving medical problems such as Alzheimer's disease, dry eyes, cancer therapy, poison antidotes, and chemical dependency.

Yet medical technology, treatment, and research aside, the ability of St. Paul-Ramsey to serve the health care needs of the community successfully rests on its ability to compete effectively in the modern medical marketplace. The delicate balance between cost and quality requires flexible, responsive management of services, and the systems that provide them.

on education for patients, physicians, nurses, allied health care professionals, and the community at large. As members of the faculty of the University of Minnesota Medical School, Ramsey Clinic physicians serve as teachers of the next generation of doctors. St. Paul-Ramsey also offers accredited programs for nurse anesthetists, dietitians, and technologists in radiology, ophthalmology, and

Through its new public benefit corporation, the medical center has developed a governing structure to enable it to serve the needs of the region into the next century. And it has pledged to reinvest $20 million in revenues over the coming years to further improve patient care areas. The reason for these efforts and others always has been and will be the same: the residents of the city, county, and region who expect the best in medical care. Serving their medical needs with quality, dignity, and in a cost-effective manner is the commitment of St. Paul-Ramsey Medical Center.

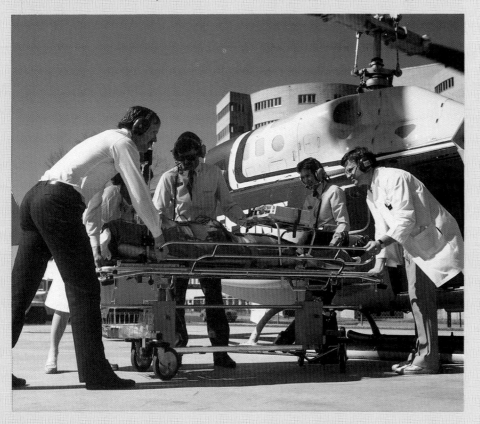

RAMSEY CLINIC

The hundreds of thousands of patients who annually seek health care through St. Paul-Ramsey Medical Center find it "a house with two doors." One door enters a modern hospital whose physical plant offers the equipment and support services needed for the full range of comprehensive general and acute medical care. The other door enters the physician offices of Ramsey Clinic, the largest multispecialty group medical practice in the city, and the third largest in the state.

For more than 100 years the medical center and the physicians' group have operated in close co-

As the regional trauma center, St. Paul-Ramsey is recognized for its emergency services, notably Room 10. Seriously injured patients are assessed briefly in the emergency room and rushed within moments to Room 10, a surgical suite that is completely equipped, fully staffed with surgeons from Ramsey Clinic, and waiting.

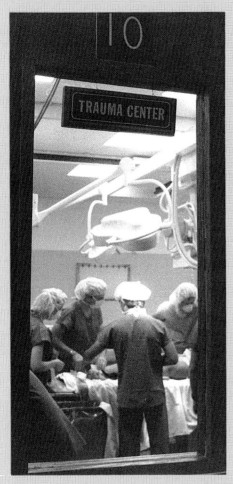

operation, one maintaining the environment for inpatient and outpatient treatment, the other providing the physician services to staff that hospital (and several specialties of Gillette Children's Hospital as well). Since 1977, when an entire wing of outpatient clinics was added to the St. Paul-Ramsey Hospital originally built in 1965, the two organizations have also operated under the same roof.

But Ramsey Clinic provides more than a physicians' group to staff the hospitals of the medical center. It also provides the financial and medical expertise needed to assure the viability of the physicians' group and the medical center for which it provides services. By assuming the executive and administrative responsibilities of modern medical practice in a highly cost-sensitive era, Ramsey Clinic frees its more than 160 physician members to do what they do best: practice medicine with an emphasis on quality and personalized patient care.

The association between physicians and medical center can be traced back to 1872, when City and County Hospital was founded in a stone mansion overlooking the Mississippi River. As the city grew, so did the medical staff and its range of in-hospital, office, and clinic services. To better coordinate the activities of this increasingly varied group of specialists, Ramsey Clinic was incorporated in 1979. Five years later a reorganization brought it into a formal working relationship with the St. Paul-Ramsey Foundation, which had existed since 1966 to support and direct research efforts at Ramsey Clinic and St. Paul-Ramsey Medical Center.

In addition to its services on the St. Paul-Ramsey campus, Ramsey Clinic also operates a growing network of satellite clinics in Minnesota and western Wisconsin to bring modern, specialized health care home to the communities

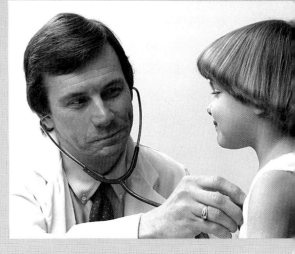

It is, above all, the personal relationship between physician and patient that makes the healing happen. Ramsey Clinic's highly skilled and experienced physicians care for the personal as well as the medical needs of their patients.

where people live and work. Its physicians provide medical education both in St. Paul and for general practice physicians outstate, and maintain a close working relationship with the University of Minnesota Medical School.

Specialized services and related research include the Alzheimer's Treatment and Research Center, the metropolitan area's first comprehensive breast cancer treatment and education center, the Center for Reproductive Medicine, diabetes treatment and management, a Dry Eye and Tear Research Center, an International Clinic for refugees and immigrants who encounter language and cultural barriers in seeking medical care, and services to meet the special needs of women, the hearing-impaired, seniors, and international travelers.

Ramsey Clinic's mission is to provide the best in individualized patient care within an organization that also offers the combined innovation, efficiencies, and support of group practice, and the modern physical resources of St. Paul-Ramsey Medical Center and Gillette Children's Hospital.

GILLETTE CHILDREN'S HOSPITAL

Arthur Gillette was just 37 years old in 1897, one of the first orthopedic surgeons at the University of Minnesota's new medical school, when he volunteered his services to the State of Minnesota for the care of the young. In return, the state appropriated $5,000 per year for two years to back his new experiment in health care—the first publicly supported hospital in the nation dedicated solely to the needs of children with handicaps. Dr. A.B. Ancker of what was then the City and County Hospital in St. Paul (now St. Paul-Ramsey Medical Center) provided a small ward, and later a building on the hospital campus, for Gillette's patients.

Ten years later the St. Paul Commercial Club, the Business League, and a number of St. Paul citizens obtained 23 acres of land at Phalen Park and raised the seed money for the construction of the Minnesota State Hospital for Indigent, Crippled and Deformed Children. Renamed in memory of its founder in 1925, Gillette offered care and support for children whose conditions in those days were often hidden away and left untreated—and for parents who not only needed help to care for their children, but also support against the superstition and lack of information of the time.

Today Gillette Children's Hospital is internationally known as a regional health center for young people with disabilities, especially those involving spine disorders. It has been a self-supporting, non-profit corporation since 1975. Since 1977, when it moved from the residential setting of Phalen Park, Gillette again has been co-located with St. Paul-Ramsey, its own staff of child-care specialists working in close cooperation with the physicians of Ramsey Clinic, who staff both hospitals.

Through almost a century of specialized treatment, research, and counseling for disabled chil-

dren, their families, and concerned professionals such as teachers, family physicians, and social workers, Gillette's services have evolved to meet new challenges. In the beginning, deformities and chronic diseases such as tuberculosis were common. The Phalen Park years saw an emphasis on extended, institutional care for birth defects and diseases such as polio.

As those traditional childhood cripplers have been conquered, new challenges have been met— spina bifida, cerebral palsy, scoliosis, epilepsy and head injuries, mental retardation, and learning disorders—but with a new emphasis on "mainstreaming" designed to keep children and their families together in integrated community settings. Gillette specialists have designed and built orthoses, prostheses, and adaptive equipment, and pioneered surgical and therapy procedures toward that objec-

tive, combining experience and technology. Extending those resources even further is the new Motion Laboratory, the first in the Midwest, which uses advanced electronic image processing technology to help physicians analyze, diagnose, and treat movement disorders in children.

Arthur Gillette's pioneering work has been continued by many others:

by Drs. Carl Chatterton and Wallace Cole, who guided Gillette from its founder's death through the 1950s; by Dr. John Moe, who established Gillette's reputation for spine surgery, and Dr. Robert Winter, who continues that work; by Elizabeth McGregor, Jean Conklin, and now Norman Allan, key administrators in the hospital's history; and by a dedicated staff of some 125 physicians and 300 nurses, therapists, counselors, and support staff.

From a borrowed ward in a turn-of-the-century hospital, Gillette Children's Hospital has grown to a world-renowned pediatric specialty hospital for children, adolescents, and young adults, its success proof of the essential need identified by its founder.

Meeting the needs of children with disabilities involves not only sophisticated surgery at times, but also individualized therapy and family support.

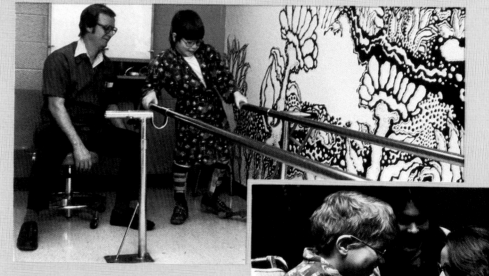

Right: *Children's Hospital of St. Paul started out in 1924 in a converted house at the corner of Smith Avenue and Walnut Street. Courtesy, Children's Hospital*

Below: *Patients and nurses at Children's Hospital enjoy sunlight on an outdoor terrace in 1932, four years after the opening of the Pleasant Avenue hospital building. Courtesy, Children's Hospital*

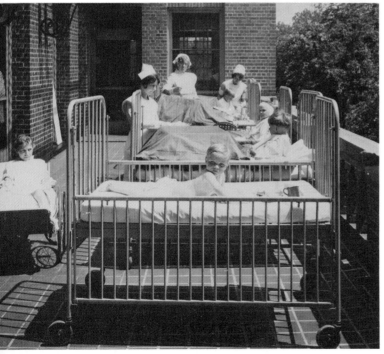

County Board of Control named Ancker its administrator.

Ancker was a charity hospital, its patients the unemployed and working poor—farmhands, laborers, domestics, and the contagiously ill. The hospital was crowded almost from the start, and early conditions were primitive. Water came from a well, light from kerosene lamps, heat from wood stoves. Operations, assisted by a nurse who was cook, laundress, and housekeeper, were performed behind a screen in a ward where other patients lay. The cellar was the morgue.

Over the years this hospital, where the Foley catheter was developed in 1927 and the original Burn Center was established in 1963, grew into a 615-bed hospital. In 1965 Ancker moved into a new and modern facility on Jackson Street and University Avenue, east of the state capitol. Now known as St. Paul-Ramsey Medical Center, it still serves the sick indigent. Its Burn Center is the leading burn-treatment center in the Upper Midwest. A training hospital, St. Paul-Ramsey has also focused on treatment of cancer and leukemia, drug and chemical abuse, Alzheimer's disease and geriatric medicine. Gillette Children's Hospital is also located in the Medical Center complex. This is an association of long standing. Gillette was established in 1897 by the state legislator as the Gillette State Children's Hospital. The first hospital in the nation to provide free care to crippled children of low-income families, Gillette was housed for its first eleven years at the city-county hospital. Gillette grew into a ten-building complex built between 1914 and 1946 on East Ivy, before its move in 1977 to the St. Paul-Ramsey Medical Center.

Gillette Children's Hospital offers a program for children, teenagers, and young adults with severe head injuries and provides acute and chronic care, rehabilitation training, family support, counseling, and education.

Other hospitals serve the St. Paul area—Bethesda Lutheran Medical Center behind the state capitol; Midway Hospital midway between Minneapolis and St. Paul; Mounds Park and St. John's Eastside on Dayton's Bluff; Samaritan Hospital, founded by the Northern Pacific Railway north of downtown St. Paul; Divine Redeemer Memorial Hospital in South St. Paul; St. John's Northeast in Maplewood.

Hospitals are now big business for St. Paul, generating 355 million dollars in revenues, employing 9,500 people, and paying 174 million dollars in salaries annually. Driven by a changing market, St. Paul's hospitals, like others around the country, are developing special services to create market niches for themselves by drawing upon late twentieth century technology for diagnosis and therapy.

Bethesda, founded more than a century ago, has a national model hospice and a special unit for patients who need respiratory help, in addition to therapy that will allow them to live at home or at least outside the hospital in a nursing

Bethesda Lutheran Medical Center is just one of many medical treatment centers in the St. Paul area. Photo by Kay Shaw

AMERICAN HOIST & DERRICK COMPANY

When the forerunner of Amhoist opened its doors at 459 North Robert Street on September 4, 1882, its business was repairing the heavy equipment used in Minnesota's timber and iron ore industries. Within a year, however, co-founders Frank J. Johnson and Oliver T. Crosby had started manufacturing their own line of hand- and horse-powered hoisting equipment.

Today lifting requirements for projects ranging from building construction to offshore drilling platforms is a complex operation accomplished by sophisticated, powerful equipment. The technology has changed—and so has the St. Paul-based company that has been using it for more than a century: American Hoist & Derrick Company, better known as Amhoist.

The Amhoist of today is a far cry from that once-simple manufacturing company. In 1883, when the firm was called the American Manufacturing Company, it was one of the first manufacturing companies to use those new technological wonders—steam and electricity—to produce its line of construction hardware and hoisting equipment.

Within 10 years of its founding, the business had outgrown its original wood-frame building and moved to 63 South Robert Street, an address that in 1987 will have been home to part of the firm's operations for a full century. But only part. By 1892 the growing enterprise had opened a second office and distribution facility in Chicago and changed its name to American Hoist & Derrick Company to better reflect its business specialty.

Today Amhoist has grown to become a worldwide leader in the manufacturing of capital goods and industrial products as well as a wholesale distributor of hardware. Through it all, however, it has continued to call St. Paul

Two Amhoist revolver cranes on the SSCV (semisubmersible crane vessel), the world's largest, are each capable of lifting more than 7,000 metric tons.

home. And while the firm's profile in the city has changed over the years, its presence remains significant. Approximately 800 of Amhoist's 3,200 employees worldwide are spread among five different St. Paul-based operations.

The most visible is the worldwide headquarters atop the glittering Amhoist Tower in the heart of downtown. In addition, four of the company's six divisions (American Crane, Harris Press & Shear, Waterous, and FOK, which stands for Farwell, Ozmun, Kirk & Co.) are headquartered in the city, as are the parts and service operation for American Crane and the manufacturing plant for the Waterous division.

American Crane remains the world's leading manufacturer of lattice boom cranes, as well as other cranes and hoists for construction, transportation, energy,

and marine industries. Amhoist's other divisions are also leaders in their fields: Harris Press & Shear in the scrap steel industry and the growing solid waste- and paper-recycling industries worldwide; the Crosby Group in high-quality industrial fittings and lifting accessories; Waterous in the manufacture of pumps, hydrants, and valves for the fire and waterworks industries; FOK as one of the nation's largest independent distributors of hardware and home-improvement products, marketed in Trustworthy Hardware Stores; and Vac-Tec Systems, which designs and manufactures equipment for vacuum coating thin films onto a variety of surfaces for industrial and electronic uses.

Through its first 104 years and the major restructuring of the corporation that has been accomplished in the 1980s, continuity has been a hallmark of Amhoist. Robert H. Nassau, president and chief executive officer since 1982, is only the seventh chief executive officer to guide the company since that first eventful day back in 1882.

SAMARITAN HOSPITAL

The changing nature of health care in America has brought with it substantial changes in the hospitals formed to provide that care. Samaritan Hospital of St. Paul exemplifies that trend. Founded in 1921 as the base hospital for the Northern Pacific Railroad System, Samaritan today is a short-term, acute care surgical hospital offering a growing array of specialized medical and health care services. A member of American Healthcare Management's nationwide family of hospitals, Samaritan provides a state-of-the-art combination of medical professionals and technology in a peaceful neighborhood setting.

When the Northern Pacific moved its hospital facilities to the Midway district from Brainerd in 1921, it created Samaritan to provide a unique combination of public and private hospital care. The first priority was caring for the employees and families of the railroad itself, but the community was also to benefit from the facility's

A Second Look™—cosmetic and reconstructive surgery at Samaritan.

emergency room, general, and acute care services.

The railroad era officially ended before Samaritan was acquired by American Healthcare Management in 1981, but the philosophy of public service has been renewed. A major renovation of the institution was undertaken to bring the physical facility up to date. A three-story medical office building

and attached parking ramp have been added, both connected to the hospital itself through a climate-controlled skyway. And a variety of specialty services and programs are available to the community.

As a railroad hospital, Samaritan was the area's first industry-sponsored HMO-style organization. Its Industrial Medicine program includes complete prevention, control, and rehabilitation services for businesses. It also provides wellness screening and educational activities for companies and their workers.

The Women's Health Network is designed to offer coordinated inpatient and outpatient health services for women in a distinctly feminine environment. Services include A Second Look™, a cosmetic surgery program; fitness testing; dietary programs; chemotherapy; OsteoProtection (testing for osteoporosis); educational seminars; and treatment programs for women's health problems.

In addition, the Balance™ program treats the eating disorders of anorexia nervosa and bulimia.

The Hospitele program is a "hotel within the hospital." Patients may stay in hotel-style rooms with the reassurance of nearby medical support services. Family members of patients also use Hospitele, which is particularly well suited to the recovery needs of cosmetic and reconstructive surgery patients.

Former Minnesota Viking Carl Eller provides drug screening, chemical dependency outpatient counseling, and special education programs for athletes through his Triumph Life Center at Samaritan.

The new Samaritan is a community hospital, with a special mission of small-town service within the metropolitan health care marketplace.

A room in Hospitele, the "hotel in the hospital."

home. The first bipolar pace-maker in medical history was implanted successfully at Bethesda in 1959.

Midway Hospital, established in 1920 by the Baptist Hospital Fund, is linked with Mounds Park and St. John's Eastside and Northeast hospitals in Health East. This is a joint venture corporation formed by Health Resources, Inc., and Baptist Hospital Fund to offer the hospitals a network approach. Part of the hospitals' emphasis is on preparing young people for careers in health services.

Children's Hospital of St. Paul has a new twelve-bed Pediatric Intensive Care Unit and extensive outpatient services. Divine Redeemer Hospital in South St. Paul has programs in psychiatry, chemical dependency and occupational medicine. It also provides an occupational health program for employers that includes pre-employment physicals and health and fitness programs. Samaritan Hospital offers an eating disorder program for people suffering from anorexia and bulimia. United Hospital's quality assurance program is based on a computerized evaluation of quality, effectiveness, and appropriateness of patient care. University of Minnesota Hospitals is world-famous for the organ transplant surgery performed by Dr. John Najarian, chief of surgery at the university since 1967.

Perhaps the most startling changes in health care, at least those that have affected the general public the most profoundly, have not been in the glossy new hospitals or the technology of implants, but in the emergence of health and hospitalization insurance plans and health maintenance organizations. Blue Cross and Blue Shield of Minnesota (BCBSM) was the second nonprofit health-care plan in the United States. The Blue Cross symbol originated in St. Paul in 1934 when E. A. van Steenwyk, Blue Cross manager and executive director from 1933 to 1939, commissioned a Viennese artist, Joseph Binder, to paint a poster with a blue cross on it.

Blue Cross grew out of the health-care crisis of the late 1920s, when some 55 percent of working Americans (26 million people) bore the brunt of medical costs that they often could not afford. Hospital beds stood empty, some hospitals folded, others operated at a loss, and by the early 1930s the worst Depression in the nation's history had begun. A system that allowed people to pay in advance for hospital, medical, and surgical care was desperately needed. Thus it was the reapplication of the idea of group insurance that was the origin of the Blue Cross movement.

Now, more than fifty years later, BCBSM, representing the traditional fee-for-service insurance coverage plans, has with its newly formed HMO Minnesota joined the newest revolution in health care: the health maintenance organizations launched in 1957 by Group Health Plan, the oldest HMO in Minnesota. Group Health grew out of the same era and some of the same circumstances—the need for affordable health care for working people—that produced Blue Cross.

Group Health's origins also go back to the 1930s and to a group of Twin Cities men and women who shared a common background in the cooperatives and in the credit-union movement of that period. Aware that most credit union loans went to pay medical bills, members of thirteen Twin Cities credit unions banded together in 1937 to found the Group Health Mutual Insurance Company, the forerunner of Group Health Plan. It was a pioneering concept—an organization that would be owned by its members and staffed by doctors paid in advance to provide medical care and to practice preventive medicine and health maintenance.

Today almost half the residents of St. Paul and Minneapolis belong to the nine HMOs serving the Twin Cities. They are led by Physicians Health Plan (PHP), the largest HMO in Minnesota, and include, besides Group Health and HMO Minnesota, Coordinated Health Care, MedCenters Health Plan (Park Nicollet), Medicare Partners, Metropolitan Health Plan, Senior

HEALTHEAST

For the 600,000 residents of the East Metro area—a region that includes Ramsey, Dakota, and Washington counties—the newest name in health care is HealthEast. Drawing on well-established resources and institutions serving the city's east side and surrounding suburbs, this new management company was formed in March 1986 in recognition of the changing health care marketplace and the growing need to create a more broadly distributed set of health care services while avoiding costly duplication of efforts.

HealthEast is a joint venture of Health Resources and Baptist Hospital Fund, Inc. It has three primary missions. On an operational level, it unites the health care operations of St. John's Eastside Hospital and Mounds Park Hospital on the east side of St. Paul. It also coordinates activities and negotiates third-party contracts on behalf of those two hospitals plus St. John's Northeast Hospital in Maplewood and Midway Hospital in the city's Midway district. And it provides corporate staff functions, including financial, legal, strategic planning, marketing services, and business development and public affairs for the respective owning organizations.

Baptist Hospital Fund was the first multihospital system in the Twin Cities. It owns and operates Midway Hospital on University Avenue, a general and acute care institution that has served the city's Midway district since 1920, and Mounds Park, an acute, psychiatric, and chemical dependency facility established in 1907 on the bluffs above the Mississippi River in east St. Paul.

Health Resources was the first health care corporation in the Twin Cities to reorganize itself in response to the deregulation and changing financial realities of medical care. Its family of services includes St. John's Eastside Hospital, an acute and general care hospital

HealthEast facilities are noted for the excellence of their specialty services from obstetrics and gynecology to care of the senior citizen—plus orthopedic care, digestive diseases, and oncology. Photos by Leo Kim

offering medical/surgical, obstetrics, and pediatric services, and St. John's Northeast Hospital, an acute care institution that opened in Maplewood in 1985.

By uniting their separate strengths, HealthEast is able to provide the most vertically integrated system of comprehensive health care in the Twin Cities. In addition to three general acute care medical/surgical hospitals and a psychiatric/chemical dependency facility, the HealthEast umbrella encompasses two long-term care facilities, two transitional care units, home health care services, an ambulance and transportation service, two free-standing surgical centers, senior housing projects, child development services, and medical real estate development

and management.

HealthEast facilities are noted for the excellence of their specialty services in the areas of digestive diseases, orthopedic care, senior care, obstetrics and gynecology, and oncology treatment. The organization also provides services to business and industry and is deeply involved in medical education.

HealthEast hospitals, clinics, and related services are affiliated with more than 600 physicians in private practice in the East Metro area and are staffed by more than 3,000 highly trained employees. Nearly one out of every three individuals who receives health care in the East Metro market in the next 12 months will receive it through a HealthEast facility.

BLUE CROSS AND BLUE SHIELD OF MINNESOTA

Andrew Czajkowski, president, and James Shaw, chairman of the board.

For more than 1.5 million people in communities from metropolitan St. Paul to the small towns of outstate Minnesota, the most important color in health care is blue. Through local, federal, and national programs, Blue Cross and Blue Shield of Minnesota serves one in three residents of the state each year—processing some seven million medical claims annually and paying well over one billion dollars for the individuals and families they cover.

But the modern Blue Cross and Blue Shield is much more than a bill-paying organization. Through nine interrelated affiliate corporations, "the Blues" have become a full-service health care system that now offers life insurance, health maintenance organization (HMO) benefits, dental coverage, preferred provider organizations, and disability plans, as well as third-party claims administration. What's more, the comprehensive information base created through years of conscientious service to Minnesotans and their families has become an increasingly valuable resource in the continuing quest for high-quality, yet cost-effective, health care.

It was a health care crisis of a different era that gave rise to the first Blue Cross organizations. In the years just prior to the Great Depression, doctors, politicians, and other health care officials wrestled with a grim dilemma: how to assure that the 26 million working Americans with incomes between $1,500 and $5,000 per year—55 percent of all working people in 1928—could afford the staggering cost of illnesses that required hospitalization.

Group insurance plans had been tried, but most programs of that time had broad cancellation provisions, restrictions on the injuries and illnesses covered, and policies that excluded women and those working in hazardous occupations. Individual plans were simply too expensive for middle-class families. Because their ability to pay was so limited, many people simply avoided hospitals—and hospitals accordingly suffered from low occupancies that threatened their ability to stay in business. Then came the Depression, and what had been a dilemma became a national crisis.

In 1932 seven St. Paul hospital administrators formed a prepaid hospitalization plan based on a model that up to that point involved agreements with only one hospital at a time. The nonprofit Hospital Service Association of St. Paul initially included Bethesda, Midway, Miller, St. Luke's (now United), Mounds Park, St. John's, and West Side General hospitals in the city. For 75 cents per month (nine dollars per year), employees of companies in St. Paul could enroll in group coverage plans that would provide 21 days of hospital care for themselves plus (for an additional dollar per year) 25 percent coverage for their dependants. A one-room office in the Guardian Building downtown was

Blue Cross and Blue Shield of Minnesota headquarters, located on Highway 13 in Eagan.

138

Claims processing combines high technology and hometown service.

---

leased, and E.A. van Steenwyk was hired to manage the organization, which quickly became a model for other groups nationwide.

It was van Steenwyk who gave the nation the Blue Cross symbol. A former advertising salesman, he wanted a logo for the business. In 1934 he settled on the blue Greek or Geneva cross, an international symbol of relief for those struck by disaster. Within five years the blue cross had become the national symbol of prepaid multihospital plans. The St. Paul organization merged with a seven-hospital Minneapolis system in 1935 to become the Minnesota Hospital Service Association. In 1938, with the addition of a plan for two hospitals in Duluth, Blue Cross began to mature into a truly statewide organization.

Over the years the Blue Cross and Blue Shield organizations have benefited from the innovative direction and leadership of van Steenwyk's successors—Arthur Calvin, Richard Crist, Robert Johnson, James Regnier, and Andrew Czajkowski. They have guided a steady diversification designed to provide the right kind of health care coverage for virtually any circumstance. To the basic Blue Cross and Blue Shield plans have been added HMO Minnesota

and HMO Midwest (which serves residents of western Wisconsin), AWARE Gold and AWARE Dental, Coordinated Health Care (another HMO option), and the life insurance programs of MII Life. In addition, the Blues administer a number of programs for the federal government and the State of Minnesota, from Medicaid demonstration projects to the Minnesota Comprehensive Health Association, which offers comprehensive health care for state residents who cannot get regular coverage.

An enduring key to the success of Blue Cross and Blue Shield is the widespread participation of physicians, hospitals, pharmacies, and other health care providers throughout the state. Every hospital in the state is involved in Blue Cross and Blue Shield programs. AWARE Gold, founded in 1983, has already become the state's largest provider network, its first-dollar coverage for preventive care and freedom to see any doctor without a referral drawing on the active participation of some 7,000 Minnesota physicians. Nearly three-quarters of the state's dentists are members of the AWARE Dental network, and nine out of 10 pharmacies participate in drug coverage programs.

These providers offer more than health care. They also contribute their expertise as members of the organization's board of trustees and advisory groups. In addition, a network of seven district offices keeps Blue Cross and Blue Shield close to both providers and consumers.

In today's more cost-conscious health care environment, the Blues' service mission involves helping people find the best health care for their particular needs, a delicate balancing of quality and cost. In 1985 alone, cost-containment programs saved members nearly $70 million, resulting in both better benefits and more affordable rates. Some 40

percent of all claims are now received and processed electronically, further streamlining the administration of the Blues' health care coverage.

To develop comprehensive and affordable coverage for future generations, Blue Cross and Blue Shield is working with 39 major hospitals in the state in using the MEDISGRPS (Medical Illness Severity Grouping System) program to better define quality health care. As this innovative data base grows, it will provide a clearer picture of the severity of various illnesses and medical conditions, and help health care providers better match their care to patient needs.

From headquarters in the southern suburb of Eagan, and a growing network of district offices around the state, the 1,600 employees of Blue Cross and Blue Shield of Minnesota provide a unique combination of hometown service and worldwide coverage to Minnesotans throughout the state and the nation.

A 1934 poster features the Blue Cross symbol, which originated in Minnesota and became a national emblem.

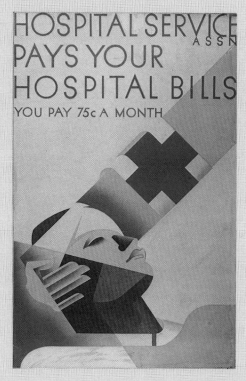

Health Plan, and SHARE Health Plan.

St. Paul's largest medical group practice is Ramsey Clinic, which includes specialists in every field of medicine who care for patients at St. Paul-Ramsey Medical Center and at six Ramsey Clinic locations in the Twin Cities area, eastern Minnesota, and western Wisconsin. A nonprofit corporation, Ramsey Clinic is primarily responsible for medical education and research, the practice of medicine, satellite clinics, and the handling of physicians' fees. Ramsey Clinic is a subsidiary of Minnesota-Wisconsin Medical Services, a holding company responsible for planning, financial policies, use of resources, networking, and diversification.

The St. Paul-Ramsey Foundation, formerly the Saint Paul-Ramsey Hospital Medical Education and Research Foundation, was incorporated in 1966 to support and direct research efforts by allocating $350,000 annually, soliciting additional grants, and administering the funds. Ramsey Clinic and St. Paul-Ramsey Medical Center representatives serve on its board, along with community leaders and consumers. The foundation is also a subsidiary of Minnesota-Wisconsin Medical Services.

The technology of the 1970s and 1980s has

been a major factor in helping the health-care industry control costs. Computers track hospital admissions and discharges, record the length of hospitalizations, and monitor types and costs of treatment, not only in hospitals but also in medical offices and clinics.

By no means all of St. Paul's economy rests on high tech, but few of the area's manufacturing firms have escaped the effect of new technology on the industrial marketplace. A fleeting glimpse of the area's industrial past can be seen in such companies as Paper, Calmenson & Company (steel products); American Hoist and Derrick (heavy cranes); Northern Malleable Iron Company (cast iron); North Star Steel (metals); Economics Laboratory (chemicals and cleaning compounds); H.B. Fuller (adhesives); Northern Conveyor (materials handling); Lindsay (water softeners); Jacob Schmidt and Stroh's (brewing); Waldorf (paper products/packaging); and Plastics, Inc. (plastics). All share a common background in St. Paul, and many have become part of national and international firms.

Paper, Calmenson & Company (PACAL) is still one of the largest family-owned businesses of its kind in the United States. It got its start in 1891 when Lewis Paper and Moses Calmenson

The St. Paul-Ramsey Medical Center still serves the sick indigent, since its founding in 1869 as Ancker Hospital. Today its Burn Center is the leading burn-treatment center in the upper Midwest. Photo by Kay Shaw

set up shop on St. Paul's East Side to buy and sell scrap iron, machinery, and metals. Their location was strategic—close to the railroad tracks—and their equipment sparse but sufficient: two wheelbarrows, three hand trucks, one railroad scale, one bale press, two stoves, a safe, and a desk. Today PACAL makes a wide range of carbon- and alloy-steel mill products—steel blades for earthmoving and snow-removal equipment, steel joints for construction—for sale throughout the United States and Canada.

Another St. Paul manufacturer began as a small Lowertown foundry specializing in repairing machinery. Oliver Crosby and Frank Johnson established American Hoist and Derrick partly on the strength of their own expertise as mechanical engineers. The evolution of Amhoist's products in the years since then illustrates how one St. Paul company adapted to a changing economy. Its American Railroad Ditcher was introduced at a time when railroads needed help in maintaining their rights-of-way. Amhoist equipment was used to build the Panama Canal and for marine deck uses during World Wars I and II. The American Revolver Crane was the right piece of machinery for public-works projects undertaken during the Depression, and its Sky Horse, capable of lifting 500 to 3,000 tons, is a response to other twentieth-century production needs. Its corporate headquarters are now located in the new Amhoist tower on Rice Park in downtown St. Paul.

Economics Laboratory and H.B. Fuller also had a pattern of family leadership. In 1923 Merritt J. Osborn, a forty-four-year-old St. Paul auto salesman, invested $5,000 in a new idea, a carpet cleaner called Absorbit. Next came Soilax, a new product for restaurant dishwashing. Sixty years later—fifty of those years under the leadership of Osborn's son, E.B.—Economics Laboratory is a multinational firm. It makes products for cleaning everything from crystal chandeliers to jet engines—none of them mixed in a mortar box with a five-pound scoop and garden hoe, as were the company's earliest products.

E.B. Osborn carried on his father's business when he joined Economics Laboratory, Inc. after graduating from Dartmouth College. Courtesy, MHS

Like Merritt Osborn, H.B. Fuller also had an idea in the 1880s. His was for a wallpaper plaster that he cooked on his kitchen stove, then sold to paperhangers and bookbinders from a third-floor office on Robert Street. Deliveries were made in a modest wagon pulled by "Davey," the workhorse. Fuller and his sons, Albert and H.B., Jr., branched out into paints and into steel scaffolding for painters and paperhangers. In the early 1930s Fuller hired a young advertising director, Elmer L. Andersen, who eventually bought out the business. He became Minnesota's governor in 1961. With

H.B. FULLER COMPANY

Stockholders and shareholders of the H.B. Fuller Company long ago became accustomed to a rare form of mathematics for a publicly held corporation. On the firm's list of priorities, they rank third, not first. Ahead of them are H.B. Fuller's employees and, in the top spot, the company's customers the world over.

If it's a rare operating philosophy, it also has been proven a successful one. The firm, which celebrates its 100th anniversary in 1987, has grown from Harvey Benjamin Fuller's kitchen stovetop wallpaper paste business in St. Paul to a diversified, multinational manufacturer of specialty chemicals, including adhesives, sealants, coatings, paints, specialty waxes, and sanitation chemicals that ranks among the *Fortune* 500.

With more than 50 plants and technical service centers in 30 U.S. cities, as well as operations in 29 countries around the world, H.B. Fuller is a major force in the packaging, graphic arts, paper converting, construction, automotive, and consumer products industries. As one stock market analyst once noted, when someone needs something wet, something sticky, or something gooey, he

comes to H.B. Fuller.

In its first half-century H.B. Fuller was an essentially regional company. Fuller and his sons, Albert and Harvey, expanded from wallpaper paste to other kinds of adhesives. In the 1930s they made another significant addition to the firm, hiring Elmer L. Andersen as advertising manager. Andersen, current chairman of the board (and governor of Minnesota from 1961 to 1963), and his son Tony, president and chief executive officer, have guided H.B. Fuller through most of its second 50 years. During that time the elder Andersen bought the firm from the founding family and, in 1968, took it public.

The Andersen years have been years of steady growth and expansion, first throughout the United States, then worldwide. The original growth was on a decentralized level, creating small plants close to customers around the country to respond quickly to specific needs. The emphasis was on rep-

---

Anthony L. Andersen, president and chief executive officer (left), and Elmer L. Andersen, chairman of the board, have directed H.B. Fuller through its dramatic half-century of growth in the United States and around the world.

licating the success H.B. Fuller had experienced in St. Paul. When the company began expanding into foreign markets—in Canada, then Central and South America—that attention to meeting the specific needs of customers close to their own markets continued.

In more recent years H.B. Fuller has widened its focus to develop operations in Europe and the Pacific, including the 1986 opening of a new manufacturing facility just outside of the city of Canton in the People's Republic of China. The plant is a joint venture with agencies of the Chinese government. It will produce a wide range of specialty chemicals, including adhesives and sealants for the construction and industrial markets in Guangdong Province, which has a population of 60 million.

The company's decentralized emphasis has been modified somewhat in the 1980s to focus on industry-specific needs. In the United States, that has meant merging together three previously separate groups—the Packaging Adhesives, Assembly Products, and Polymer divisions—into a combined Adhesives, Sealants and Coatings Division (known as ASC), with sales forces organized along industry lines. ASC's 25 local manufacturing plants and six service centers serving industries ranging from containers and envelope manufacturing to telecommunications and aerospace, from automotive to nonwovens and graphic arts.

In addition, five specialty divisions serve distinct markets: supplies for the construction contractor and the do-it-yourselfer (Building Products Division); sanitation chemicals for the food and dairy industries (Monarch Products Division); decorative and protective powder coatings for metal products (Industrial Coatings Division); adhesives, sealants, mastics, and coatings for insulation (Foster Products Division); and hot-melt-

coated string for specialty applications in plywood and packaging (Linear Products Group).

Internationally, the 1982 acquisition of Isar-Rakoll Chemie of Germany (FRG) more than doubled H.B. Fuller's presence in Europe, making the continent the center of the company's largest overseas operations. In Latin America, the Kativo Chemical Industries subsidiary continues a tradition of industrial activity and involvement that began some 20 years ago. H.B. Fuller plants operate in 14 of the region's 21 countries, and serve the rest through exports. Other international operations are located in Canada, Australia, New Zealand, Japan, and Taiwan.

The corporate headquarters on Energy Park Drive in St. Paul coordinates this growing array of international business activity. In all, about 600 of the company's 1,700 U.S. employees—there are more than 4,000 worldwide—are concentrated among the six H.B. Fuller office, research, and manufacturing locations in the Twin Cities.

In addition to the headquarters and a St. Paul production plant, other operations include the headquarters of the ASC, Industrial Coatings, and Monarch divisions, a manufacturing plant in Fridley, and the Willow Lake Research

Situated in a 100-acre nature preserve, the Willow Lake Research Center in Vadnais Heights spearheads H.B. Fuller's new product development efforts.

Center, the firm's research and development laboratory, located on a 180-acre site in Vadnais Heights. One hundred acres at Willow Lake have been left undeveloped as a wildlife refuge, while the three-story building is earth-sheltered on three sides and makes use of the latest innovations in energy technology to intrude as little as possible into its unspoiled natural setting.

The H.B. Fuller philosophy has a fourth priority: the communities in which it operates. Employees at every level of the organization are involved in the Community Affairs Program that operates in their respective communities. The program combines the time contributed by employee volunteers with company support and financing through 34 local Community Affairs Councils. Each council (there is one in every U.S. city where H.B. Fuller operates a plant or technical center) develops its own ideas, elects its own leadership, and decides how its support will be allocated. The program is being expanded to international locations as well.

In recent years the councils have emphasized programs that deal with domestic violence. The St. Paul group helped start shelters for battered women. A group in Minneapolis developed a program to station a legal advocate at the courthouse to help women

who decide to prosecute their rapists. Other programs have included shelters for runaways and victims of child abuse, plus broader ranging activities in support of the Special Olympics, senior citizens, and excellence in education.

The mathematics is interesting—and inspiring. Combine an emphasis on meeting the needs of the customer with a concern for employees and the communities where they (and their customers) live and work, and you create a company whose success is shared by all. That's a sound investment, any way you look at it.

At the Willow Lake Research Center, H.B. Fuller chemists and technicians focus their efforts on solving industrial problems through the development of adhesives and specialty chemical products.

Quality—the conformance of product to end-use requirements—is an essential ingredient at H.B. Fuller adhesive and specialty chemical plants around the world.

BETHESDA LUTHERAN MEDICAL CENTER

One of St. Paul's oldest hospitals is also one of its newest and most up-to-date medical service providers, an emerging leader in acute and long-term health care throughout the state of Minnesota.

Bethesda Lutheran Medical Center, which celebrated its centennial in 1983, began as a "home for the sick" on a rise of land two blocks east of Lake Como. It subsequently moved to downtown St. Paul before settling in at its third and current location, a multiple-care medical campus just two blocks north of the state capitol.

The medical center includes the hospital itself, with 298 acute care beds, and 138 additional beds dedicated to providing a skilled care center. It includes Hospice St. Paul, Minnesota's oldest hospice program for the terminally ill, the nationally recognized Prolonged Respiratory Care Unit, Surgaday (one-day surgery), crisis intervention programs, and a growing number of community health education initiatives—postoperative cardiac care, prepared childbirth classes, a quit-smoking program, and bereavement outreach.

Bethesda Lutheran is also a primary teaching hospital. It is the site of a University of Minnesota Family Practice Residency Program. Bethesda provides valuable clinical experience for students training to become registered nurses through Gustavus Adolphus College. And it is a national focal point for Clinical Pastoral Education, a program for clergy of many denominations as they train for work in today's complex health care environment.

The modern, multifaceted medical center in the bustling Capitol Heights section of St. Paul has come a long way from the 20-bed, indigent-care hospital opened more than a century ago in a renovated house near Lake Como by an arm of the Swedish Lutheran Minnesota Conference. In its early days Bethesda Hospital was an

Bethesda Lutheran Medical Center was founded more than a century ago as a 20-bed, indigent-care facility near Lake Como. Today's hospital, at 559 Capitol Boulevard in St. Paul, is a leader in acute and long-term health care throughout Minnesota.

important resource for newly arrived immigrants to Swede Hollow on St. Paul's East Side, home to most of the city's Swedish population in the latter days of the nineteenth century.

By 1892 the hospital had been moved from the then-remote Lake Como site (today again a private home on North Victoria Avenue) to the former Upham mansion at Ninth and Wacouta in the downtown area (right next door to railroad baron James J. Hill's first home). There it served more than 100,000 patients, from St. Paul and the surrounding region, over the next four decades.

In 1931, in the face of the ravages of the Depression, ground was broken at the current site for the new Bethesda, a modern hospital constructed on a budget that seemed astronomical for the time: $500,000. More than 5,000 people attended the dedication a year later. The keynote speaker: Dr. William J. Mayo.

The original exterior of the hospital still exists, with additional wings having been added through

New parents can enjoy their babies in the homelike setting of the Family Suite, one of many innovations for patient comfort.

the years. In the last year the entire interior has been completely renovated. It is being joined by the Capitol Heights housing development, designed to provide more than 200 apartments for the elderly on the Bethesda campus, and visible evidence of Bethesda's continuing involvement in the rebirth of St. Paul.

Today Bethesda Lutheran Medical Center remains true to its original mission—a home for those in need, whether in a traditional hospital facility, in a longer-term nursing or senior care setting, or in the comfort of a private home. Its birth, development, and rebirth mirrors that of St. Paul itself, a modern health care provider that has served the needs of the city for most of St. Paul's history.

144

NORTH STAR STEEL COMPANY

Rebirth and redevelopment are themes that apply to many aspects of St. Paul's economic profile. They apply, as well, to America's steel industry, where the larger, centralized mills of years past have given way to newer "mini-mills" more closely oriented to regional and specialized markets. A leader in that movement is North Star Steel Company, Minnesota's only steel mill and a wholly owned subsidiary of Cargill Company.

What is now a growing network of mini-mills in six states began in St. Paul in 1965 as a joint venture between Canadian and Twin City business interests. From the Canadian side came G.R. Heffernan, a man who had built and operated two steel mills in Canada. His local counterpart was J.B. Klemp, whose background included not only steel but also a stint as an FBI agent.

The two chose to base their new business on a 200-acre site in the St. Paul Port Authority's new industrial park along Pig's Eye Lake on the city's southeast side. Ten years later W. Duncan MacMillan, a member of the Cargill family who served on North Star's board of directors, was instrumental in arranging Cargill's purchase of the business. Since then North Star has added mills and other facilities in Duluth; Wilton, Iowa; Beaumont, Texas; Youngstown, Ohio; Monroe, Michigan; and Calvert City, Kentucky. Total sales now exceed $500 million annually. More than 400 of the company's 2,500 employees work in the St. Paul plant.

It was Klemp and Heffernan who originally convinced the Port Authority to name its entire industrial park for Red Rock, a distinctive Indian landmark among the bluffs along the Mississippi River's eastern bank. And while "park" is a word seldom associated with heavy industries such as steel, it's a word that can be used to describe the bustling plant St. Paul

North Star Steel Company's arc furnaces and continuous casting lines reduce scrap, especially automobiles, into reusable steel scrap and other nonferrous and nonmetallic material.

The steel scrap is melted down in electric arc furnaces.

drivers see from Highways 10 and 61, just north of the junction with Interstate 494. Frontage landscaping and a subdued paint scheme effectively mask a mill site that annually ships 300,000 tons of finished product and 120,000 tons of "billets" (lengths of solid steel) to other mills and manufacturers in Minnesota, Wisconsin, Iowa, the Dakotas, Illinois, Kentucky, Nebraska, and Oklahoma. Fully five miles of rail serve the plant's elec-

tric arc furnaces and continuous casting lines, and trucks depart constantly for destinations throughout the Upper Midwest and beyond.

Much of the raw material used in the St. Paul mill comes from scrap, especially automobiles. A 6,000-horsepower shredder reduces yesterday's family chariots to fist-size fragments that are then separated into reusable steel scrap and other nonferrous and nonmetallic material. The steel scrap is melted down in electric arc furnaces that allow precise controls for desulfurization and alloying, yielding billets of uniform quality and purity.

North Star Steel Company's continuous casting method transforms the molten steel into a solid billet in about seven minutes. So precise is the process that seven different grades of scrap, based on purity and density, can be selected and blended to make new steel to custom specifications. Much of the mill's finished product is used in construction, oil country goods, and general equipment.

worldwide sales, H.B. Fuller is widely diversified, and widely known as one of the Minnesota corporations cited as national models for charitable contributions across the country ranging from 2 to 5 percent of pretax profits. Fuller, however, may be the first American corporation to export its giving; in fact, charitable gifts among its Latin American subsidiaries now stand at 2 percent and are heading for a goal of 5 percent.

GNB Batteries, Inc. (Gould National Batteries) has come full-circle since its founding in St. Paul in 1910 as Electric Manufacturing Company. Now the world's largest independently owned battery company and manufacturer of lead-acid batteries for cars, trucks, and construction equipment, GNB pioneered private label marketing. In 1922 the company had been reorganized as National Lead Battery Company; eventually it became a subsidiary of Gould, Inc., the Chicago electronics firm.

In 1984 GNB's senior managers bought GNB Batteries from Gould and reestablished it as an independently owned and managed company. Two of GNB's three divisions and its corporate headquarters are located in Mendota Heights in suburban St. Paul.

Switching from casting malleable iron for horse-drawn farm machinery to producing ductile iron for trucks, auto parts, and computerized farm machinery, Northern Malleable Iron Company is the only company of its kind in Minnesota today, just as it was in 1905 when it was founded. Metal in those days was melted in hand-fired, coal-burning furnaces, and employees included so many immigrants from Europe that company rules were printed in seven languages. Today electric induction furnaces have replaced coal, and highly mechanized equipment operated with electricity has taken over some of the tasks once performed by labor.

Standard Conveyor has for the past eighty years manufactured systems for handling products that stem from an invention Charlie Lister hammered together from two-by-fours and the tops of baking-powder tins. Another inventor with an idea was Lyn G. Lindsay, Sr. In the 1920s Lindsay worked at improving the cumbersome water-conditioning equipment that rid water of hardness, iron, acidity, bad taste, and odor. Sales skyrocketed with the post-World War II building boom and the development of smaller and more efficient water softeners. Now a division of Ecodyne Corporation, Lindsay is the largest manufacturer of automatic water conditioning in the country.

Waldorf Paper Products has also come full circle in the 100 years since H.L. Collins produced labels and pill boxes in a modest plant at Fifth and Minnesota in downtown St. Paul. The company moved from making labels, shipping containers, and shopping bags to recycling paper and wood. St. Paul residents who were children during the early 1920s remember the huge paper drives involving thousands of children that the company organized. Waldorf became Hoerner Waldorf, then merged with Champion International of Stamford, Connecticut, and now it has been purchased by a group of local executives and is once again a St. Paul-based and locally owned corporation.

Then there is Plastics, Inc., chartered in 1940 and expanded under the leadership of Paul K. Schilling (inventor of the disposable plastic glass) until its acquisition by Anchor-Hocking. High tech, which brought about the microwave oven, created the need for microwave products, which Plastics, Inc., also manufactures.

Nowhere can St. Paul's industrial past be seen more clearly than in the story of its breweries, a proud tradition inherited by Stroh Brewery Company, which has spent thirteen million dollars to renovate the old Hamm's Brewing Company plant on the East Side. On the opposite side of the city is the crenellated Jacob Schmidt Brewery on West Seventh Street, now owned by G. Heileman Brewing Company of La Crosse, Wisconsin.

As the *St. Paul Pioneer Press* observed in 1887, "the five prominent institutions in every new-born Western town are the school house, the church, the general store, the newspaper and the saloon." In a city with a predominantly German population, the corner taverns became the neighborhood gathering places and the cornerstones of small businesses, just as the breweries that kept the taverns supplied were an essential factor in the city's cultural and business life.

Once there were twelve breweries in St. Paul, the brewing center of a state that in 1887 had 112 breweries. The Germans who flocked to Minnesota in the nineteenth century brought with them lager beer, the German invention that revolutionized brewing in America. Created by a different type of yeast and a different preparation method (aging in a cold place), lager beer had a cool, light, foaming quality. St. Paul held a particular attraction for brewers—its aging caves.

"In the pre-electric world of 19th century brewing, underground refrigeration was a necessity," Gary J. Brueggemann wrote in *Ramsey County History* magazine, published by the Ramsey County Historical Society. "St. Paul's Mississippi River bluffs not only provided a number of deep caves, but the soft texture of these sandstone terraces made it relatively easy to artificially create cooling caverns . . . At least fourteen different breweries took advantage of St. Paul's sandstone terraces." Some of these caves still exist under West Seventh Street. An 1883 business publication described them as "a perfect labyrinth of rooms and cellars and under cellars three deep, reminding one of the catacombs of Rome, for none unacquainted with these subterranean vaults, without a guide, could grope their way through them and find their way out to daylight."

The Jacob Schmidt Brewing Company dates back to 1884, when Schmidt, a native of Bavaria, took over control of the old North Star Brewery, the second-largest brewery west of Chicago that was producing 16,000 barrels of beer a year. In 1890 Schmidt hired as his bookkeeper

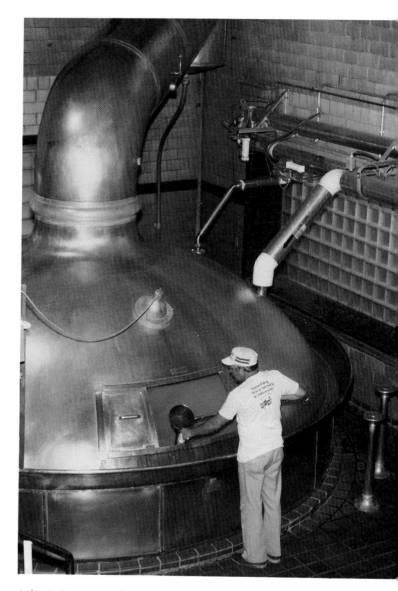

A Stroh Brewery worker takes a sample from a vat, which holds 500 barrels of beer. The 120-year old St. Paul plant produces three million barrels of beer per year. Photo by Leighton

Adolph Bremer, another German, who married Schmidt's only child, Maria, in 1896. Bremer became company president in 1899 and twelve years later, after Schmidt's death, assumed control of the brewery.

Meanwhile, Theodore Hamm had established Hamm's Brewery on the bluffs above St. Paul's

PLASTICS, INC.—ANCHOR HOCKING CORPORATION

For more than 48 years one of St. Paul's most innovative and productive manufacturing plants has been located just off Fort Road near Irvine Park—today within a few blocks of the St. Paul Civic Center.

The St. Paul home of Plastics, Inc., a wholly owned subsidiary of Anchor Hocking Corporation, is the point of origin for the dinnerware used by most airlines, the plastic serving cups ultimately filled with the taste-tempting creations of thousands of Dairy Queen and other fast-food stores, the upscale microwave meals found in the frozen-food sections of the nation's supermarkets, and the microwave cookware used more and more often in modern households. In all, the 1,100 employees of Plastics, Inc.—approximately 450 of them at the St. Paul plant, which also serves as headquarters for sales, marketing, and product engineering—manufacture some 3,500 products for food-related uses.

The company was officially chartered in 1938, and has been located at its current 224 Ryan Avenue address since 1944. In recent years rapid growth sparked by continual product innovations has made the St. Paul location the hub of a network of three other plants in Minnesota and Illinois, plus a major warehousing and distribution center on Vandalia Avenue.

The success of Plastics, Inc., is due largely to its tradition of taking a market-driven approach to existing and developing business specialties. The firm began as a maker of compression-molded plastic products during the World War II years, but it was the postwar prosperity and commercial opportunities of the late 1940s and early 1950s that set the stage for its growth.

In those years the nation discovered commercial air travel. A new industry was born to convey busi-

Under the leadership of Paul K. Schilling (left) and current president and general manager Robert H. Horn, Plastics, Inc., has become a diversified producer of custom and commercial food-service products.

ness executives and pleasure travelers to destinations all across the continent, and beyond. New systems had to be devised to meet the needs of those travelers—including ways to feed them onboard the era's propeller-driven airliners.

Plastics, Inc., actually introduced its first plastic dinnerware for the airline industry as early as 1948. It was made through compression molding of urea, the only food-grade plastic material then available. Within a few years, however, melamine made its debut, offering lighter weight and greater durability. Just as significantly, the bowls, plates, cups, and trays designed and manufactured by Plastics, Inc.—typically to the individual specifications of each separate airline—could be stacked easily, saving valuable space in an airliner's cramped galley.

As air travel literally took off in the 1950s with the introduction of jet aircraft, the fortunes of Plastics, Inc., soared as well. Over the next several years its dinnerware products became industry standards for excellence and efficiency.

By 1958 the company had introduced a new, two-color process that allowed the creation of custom dinnerware that was white on the inside and colored on the outside. At the same time Plastics, Inc., introduced a new cup design featuring an open handle, for the first time allowing cups to be stacked conveniently to further economize on galley space. To make the new cups, injection-molding processes were added to traditional compression-molding techniques.

If the 1950s were characterized by growth based on airline food service, the 1960s brought growth founded on airline beverage service. Under the leadership of St. Paul native Paul K. Schilling, Plastics, Inc., continued to identify and capitalize on developing market areas, initially serving the airline industry, but ultimately growing into other food-service sectors.

It was Schilling who invented the disposable plastic glass now commonly used not only by the airlines, but also by hotels and motels, restaurants, fast-food stores, and people entertaining at home. The injection-molded plastic tumblers were introduced by Plastics, Inc., in 1952, making convenient in-flight cocktail service possible for the first time. Over the next few years custom-designed decorator drinkware and two-piece stemware (allowing compact stacking of separate container and base pieces prior to use) were added to the firm's product lines.

It was also Schilling who began diversifying the company's marketing. The Hi-Heat® line of casserole dishes introduced for airline service in the mid-1960s quickly proved popular in hospitals as well, where a new form of cooking—by microwave—was gaining acceptance. By virtue of its early identification of this new market area, Plastics, Inc., was well positioned to ride the next growth wave in the food-service industry.

In recent years Plastics, Inc., has expanded its product lines (clockwise from lower right), from the airline industry, where it has long held a dominant position, to the commercial food-processing market, food service, and the microwave cookware used in more and more modern homes.

Its strengths and positioning led to its acquisition as a wholly owned subsidiary of Anchor Hocking Corporation of Lancaster, Ohio, in 1968. Benefiting from Anchor Hocking's strengths as a major supplier of household, hardware, and packaging products, the firm pioneered the emerging market for cookware that could be safely used in a microwave oven.

Today its Microware® line—developed from the company's Hi-Heat® product technology as the first full line of plastic microwave cookware that can be used in a microwave or conventional oven to 400 degrees—is the largest selling line in the industry. Meanwhile, the Hi-Heat® line continues to serve the airlines as well as major food processors who supply preplated frozen meals to institutional food-service operations. In the late 1970s this product line also began to enter households when major food companies began marketing upscale frozen entrees and dinners through grocery stores.

In 1985 a companion microwave line debuted: Freeze, Heat & Serve™, lightweight plastic cookware that can safely go from freezer to oven to table. Through a $4.5-million capital investment program, including involvement by the state and the Port Authority of the City of St. Paul, new production capacity has been added to the St. Paul plant to produce the newest line called FoodKeepers™.

Under the leadership of Schilling, and now Robert Horn, Plastics, Inc., has grown from an airline-based dinnerware maker to a diversified manufacturer of custom and commercial plastic products intended for food-service, food-packing, retail microwave cookware, premium, and airline markets. As a consequence of diversification and the rapidly rising popularity of microwave cooking, sales have mushroomed from $18 million in 1979 to $110 million in 1986. Approaching its 50th anniversary in St. Paul, Plastics, Inc., looks forward to continuing growth and success.

WALDORF CORPORATION

One of St. Paul's newest companies celebrated its first and its 100th anniversaries in 1986. Impossible? Not for Waldorf Corporation. The paperboard and folding carton manufacturer grew out of a small business that began in St. Paul in 1886, and for many years was better known around town as Hoerner Waldorf. On July 17, 1985, it reemerged as an independent company after eight years as part of the consumer packaging group of Champion International.

The new Waldorf is a vertically integrated producer of paperboard packaging for a variety of uses: food and beverage containers, wet and dry product cartons, heat-resistant cook-in cartons, and special structures for nonfood products. It operates three paperboard mills (the largest two are just off I-94 in a 46-acre complex in St. Paul's Midway District, the third is in Michigan) and six folding carton plants (the St. Paul operation plus facilities in Illinois, Iowa, Massachusetts, North Carolina, and Wisconsin), all purchased from Champion.

The heart of the business is recycling. The paperboard that will become boxes for everything from Cheerios® to Crayolas® begins as bundled-up newspapers, outdated computer forms, and trimmings from other paper packaging and publishing operations. At the

St. Paul plant, more than 300,000 tons of wastepaper are converted into useful forms each year. For that still-useful raw material, Waldorf pays out more than $20 million per year to recyclers, commercial suppliers, and the approximately 600 church, civic, and community groups in the area that conduct paper drives to raise funds.

And that's nothing new. It was the original Waldorf Boxboard Company that "invented" the paper drive way back near the turn of the century. The oldest of 21 children, Michael W. Waldorf joined the H.L. Collins Company in 1895 as a salesman for the business, which in those days made stationery, labels, and small boxes. One of his first big sales was to Washburn Crosby Company (now General Mills): 50 million labels for cans of Gold Medal® flour. By 1907 he not only was a part owner of Collins, but also had opened his own mill that operated on the wastepaper typically burned in backyard barrels all over the Twin Cities.

In 1917 the separate businesses were united as Waldorf Paper Products Company. Hoerner Wal-

The original Waldorf Boxboard Company "invented" the paper drive back near the turn of the century, and recycling has remained the heart of the business throughout the firm's history.

Today Waldorf Corporation paperboard mills purchase 400,000 tons of wastepaper a year, producing boxboard and packaging for many well-known consumer products.

dorf Corporation was formed in 1966 through a merger with Hoerner Boxes of Keokuk, Iowa. At the time of its acquisition by Champion in 1977, the company was one of the nation's foremost packaging firms. After eight years in the Champion family, Waldorf Corporation was purchased by local investors who have returned its business focus to the specialized niche it helped invent some 80 years ago. Eugene U. Frey, a 30-year veteran of the company, serves as president and chief executive officer. Richard E. O'Leary is chairman of the board.

For the new Waldorf, the city is a forest. Its mills draw on the most extensive recycling network in the nation, a 500-mile sweep that provides more than 1,000 jobs at the St. Paul plant alone. In addition to paperboard, Waldorf produces more than three billion folding cartons annually—more than a dozen for every man, woman, and child in the country. About 80 percent of the products manufactured in St. Paul are shipped to customers outside Minnesota. In the process Waldorf saves various communities more than four million dollars per year in landfill costs by diverting wastepaper into useful packaging. Waldorf Corporation, St. Paul's youngest 100-year-old company, is clearly one of its most innovative.

historic "Swede Hollow," the Phalen Creek valley. His only son, William, inherited his father's business, and he worked there as an executive for forty years. In 1972 Schmidt's became a division of G. Heileman, and in 1975 Hamm's, the last of St. Paul's local breweries, became part of Olympia Brewing Corporation and later part of Stroh's. Even so, some of the beers that made St. Paul famous—Schmidt's and Hamm's—are still being produced in St. Paul.

Labels, so important to the breweries, have become big business for Tapemark, founded in 1950 and now operating out of a plant in West St. Paul. Formed originally to print pressure-sensitive labels for 3M, Tapemark has branched out into making pressure-sensitive adhesive pads for medical tests, decorative labels for children's toys, even labels that were attached to space-exploration equipment and sent to the moon. Tapemark is an example of how new technologies shape industries.

This is particularly true of printing and publishing, Minnesota's fourth-largest industry. Of the top 156 printing and publishing companies in the country, as listed by *American Printer* magazine, six are in Minnesota and three of those—Deluxe Check Printers, Brown and Bigelow, and The Webb Company—are in St. Paul. Between 1977 and 1982 the state's printing industry posted a 21 percent increase in the value of shipments, most of it in commercial printing. Employment was up 23 percent. Almost half of the industry's shipments leave Minnesota, indicating a market fueled by national demand for Minnesota's printing products.

With 78 percent of Minnesota's printing and publishing companies employing fewer than twenty workers, the industry is typically small business, according to PIM (Printing Industry of Minnesota, Inc.), its statewide association. The industry has a "seedbed" function, that of giving entry-level employees the training and experience needed to establish themselves.

Minnesota has about 125 publishers and 623 printers. While many publishers also do com-

mercial printing, most publish book manuscripts, magazines, and periodicals for specific industries. Bolger Publications, St. Paul, is both a commercial printer and publisher. On the other hand, Deluxe Check Printers, located in suburban Shoreview—and a fixture of the St. Paul area's economy since the 1920s—is the nation's largest supplier of checks and other magnetic-ink-encoded financial forms. Deluxe produces half the checks used in America today.

Not all of the paper the state's printers use comes from Minnesota's trees, or even from American trees, PIM points out. Much of it comes from Canada's forests. Pentair, Inc., a St. Paul-based Fortune 500 company, and Minnesota Power of Duluth have broken ground for a new paper mill in Duluth that will produce lightweight, clay filled, semiglossy paper.

The printing industry has perhaps seen greater changes in the past twenty-five years than it

The Webb Publishing company staff, circa 1912, stand in front of their building at 10th Street and Cedar. Today the Capitol Square Building stands on the site. Courtesy, The Webb Company

DELUXE CHECK PRINTERS INC.

One hundred million times a day, Americans engage in a practice that may date back to the ancient Romans. For business or pleasure, close to home or far from it, they write a check. It is, far and away, the most popular method of payment in our society today. And it forms the foundation of one of the country's most successful businesses: Deluxe Check Printers.

There's more to the modern, innovative company based in the northern suburbs of St. Paul than just checks, however. Deluxe today includes more than 60 production facilities nationwide, in which some 12,500 "Deluxers" (as the firm's employees refer to themselves) produce and market checks, deposit tickets, and related business forms for financial institutions and their customers. In addition, Deluxe offers new-account verification services and markets a diverse line of related products, such as fabric and leather checkbook covers, installment loan coupons, internal transaction forms, self-inking stamps, computer forms, pegboard systems, and medical and dental forms.

When W.R. Hotchkiss founded Deluxe Check Printers in 1915, the personal check was all but unknown, and even the most imaginative of futurists could not have foreseen the changes in the financial payment system on the horizon. Hotchkiss drew on his knowledge of printing (he published small newspapers in Wisconsin) in opening a small shop to manufacture bank checks. He had $300 of borrowed money behind him, a small press, paper cutter, and a few fonts of type to work with, and three employees (all sisters). One of the sisters, Katherine Sander, became his wife.

The first orders came from outstate Minnesota. Then came business from the People's Bank and the Western State Bank in St. Paul, followed by the Merchant's National Bank (now part of First

Bank System), which became the first large bank to give its check-imprinting business to Deluxe. By 1918 the firm had grown large enough to print something else— a first-of-its-kind catalog of bank checks, including the first stock checks that could be personalized for the individual customer. The little storefront print shop was becoming a going business concern, moving to larger quarters in 1919 and incorporating the following year.

It would be another couple of years before Deluxe would print the first personalized, register-style checks for individual accounts—the design of choice for 75 percent of all checking account holders today—but Hotchkiss had correctly foreseen the coming of a new era of consumer banking, when people as well as businesses would employ checks for their financial convenience. As this new form of personal banking grew, Deluxe grew with it. A first branch plant opened in Chicago in 1921, joined by facilities in Kansas City, Cleveland, and New York by the end of the decade.

Deluxe Check Printers, which began with one small plant in St. Paul, now employs more than 12,000 people at more than 60 locations nationwide.

Deluxe founder W.R. Hotchkiss honored members of the company's 25-Year Club in 1948.

Deluxe did more than print checks. It also developed much of the equipment needed for this specialized business, a pattern of innovation that continues through the present. The first Hotchkiss Imprinting Press, which printed

three checks on a page with only one set-up of type, was made for Deluxe by Carl Hawkinson of St. Paul in 1923. Five years later the patented Hotchkiss Lithograph Press debuted, introducing lithography to the check-printing industry.

Through the worst of the Depression, Deluxe struggled but never laid off an employee—a people-oriented tradition that also continues to the present. The company's future was enhanced by the Social Security Act of 1936, which created a need for specialized payroll checks. By 1938 George McSweeney, the firm's second president (there have been but five in more than 70 years), had launched the Personalized Check Program, a marketing strategy designed to sell banks on sell-

Deluxe used this truck to deliver orders to area banks during the company's early years.

ing checks to their customers. When that market faltered during World War II, Deluxe compensated by printing government sugar ration coupons. After the war the renewed growth of personal checking doubled sales volume every five years for many years.

In the 1950s technology again brought change—and growth—to Deluxe. To help banks process

the ever-increasing numbers of checks in use, Deluxe began printing account numbers on the checks in 1955. In the ensuing years the firm worked with others in the banking industry on the introduction of Magnetic Ink Character Recognition (MICR), further improving the speed and efficiency of check handling.

After 50 years as a private company, Deluxe went public in 1965 under its third president, Joe Rose. Under his leadership, Deluxe installed four-color presses and led a movement to change U.S. postal regulations so bank stationers could use an improved check-mailing procedure. His successors, Gene Olson and Harold Haverty, have managed a period of steady growth and well-planned diversification, moving Deluxe into non-check products and computer forms—the latter designed for the special needs of small businesses using microcomputers—while adapting to such major financial changes as the advent of NOW and money market accounts.

Through Delmart, a direct marketing division, Deluxe has become a leading supplier of the self-inking stamps used for endorsements and return addresses. Through its Business Systems Group, the firm has moved into the production of One-Write bookkeeping systems for small businesses and encoded products for investment houses, mutual funds, insurance companies, and other financial institutions.

Acquisitions have added other companies to the Deluxe family, including Colwell Systems, the nation's leading supplier of business forms and related products to the medical and dental markets, and Chex Systems, a new-account verification service used by more than 32,000 financial institution offices.

The concern's roots in St. Paul, where 2,000 Deluxers are employed, have had their effect on its

In addition to checks, Deluxe produces items such as loan coupon books, deposit tickets, and computer forms for small businesses.

corporate culture as well as its business. Deluxe contributes approximately 2 percent of its pretax earnings to the communities in which it operates. Equally important, Deluxers are known for volunteering their time, both paid and unpaid, in community-based social programs. The Deluxe Check Printers Foundation is a primary channel for corporate contributions to national and community organizations. The W.R. Hotchkiss Foundation awards scholarships to the children of Deluxe employees.

Through it all, quality and service have remained hallmarks of the firm's business. More than 96 percent of the nearly 400,000 orders received each business day are shipped within two days from receipt of the order—and nearly 99.5 percent of the 100 million document orders received each year are printed without error. Both figures reflect the high levels of commitment and care Deluxers bring to their jobs.

PENTAIR, INC.

There were five of them—hence "penta"—when it started. And "air" is what their little company was going to be about. They were leaving their jobs with Litton Industries in the Twin Cities to launch a new venture that would make high-altitude balloons for military and aerospace research. But then, just five days before they opened their doors, the government threw them a curve: Because of the increasing commitment of military resources to the developing war in Vietnam, research spending would be concentrated on weaponry. It looked like the air had been let out of Pentair before it could even get off the

Of the five founders, only Harpole was still with the struggling company in 1968 when, down to its last $10,000, Pentair purchased a money-losing toilet tissue mill in Ladysmith, Wisconsin. The balloon business had been a bust. So, too, had attempts at relaunching the firm around canoes and large plastic items. But with toilet tissue, the company's fortunes turned around. In addition to conventional toilet paper, the plant made the absorbent tissue needed for a new product being launched by giant Procter & Gamble: Pampers disposable diapers. The mix of raw materials used in the plant was adjusted to be more cost-effective,

Electric power tools for the professional made by Porter-Cable Corporation in Jackson, Tennessee.

No. 3 and No. 4 paper machines producing coated paper for magazines at Niagara, Wisconsin.

ground.

Yet start it did. And in the scant space of just 20 years, it grew literally from flat on the ground to a member of the prestigious *Fortune* 500, with sales approaching three-quarters of a billion dollars annually and more than 5,000 employees worldwide. On July 6, 1986, from its modest international headquarters near Rosedale in St. Paul, Pentair began its second 20 years of life—but the first without founder and chairman Murray Harpole, who retired on the 20th anniversary of the company's founding at the mandatory age of 65 he himself had established.

and labor relations were improved to increase productivity. As Pampers became a successful addition to its product line, Procter & Gamble contracted for the plant's entire production for three years. Pentair was on its way at last.

The purchase and revitalization of the paper plant in Ladysmith set a pattern that Pentair would follow, and successfully, for nearly 20 years. The company grew steadily through acquisi-

tions of nonperforming paper-manufacturing plants and industrial products that it believed could be reworked and made productive. For example, Niagara of Wisconsin Paper Corporation, Pentair's largest paper mill operation, was once a money-loser for Kimberly-Clark; the successful line of Porter-Cable professional and industrial power tools that anchors Pentair's Industrial Products Group was resurrected from Rockwell International's larger, consumer-oriented power tool division.

In addition to its penchant for making savvy acquisitions, Pentair has brought a stable, decentralized management style to its various operations. Corporate staff in St. Paul numbers only about 30, including D. Eugene Nugent, for 10 years Harpole's close associate as president, and chairman and chief executive officer since his retirement; S.A. "Tony" Johnson, current president and chief operating officer; and John H. Grunewald, chief financial officer and treasurer. The firm's strategy has always been to support managers and executives of Pentair's subsidiary companies without meddling in their day-to-day operations. The autonomy and streamlined decision-making process that results has kept Pentair competitive in smokestack industries where many larger concerns have found it difficult to remain profitable.

Pentair's management style and a strong code of business conduct were key ingredients in its most recent acquisition, a friendly tender offer in mid-1986 for McNeil Corporation, a strong, St. Louis-based manufacturer of lubrication equipment and fittings, and industrial pumps. With the addition of McNeil's operations in Missouri, Arkansas, Ohio, Canada, and

Canada, and Brazil.

The Paper Group includes four paper companies with five mills: Niagara of Wisconsin, Flambeau Paper Corporation (Park Falls, Wisconsin), Miami Paper Corporation (West Carrollton, Ohio), and Port Huron Paper Corporation (Port Huron, Michigan). Together, these firms produce printing, writing, and packaging papers used in magazines, books, commercial printing, office papers, food packaging, and specialty products. Pentair papers are used in Bibles; dictionaries; the *Encyclopaedia Brittanica;* magazines such as *The New Yorker, Bride,* and *Travel and Leisure;* books (including Garrison

Pentair executives (back row, left to right): John H. Grunewald, vice-president/finance, and D. Eugene Nugent, chairman and chief executive officer. In the front row (left to right): Murray J. Harpole, chairman emeritus, and S.A. "Tony" Johnson, president and chief operating officer.

West Germany, Pentair's Industrial Products Group became approximately equal in size to its Paper Group.

In addition to McNeil, the Industrial Products Group includes Porter-Cable Corporation of Jackson, Tennessee, a major manufacturer of portable electric power tools with more than 40 service centers throughout the United States and Canada, and Delta International Machinery Corporation of Pittsburgh, Pennsylvania, the nation's largest maker of general purpose woodworking machinery. Delta operates plants in Mississippi,

An artist's view of the Lake Superior Paper Industries' mill for supercalendered paper in Duluth, Minnesota.

Keillor's *Lake Wobegon Days);* U.S. postage stamps; Mr. Coffee coffee filters; xerographic copy paper; and single-service sugar packets.

In late 1987 the company expects to put into production its first built-from-scratch paper mill. Under a joint venture between Pentair and Minnesota Power of Duluth, headed by Ronald Kelly,

formerly Pentair's vice-president of corporate development, the new Lake Superior Paper Industries plant will be a world-class facility specifically designed for the manufacture of "supercalendered" paper, a semiglossy stock increasingly used in catalogs, newspaper supplements, magazines, inserts, and other commercial printing. The $350-million plant will employ technology new to the United States and provide a dependable domestic source for a type of paper largely imported from overseas. It will produce up to 235,000 tons of high-quality publication paper per year when it begins deliveries in 1988.

Lake Superior Paper represents the largest industrial investment in Duluth since 1916 and a dramatic boost to the Arrowhead Region's economy. It will draw on renewable sources of native Minnesota woods for pulp and fuel, and will provide more than 300 permanent jobs for the city in addition to some 1,600 construction jobs during the peak building period.

It will also likely push Pentair's annual sales over the billion-dollar mark—a high point indeed for Murray Harpole's revamped balloon business.

155

has in all the years since 1456 when Gutenberg invented his printing press. Much of that change involves color printing, which, in turn, is linked to color television and the profound appeal color has for consumers. It is ironic that it was the printing industry's major competitor, telecommunications, that developed the technology the print media use to produce fast color printing of high quality. Electronic technology has also created new systems for preparing and proofing manuscript copy and new press and distribution capabilities through such exotic techniques as laser imaging, robotics, and satellite transmission.

All of this would have astounded James M. Goodhue, who brought Minnesota's first printing press to St. Paul and founded the settlement's first newspaper, the *Minnesota Pioneer*, in 1849.

By 1858, when Minnesota became a state, St. Paul had eleven newspapers. Their colorful editors helped shape the settlement of the city and the state and the political life of the area. One of the realities of publishing on the frontier was that it could not survive without commercial printing, and the city's early printer-publishers were devastatingly honest about that.

"In politics we shall be Democrat or Whig, just as may best serve our interest," one declared bluntly. "We are after the public printing, and everything else out of which money can be made." Fiercely competitive, sparing no invective, they fought the great journalistic battle of those years, the scramble for the appointment as government printer. Once appointed, they hung onto the job with determination and ingenuity.

D.A. Robertson, who established the *Minnesota Democrat* in 1859, accused Goodhue of threatening "to fight and whip members of the Legislature . . . " to obtain public printing. J.P. Owens, editor of the Whig paper, the *Minnesotian*, accused Robertson of "whining around certain Whigs to get votes in the Legislature for the printing." Joseph R. Brown was especially

creative during his 1853-1854 tenure as territorial printer. Also a senator in the territorial legislature, Brown sat up all one night writing a "Bill to Suppress Immorality," which he introduced into the senate the next day, at the same time moving that it be read and printed. The bill called for the suppression of liquor in the bars of steamboats, listed other elements of immorality, and asked that no person be permitted to hang the undergarments of either sex on a public clothesline, describing such an act as detrimental to public morals. While the bill was understandably laid over indefinitely, Brown in the meantime had published it and netted $100 for one night's work.

Violent encounters between newspaper editors and angered readers were not unheard of during those years of unfettered editorial comment. An editorial Goodhue wrote excoriating Judge David Cooper resulted in a duel between Goodhue and Cooper's brother on a downtown street. Both men were seriously injured.

Despite their preoccupation with their internecine warfare, St. Paul's early publishers were ardent promoters of immigration to the state and the blossoming city. It was Goodhue who first spoke of St. Paul as the New England of the West. As the late historian Theodore Blegen pointed out, America's editors were in the vanguard of the western movement and were immediately influential in giving direction to the early communities.

Today's *St. Paul Pioneer Press Dispatch* is, through a series of mergers, a descendant of several of those territorial newspapers, as are a number of present-day printing firms. In 1875 Joseph A. Wheelock and Frederick Driscoll, publishers of the *St. Paul Daily Press,* bought the *Pioneer* and created the *St. Paul Pioneer Press.* In 1909 George Thompson, owner of the *St. Paul Dispatch,* bought the *Pioneer Press* and combined the two papers as evening and morning editions. Ownership changed hands again in 1927 when Bernard, Joseph, and Victor Ridder of New York bought the newspapers,

and yet again in 1974 when the newspapers merged with the Knight Newspapers to form the Knight-Ridder Newspapers of Miami, owner of thirty-one other dailies around the country.

In 1983 the *Pioneer Press Dispatch* dedicated its new $44-million, 160,000-square-foot production and distribution plant across the river from downtown St. Paul. Newspaper analysts have called it one of the most sophisticated plants of its kind in the country. About thirty-three million dollars of that investment was for state-of-the-art equipment, including an eighteen-unit Gore offset printing press, computer- controlled and capable of producing 70,000 papers an hour, and a $5.8-million Swiss-made inserting machine for stuffing news and advertising sections.

The new plant replaces the old Mechanical Annex in downtown St. Paul, where the newspapers had printed and shipped their editions since 1895. However, the *Pioneer Press Dispatch*'s commitment to downtown St. Paul was

Top: *The* St. Paul Pioneer Press *staff poses outside of the paper's headquarters. The* Pioneer Press, *dating back to territorial newspapers, merged with the* Dispatch *in 1909 and became the morning edition.* Courtesy, MHS

Above: *Around the turn of the century, linotype machines at the* St. Paul Dispatch *replaced the earlier hand-set type method of composition. Today computers have again revolutionized the printing industry.* Courtesy, MHS

ST. PAUL PIONEER PRESS AND DISPATCH

The rebirth and renewed spirit of optimism in St. Paul is both a local story and a national one. Fittingly, it has been chronicled by a local newspaper whose own actions parallel that rebirth and renewed sense of energy and commitment. Each day more than one-half million readers turn to the *Pioneer Press and Dispatch* for news of their city and their world.

The editorial excellence of the *Pioneer Press and Dispatch* has attracted a highly motivated and professional staff, and has earned it numerous honors in recent years, including journalism's most prestigious award, the Pulitzer Prize, in 1986. That emphasis on excellence has been mirrored on the production side, culminating in 1983 with the dedication of a new, $45-million production plant to further enhance the paper's printing and distribution.

Editorially, the publication has actively supported the rebirth of the city. What's more, it has backed that editorial encouragement by its own actions. In addition to the major downtown investment represented by the new printing and distribution facility in Northport Industrial Park near Holman Airport just outside the Loop, the *Pioneer Press and Dispatch* moved its editorial, production, advertising sales, and administrative staffs into improved facilities at 345 Cedar Street in 1984. That move, one block away from the offices on East Fourth Street that served as the newspaper's home since 1941, kept the publication downtown in the heart of the city it covers.

The original *St. Paul Pioneer Press* was created in 1875, when the publishers of the *St. Paul Daily Press* purchased the *St. Paul Pioneer*—the successor to the *Minnesota Pioneer,* the state's first newspaper, founded in 1849—and merged the two into one daily publication. The *St. Paul Dispatch* was founded in 1868 and operated as a competing paper until its pub-

lisher bought the *Pioneer Press* in 1909. From that point, the *Pioneer Press* became established as the city's morning newspaper, and the *Dispatch* as the afternoon daily.

In 1927 three brothers—Bernard, Joseph, and Victor Ridder—from a New York newspaper family whose roots in publishing went back to 1875, bought the two publications. During the Ridder years the *Pioneer Press and Dispatch* grew to become a major force for progress in the city, just as Ridder Publishing grew to become the nation's eighth-largest newspaper group. Bernard H. Ridder, Jr., who served as publisher from 1958 to 1973, was a member of the Metropolitan Improvement Committee that brought the Hilton to downtown St. Paul and helped launch and nurture the city's revitalization efforts. His active involvement in civic affairs followed a tradition begun by his father, who became publisher in 1938, and was continued by his two brothers, Herman and Dan, during their years as publisher of the papers.

The merger of Ridder Publishing and the Knight group of newspapers that created Knight-Ridder Newspapers, Inc., in 1974 broadened the resource base of the *Pioneer Press and Dispatch* while reinforcing the commitment of its editors and managers to in-depth and insightful coverage of the city, the nation, and the world.

To meet the changing needs of its readers in the city and the surrounding communities of the Twin Cities metropolitan area, the paper created new special sections such as "EXTRA" and "Business/Twin Cities," the latter Minnesota's first weekly in-depth newspaper business section. Coverage of state government, the arts, sports, and religion was expanded. The paper's editorial page strengthened its commitment to balanced commentary on concerns of both local and national importance, and reader access to the section was en-

hanced. Greater resources were allocated for personnel, equipment, and "newshole"—the amount of the paper devoted to news coverage. With top newsroom managers in place as the 1980s began, renewed emphasis was placed on writing and editing quality, photographic excellence, and creative newspaper design. Four-color photography and illustration was added to brighten coverage of local and national events.

Publishers Thomas Carlin, and now John T. Henry, have continued the paper's strong tradition of active involvement in civic and community affairs. The newspaper's managers, editors, and reporters have made substantial contributions to their profession through local and national journalism organizations. Other key members of the paper's management include senior vice-president/editor John R. Finnegan, nationally recognized for his work on First Amendment concerns, and Mary Junck, senior vice-president/general manager, who administers the business side of the newspaper.

Today's all-day *Pioneer Press and Dispatch* is a bright, reader-oriented newspaper whose mission is to be an involved and positive force in the community it serves and whose quality is recognized as among the best in the country. The number of awards won by the newspaper in recent years for writing, editing, photography, design, and reproduction is large and impressive, and attests to the overall commitment to quality renewed every day by its more than 800 employees.

A Record of Excellence

These awards given to members of the editorial staff in 1986 reflect the commitment to quality of the *Pioneer Press and Dispatch*

Pulitzer Prize—John Camp

American Society of Newspaper Editors Award—John Camp

Farm Writer of the Year—Lee Egerstrom

Frank Premack Award—Allen Short

Gene O'Brien Excellence in Journalism Award—Jacqui Banaszynski, Jean Pieri (The Soudan)

John Peter Zenger Award— John R. Finnegan

Minnesota Sportswriter of the Year—Charley Walters

Editorial Writing, Minnesota Education Association/Society of Professional Journalists—Ann Goodwin

Four Awards of Excellence, Society of Newspaper Design

Nine First Place Awards, Associated Press (Minnesota)—Photo Staff

15 Awards (3 Firsts), Minnesota Newspaper Photography Association—Photo Staff

H.M. Smyth executives examining a sheet of labels. Courtesy, H.M. Smyth Printing Company

reaffirmed in 1984 when the newpapers bought Minnesota Mutual's former building at Fourth and Cedar streets and moved their offices there. In 1985 the Pulitzer Prize for feature writing went to the newspaper's John Camp for his five-part series, "Life on the Land," which dealt with the farm crisis.

McGill-Jensen, Inc., also traces its origins to the Pioneer Press Printing Company and to James M. Goodhue. In 1899 Eli S. Warner and Charles H. McGill, the son of Minnesota Governor Andrew R. McGill, bought an interest in the printing company and ten years later acquired the rest of it. Located at Ninth and Sibley—the heart of the Lowertown printing district—McGill-Warner became McGill-Jensen, then was acquired by Norman B. Mears of Buckbee-Mears (now BMC) in 1963; it is now one of the ten area printing companies under one management.

H.M. Smyth Printing Company is another old-line family-managed firm that emerged from Lowertown's "printer's row." As early as 1877, H.M. Smyth, the company's founder, was printing business cards, letterheads, and invoices for his St. Paul customers. The first company west of Chicago to use lithography, Smyth was managed by men like G.G. (Mac) McGuiggan,

who rose from shop foreman to president, treasurer, and general manager. William Hickey, Sr., McGuiggan's son-in-law, followed him into the business, as did his son and his grandsons. Today the firm designs and prints point-of-purchase displays and colorful labels and packaging for products.

West Publishing was founded in St. Paul in 1876 by John B. West, who had arrived from Massachusetts in 1870. For a time he sold books, including law books and legal forms, both of which were scarce on the frontier. Then the problems lawyers had in keeping abreast of legal decisions captured his attention. Operating out of a basement room at 11 Wabasha Street, West and his brother, Horatio, began to publish a weekly legal news sheet, *The Syllabi,* in 1876. This was a digest of decisions by the Minnesota Supreme Court and the federal courts in the state. Within weeks West had added Wisconsin to his coverage. Its purpose, as described in its first issue, was to publish "prompt and reliable intelligence as to the various questions adjudicated by the Minnesota Courts at a date long prior to the publication of the State Reports." Before *The Syllabi,* the contract for published court decisions often was a political plum, and lawyers and judges sometimes waited months

Above: *West Publishing, founded in St. Paul in 1876, is now the world's largest publisher of law books. Its corporate headquarters nestle along the bluff on the Mississippi River. Courtesy, West Publishing*

Above: *Text copy is created at West Publishing by computers which utilize laser technology to increase speed and efficiency. Courtesy, West Publishing*

Left: *West Publishing's web press is capable of printing up to 1,200 feet per minute. Courtesy, West Publishing*

for published decisions. Accuracy was also a problem.

West's little news sheet changed all that. Within six months West had replaced *The Syllabi* with a new series, *The North Western Reporter.* It listed circuit court and supreme court decisions for Minnesota and Wisconsin. Later *Reporters* published the full texts of all current decisions from Iowa, Michigan, Nebraska, and the Dakota Territory, in addition to Minnesota and Wisconsin. By 1888 the company was publishing *Reporters* in all sections of the country. The *National Reporter System* was the first of West's two great entrepreneurial ideas. The second was the *American Digest System.* The digests indexed court decisions through the use of headnotes and keynumbers. In 1924 Congress asked West Publishing Company to join with the Edward Thompson Company, another legal publisher, in preparing a new compilation of all existing laws. The new work was adopted by Congress on December 7, 1925, as the "United States Code."

Now, in the 1980s, the company that once operated with a single press in the basement of a building on the site of the present Ramsey County Courthouse is the largest publisher of law books in the world. West's ten-story corporate headquarters are perched on a bluff overlooking the Mississippi River in downtown St. Paul, and its twenty-four- acre printing, bindery and shipping plant in suburban Eagan produces more than fifty million books and pamphlets a year. State-of-the-art technology includes ten web presses capable of printing more than 40,000 thirty-two-page signatures an hour. WESTLAW, West's computerized legal-research service, lets courts, lawyers, and researchers gain instant access to millions of documents stored in the company's data bases. Long committed to downtown St. Paul's redevelopment, West has given the city its old printing, bindery, and warehouse for use as a small-business incubator.

Several blocks down Third Street from West,

Edward A. Webb was publishing, in the 1890s, a monthly tabloid he called *The Northwestern Farmer and Breeder.* It was, as the masthead stated, "for the farm field, stock and home." Its subscription price was pegged for years to the price of wheat, and it became *The Farmer,* now the most widely read farm publication in this area and the flagship of The Webb Company, one of the largest printing and publishing companies in the U.S. The journal designed for farmers in Minnesota and North and South Dakota was being read in 45,000 farm homes by 1895. Webb boosted its publication to twice monthly, added *Poultry Herald* and, in 1905, *The Farmer's Wife,* which carried columns on recipes, sewing, gardening, and health. The publication had a lasting effect on the company. When a reader suggested that its recipes be collected in book form, the result was *The Country Kitchen,* one of America's early cookbooks, still in print and revised many times. Publishing wasn't Webb's only interest. With Thomas F. Shaw, *The Farmer's* editor, he established an experimental farm south of St. Paul in Rosemount, where new crop varieties, seeds, machinery, and crop management procedures were tested.

Located for many years on Tenth and Cedar Street in St. Paul's "printer's row," Webb so outgrew its quarters that by 1962 it had moved to a new $5- million plant near downtown St. Paul. Here computers set type, make up pages, bill customers, and pay employees. Copy is edited with electronic cursors on video display tubes.

Webb delivers seventy-six million magazines to readers around the world. The magazines range from agriculturally related publications that were the company's mainstay to *The Family Handyman,* a magazine with a circulation of 1.2 million. Webb prints advertising supplements, and telephone directories (sixty million in five years). There are magazines on home maintenance and renovation, and they include two million copies of *TV Guide* printed on a

The Webb Publishing Company's magazine The Farmer *has been one of the most widely read agricultural publications since Edward A. Webb started it in the 1890s. Courtesy, The Webb Company*

custom-built, computer planned and driven press. Text and pages are computer-sent and received by telephone.

The sophisticated equipment Webb uses is as far removed from its first self-feeding press as Webb's early seed experiments at Rosemount were from the complex plant engineering that characterizes much of agribusiness today. Agriculture still is Minnesota's largest industry. Although St. Paul has been urban rather than rural from its early years as part of a growing metropolitan area, agriculture has played an important role in its economy since the 1850s, when the first two-horse power thresher arrived by steamboat. In 1874 the St. Paul Harvester Works northeast of the city limits was making farm machinery. More than 200 men worked in the plant.

Today, more than 100 years later, the state's urban dwellers who visit the Minnesota State Fair in St. Paul see huge machines as colorful as the vermillion-gold-and black machinery that Harvester's workers turned out, but guided by on-board computers that control a machine's progress as it lumbers along the farm furrows. Seed used in the field crops of the out-state regions and for the vegetables grown by market-garden farmers living closer to St. Paul bears little resemblance to that used for nineteenth-century crops. While hybrids and disease-resistant strains are commonplace now, the

Above: *An old-fashioned carriage displays a form of nineteenth-century transportation at the annual Minnesota State Fair; the space-age Pioneer Building appears in the background. Photo by Kay Shaw*

Right and top, right: *Besides the many displays, the fair offers the famous Midway. Photo at right by Kay Shaw; top photo, courtesy St. Paul Convention Bureau*

Below: *Governor Rudy Perpich is a spectator at the Minnesota State Fair. Photo by Kay Shaw*

Bottom: *The Midway is another popular attraction at the fair. Photo by Kay Shaw*

BCED MINNESOTA INC.

In 1987, capping 30 years of ambitious rebirth and redevelopment efforts, St. Paul's tallest, proudest office tower will open for business. The Minnesota World Trade Center, 36 stories tall and with more than a half-million square feet of top-quality office and retail space within its granite-clad walls, provides a new cornerstone for the central business district of the city. It also sets the stage for future developments along the proposed Capitol Mall, designed to reunite the State Capitol complex with downtown St. Paul.

Many of those future developments, together with the leasing and management of the offices in the World Trade Center tower plus the neighboring Conwed and North Central Life towers of Town Square, and the continuing management of retail stores and services in the World Trade Center and Town Square, St. Paul's downtown retail heart, are being conducted by BCED Minnesota Inc. A member of the worldwide family of companies owned by Bell Canada Enterprises (BCE), BCED Minnesota is one of the most recent but already one of the largest participants in the new life of the city.

BCED Minnesota came to St. Paul in April 1986 through its parent company's acquisition of the stock and assets of Oxford Properties, Inc. In the Twin Cities, that involved the World Trade Center and Town Square complexes in St. Paul plus the IDS Center and City Center in downtown Minneapolis. As part of the acquisition, Oxford Properties was renamed BCE Development Properties Inc., and BCED Minnesota was created to manage the previous operations of Oxford Development Minnesota, Inc.

For St. Paul, the development of Town Square and the World Trade Center both serve as landmark dates in the recent history of the city. Since its opening in October 1980, Town Square has successfully proven that retail activities can thrive in a modern downtown area. Its three shopping levels and 75 shops and restaurants, including the two-story Donaldson's Department Store that serves as the retail anchor, daily attract thousands of downtown workers and residents of the surrounding east metro area.

Topping off Town Square is Town Square Gardens, a lush, fully glass-enclosed city park that offers an oasis of year-round greenery and cascading streams in the midst of St. Paul's ever-expanding skyway system. Daily entertainment and changing exhibits divert shoppers and downtown workers alike, bringing new character to the central core of the city.

BCED Minnesota will make its mark on St. Paul by fully integrating Town Square with the new retail shops and restaurants to be added across Cedar Street with the opening of the World Trade Center. Together, Town Square and the new retail core of the World Trade Center will offer more than 250,000 square feet of specialty shops and dining experiences—all of it climate-controlled and skyway-accessible, and all of it served by convenient and inexpensive parking in the below-ground, heated garages within the two multiuse developments.

Of course, there is a good deal more to Town Square than stores and restaurants. The 17-story Town Square Holiday Inn, with its 250 guest rooms and corporate meeting facilities, annually offers a home away from home for thousands of visitors to the city. Meanwhile, the twin Conwed and North Central Life office towers provide more than 425,000 square feet of office space for a broad range of businesses. Leasing and management activities for both the 25-story Conwed Tower and the 27-story North Central Life Tower are pro-

When completed this year, the 36-story Minnesota World Trade Center office tower will dominate the skyline of St. Paul. It will house the Minnesota World Trade Institute, professional service firms, companies, and agencies involved in international trade.

vided by BCED Minnesota.

The links between Town Square and the World Trade Center are many, and promise to be busy. The World Trade Center Tower will be the tallest office building on the St. Paul skyline. Its unique configuration offers up to 16 corner offices on each of 36 floors. On one of its top floors will be the exclusive World Trade Center Club, a full-service business and social facility destined to be one of the community's most prestigious locations.

Three levels of World Trade Center retail shops immediately adjacent to the existing Dayton's Department Store will be fully integrated into Town Square retail establishments. Within the World Trade Center itself, stores and boutiques will be clustered around a 100-foot-diameter crystal-domed galleria with a central fountain and colorful interior landscaping under the skylit roof.

Among the tenants taking up residency will be the State of Minnesota's Trade Office and the World Trade Board and Institute, the latter being part of the increasingly sophisticated global network of World Trade Centers that now number more than 100 cities worldwide. St. Paul will join nearly 50 other members of the movement from Abidjan to Vancouver with Trade Centers operating; more than 40 others are planned or being constructed worldwide; and 32 cities around the globe have affiliate organizations in place. The Trade Center movement seeks to facilitate expanded commerce among nations of every size and scale of development.

St. Paul's World Trade Center will be well equipped to play an active and helpful role in linking Minnesota with world markets. Advanced telecommunications

The 25-story Conwed Tower, housing the offices of BCE Development Properties Inc., and its twin, the North Central Life Tower, provide more than 425,000 square feet of office space for a broad range of businesses.

systems, and professional worldwide marketing information and referral services will be available along with display areas to showcase products and services. Businesses officed in the World Trade Center Tower will have access to conference facilities and an amphitheater capable of simultaneous translation.

In the years to come hotel, technological, and residential developments will cluster around the World Trade Center. In addition, a planned Capitol Mall development will someday arch across the I-94 corridor and reunite downtown St. Paul with the State Capitol complex three blocks to the north.

BCED Minnesota Inc. represents a strong commitment to St. Paul's future by a diversified company whose real estate assets are valued at more than $2.5 billion. Under J.E. "Jack" Poole, chairman and chief executive officer, BCE Development is an important element of Bell Canada, that nation's largest publicly held corporation. St. Paul activities are under the guidance of Richard H. Zehring, vice-president/development. Zehring, who served as vice-president/legal for Oxford, is also a former assistant city attorney specializing in real estate and economic development for the City of St. Paul.

BCE Development's Town Square is a unique shopping area. Its lower three floors house an array of shops, restaurants, and eating places anchored by Donaldson's department store. The top floor (shown) features a glass-covered city park with waterfalls, gardens, and an amphitheatre for public performances.

future lies in plant genetic engineering. Scientists working at the University of Minnesota's agricultural campus in St. Paul and in the laboratories of Twin Cities agribusiness firms are using biotechnology in experiments that they hope will improve the protein content of corn as well as increase its yield.

In the meantime the day-to-day problems of production and distribution are managed by such organizations as Harvest States Cooperative, a farmer-owned regional cooperative formed in 1936 to market grain and oil-seeds; Cenex (Farmers Union Central Exchange, Inc.), organized in 1931 and offering farmers, ranchers, and rural communities petroleum and petroleum products; Land O'Lakes, incorporated in 1921 and a processor and marketer of foods and food products; Mid-America Dairymen, the nation's second-largest dairy cooperative; and Central Livestock Association, incorporated in 1921 to buy and sell livestock.

Central Livestock in South St. Paul has been for many years the livestock-marketing and meat-packing center for the Upper Midwest. In the 1880s the Saint Paul Chamber of Commerce realized that cattle and sheep that were fattening on Dakota grasslands could be sold in St. Paul rather than in Chicago where most were shipped. In 1886 A.B. Stickney and several other St. Paul businessmen incorporated the St. Paul Union Stockyards Company. Trading, packing, and stockyards facilities were set up on land Stickney owned in South St. Paul.

At about the same time, Minneapolis businessmen led by William D. Washburn of the Washburn-Crosby Company (now General Mills) established the Minneapolis Stockyards and Packing Company in New Brighton. Competition between the two centers was lively for at least a decade. Swift and Company decided the issue when it chose South St. Paul for the major new packing plant it built there in 1897.

While Swift has now consolidated its operations in Chicago, an enduring remnant of the farming activities that have been a part of Ramsey County remains. The Schroeder Milk Company was established in 1884 by German immigrant Henry Schroeder and his brother. Their "herd" consisted of a single cow. The company is still there on the same site on Rice Street near the northern city limits, and run by Schroeder's grandsons, but their cattle are gone. Schroeder's is part of the new technology that uses machines to pipe milk directly from cows to refrigerator trucks, and descendants of families who once greeted Schroeder each morning as he delivered their milk now buy it at the supermarket.

The farming activity Schroeder's Milk represents still exists around the Twin Cities. There are more than one million acres of farmland in the metropolitan area, with agriculture taking up the largest land use, according to figures from the Metropolitan Council, which coordinates planning and development for the seven- county metropolitan area. The council is authorized by state and federal laws to plan for highways and transit, sewers, parks and open space, airports, land use, air and water quality, solid waste management, health, housing, aging and the arts. There is more acreage in corn production alone, the council reports, than in housing and commercial development altogether.

The farms in the metro area are urban fringe farms, and many still supply the vegetables, fruits, honey, and other produce for city tables that their counterparts did a century ago. The concept of urban fringe farming—farming in the shadow of the city—is not a new idea, but it is on the cutting edge of recent historical scholarship. Because of their closeness to the city, the life-style of the urban fringe farmers was more like that of city dwellers than of farmers living in the more remote countryside. Henry Schroeder was an urban fringe farmer and so were Heman Gibbs and his son, Frank, who grew vegetables on the farm in northwest Ramsey County that now is the Gibbs Farm Museum, owned by the Ramsey County Historical Society.

Dr. Russell R. Menard, professor of history at

Above, left, and right: *The Gibbs Farm Museum, owned and operated by the Ramsey County Historical Society, interprets life on an ubran fringe farm in the early twentieth century. Left photos are of an early one-room school. Photos by Kay Shaw*

KSTP was one station which heralded St. Paul's Communications industry. Left: While covering the St. Paul Open Golf Tournament, KSTP/Radio tucked a radio transmitter in a baby carriage. Below: Founder Stanley E. Hubbard, (back row, far right,) is flanked by, back row: Bert Lahr, James Cagney, Frances Langford; front row: Merle Oberon, Frank McHugh, and Pat O'Brien. Courtesy, Hubbard Broadcasting, Inc.

the University of Minnesota, offers an interesting comment on such farmers:

.. .. There was one profound similarity between urban fringe farmers and their country cousins, a similarity of myth and memory. In the late 1940s Frank Gibbs described his early years on the Gibbs farm. He invoked the myths of frontier isolation, rural self-sufficiency, and yeoman independence, powerful images of the American past. Frank told of an isolated life, said his family produced most of what it consumed and consumed most of what it produced, went for a year without seeing cash or visiting a store. Nothing could be further from the truth. The family was thoroughly integrated into St. Paul's metropolitan net, so far removed from self-sufficiency, isolation, and independence that Heman Gibbs ... regularly visited a barber for a shave and a haircut, made weekly trips to St. Paul to shop, dine, and be entertained, earned his income by producing crops for urban customers, and so on. Frank Gibbs remembers other-

wise, powerful testimony to the hold of the pioneering myth on the American imagination.

By the time Schroeder was delivering milk on Summit Avenue, his orders could be placed by a fascinating new device called the telephone. Telegraph service had been established in St. Paul as early as 1860. In 1877 Griggs and Sanders Coal Company installed the first commercial telephone line in St. Paul. It ran from the company's office to its yard. In 1878 a telephone exchange was established in St. Paul, and the following year two lines connected the central office in St. Paul with the one in Minneapolis.

By the 1880s there were more than 600 telephones in St. Paul and Minnneapolis. Newspapers published instructions on how to use them, assuring readers that "any child able to speak distinctly" could communicate over the wires as easily as "the most learned in the electrical sciences." In 1907 the Tri-State Telephone and Telegraph Company was formed out of a merger of two earlier companies. Tri- State operated in St. Paul and southern Minnesota until 1942, when Northwestern Bell and Tri-State merged into the Northwestern Bell Telephone Company.

As of the mid-1980s, Northwestern Bell, along with Pacific Northwest Bell and Mountain Bell, falls under the umbrella of U. S. West, a holding company that was formed as a result of the AT&T divestiture and provides communications services to fourteen states. St. Paul and Min neapolis are linked by a $4-million fiber network consisting of a ninety-six-fiber-optic cable around each city, interconnected by a thirty-six-fiber cable. The network provides state-of-the-art telecommunications for the Twin Cities area. Hairthin glass fibers are encased in a larger protective cable that runs inside ducts beneath the streets of both cities.

The technology of telecommunications has also pushed radio and television far beyond crystal sets and flickering images. There are four commercial television stations in Minneapolis and St. Paul: WCCO-TV, CBS; KARE-TV, NBC; KMSP-TV, independent; and KSTP-TV, ABC. Channel 4 (WCCO-TV) and Channel 11 (KARE-TV) maintain St. Paul bureaus, and KSTP-TV, the Hubbard family-owned and operated station, has long been associated with St. Paul. Beginning in 1923 with broadcasts from the Marigold Ballroom in Minneapolis, Stanley E. Hubbard's WAMD (Where All Minneapolis Dances) had become KSTP by 1928. Studios

Minnesota Public Radio serves a wide area of listeners who enjoy both local and national programming. Photo by Kay Shaw

NORTHWESTERN BELL

For more than 100 years the story of Northwestern Bell was also the history of telephone service in St. Paul. But today that story involves far more than the familiar telephone. Since the breakup of AT&T in 1984, Northwestern Bell's mission has broadened dramatically to include all manner of electronic transmission.

This "new" Northwestern Bell is a provider—and an aggressive marketer—of the computer era's full range of sophisticated information distribution services. It supplies the all-important network lines that link carriers, consumers, and intermediaries in an increasingly complex system capable of responding to a wide range of personal and business needs.

As a principal subsidiary of U S WEST, Northwestern Bell's 6,500 Minnesota employees serve more than 1.3 million of the state's residents and businesses. In all, Northwestern Bell operations include more than 13,000 workers in Minnesota as well as Iowa, Nebraska, and North and South Dakota. And, as always, that service is provided 24 hours a day, 365 days a year.

The telephone, Alexander Graham Bell's sensational addition to the nation's centennial celebration in 1876, was only two years old when the Northwestern Telephone Exchange Company was organized in St. Paul. In its first year it signed up 37 local customers and built a line to link up with the fledgling system over in Minneapolis. The first working line was strung between the office and the coal yard of the Griggs and Sanders Company. By 1880 St. Paul residents could call "long distance"—to Minneapolis, Fort Snelling, and far-off Stillwater.

The company's first switchboard room was on the third floor of the old Pioneer Press Building at Third and Minnesota streets. The wires were strung in through holes drilled in two boarded-up windows on

Northwestern Bell's Jerome B. Crary, in front of the Minnesota World Trade Center (under construction in St. Paul). Northwestern Bell is committed to the development of Minnesota's economic future as well as the quality of its community life.

On December 15, 1982, Northwestern Bell launched this hot-air balloon to celebrate the first Enhanced 911 service to the St. Paul/Minneapolis metropolitan area in cooperation with five independent telephone companies. This was the first multicounty area in the nation to receive this service.

the Second Street side, and two gravity batteries under the operators' tables provided talking current. Service lines were strung with iron wire that ran over rooftops and across pole lines, often in close proximity to telegraph wires. Static discharges and arcing between the two different systems provided a great deal of impromptu fireworks for local residents in those early days, especially during wet weather. By 1890 the firm was starting to put its

wires underground.

The first form of divestiture to hit the business occurred in 1893, when Bell's patent on the telephone expired, and a host of independent companies sprang up to offer service. One was the Mississippi Valley Telephone Company, launched to provide service to St. Paul in 1898, and reorganized three years later as the Twin City Telephone Company. In 1906 it merged into the Tri-State Telephone and Telegraph Company. The four St. Paul offices of the new enterprise formed the hub of a system that stretched from Duluth to Albert Lea, from La Crosse in Wisconsin to Grand Forks in North Dakota.

Meanwhile, Northwestern Telephone was growing as well. By 1907 its operations and those of independent companies in Iowa and Nebraska had been united under the Northwestern Group of Bell Telephone Companies, a forerunner of the modern Northwestern Bell. In 1918 Tri-State and Northwestern agreed to divide the state between them, Tri-State concentrating on St. Paul and the southern part of the state, Northwestern taking Minneapolis and the northern part of Minnesota. The agreement continued until 1933, when the Northwestern Bell Company grew out of Northwestern's acquisition of Tri-State. The latter firm continued to operate as a subsidiary of Northwestern Bell until 1942, when all operations were finally combined under one service umbrella.

Since 1937 Northwestern Bell has been a prominent part of downtown St. Paul. The first building in its complex between Kellogg and Market, just off Rice Park, opened that year, followed by the addition of a second building in 1967 and a third 10 years later. It now serves as a base of operations for the city's local electronic switching system, long-distance

The market demands higher transmission speeds and greater capacities, with the flexibility to handle all data, voice, and video needs—now and in the future. Northwestern Bell responds to these demands with Lightway 1™/fiber-optic technology.

services, directory assistance, engineering, repair, and administrative services.

In 1985 the newest form of telecommunications technology linked downtown St. Paul and downtown Minneapolis when Northwestern Bell's $4-million Twin Cities fiber-optic cable network was put into service. Part of a growing system that will ultimately link cities throughout Minnesota and throughout the nation, fiber-optic technology uses laser light to carry voice, data, graphic, and video communications.

The newest form of divestiture took effect on January 1, 1984. AT&T was split into eight companies, among them U S WEST, a diversified telecommunications holding company. U S WEST's three operating subsidiaries—Northwestern Bell, Mountain Bell, and Pacific Northwest Bell—together serve 11 million customer lines in 14 western states. Other subsidiary companies are involved in directory publishing, cellular mobile telephone systems, business communications products and services, customer leasing and financial services, and real estate development and property man-

agement.

For Northwestern Bell, it meant the beginning of a new era in terms of business operations, yet a continuation of a history of service already more than a century old. Because its business necessitates close involvement with its customers, the company has always encouraged and supported the contributions made by its employees in their communities. In Minnesota, Northwestern Bell people pledge almost one million dollars per year to the United Way and the City of Hope, and a program of company-sponsored cultural and educational matching gifts also benefits the communities in its service area.

But even more important is the time Northwestern Bell people traditionally have invested. In the firm's service area, more than 3,000 employees, joined by 4,000 retirees, carry out a tremendous variety of projects—including many designed to solve the communications problems of the disabled—as members of the Telephone Pioneers. In addition, nearly 40 Community Service Teams, each made up of from 10 to 20 Northwestern Bell employees and retirees, contribute some 15,000 hours per year toward the approximately 250 separate programs they have established and continue to help run. St. Paul area efforts have for many years been spearheaded by Jerome B. Crary, assistant vice-president of distribution—and, in recognition of his many activities, 1986 King of the St. Paul Winter Carnival.

Community involvement is basic to Northwestern Bell's philosophy that the quality of community life can only reflect the personal contributions of individual community members. The company supports and encourages that involvement in both its current and past workers, secure in the belief that such involvement ultimately benefits its business as well.

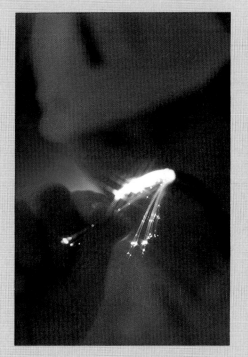

VIDEO UPDATE, INC.

In 1982 John Bedard was working for IDS; Daniel Potter was a student at William Mitchell College of Law. Intrigued by the growing popularity of videocassette recorders and driven by their own love of the movie business, they pooled $8,000 with a friend and opened a video rental store on Rice Street in St. Paul. They were 24 years old at the time.

From that first storefront, Bedard and Potter have parlayed Video Update into one of the top 10 video rental franchise corporations in the United States, a company whose familiar red-and-white signs have spread from Rice Street to the Pacific Basin. Their fast-growing network grew to nearly 100 locations in 20 states in Video Update's first four years, making the firm the largest franchiser of video-cassette rental stores in the Upper Midwest. And that is just the beginning.

Projections call for the addition of more than 100 new franchise and company-owned locations in the next few years, including pioneering larger, free-standing "super stores" for the increasingly broad-ranging tastes of today's VCR owner. From its home base of St. Paul, Video Update plans to grow into a dominant video rental presence in most major U.S. met-

Dan Potter, chairman and chief executive officer (right), and John Bedard, president, of Video Update, Inc., in the White Bear Lake store.

ropolitan areas by the end of the decade. It also is active on a growing scale internationally, both in Europe and the South Pacific.

Bedard and Potter were classmates in the sixth grade; both attended the University of Minnesota and studied film and theater in Mexico. At the time they recognized the coming popularity of video, sales and rentals of video-cassettes nationwide were under $50 million per year. Over the next four years business volume increased 100 times over, resulting in a new, $4-billion consumer industry that virtually did not exist at the beginning of the decade.

What turned Video Update from a personal storefront business into a national leader in the creation of video rental franchises was the business sense Bedard and Potter developed through their own first venture. New stores are opened only after a thorough investigation

of the proposed location and the prospective franchisee. Video Updates are located in specially selected areas; their opening inventories of at least 1,500 titles are carefully chosen and updated through the firm's own computerized management program.

In addition to Hollywood favorites, Video Update stores stock a wide variety of "how-to" programs and a large selection of movies for children. Store design, formal training, advertising and marketing services, and continuing business operational support are included as part of the franchise package.

Nearly half of Video Update's first 100 stores were opened in the Twin Cities metropolitan area, and the company's first free-standing "super store" (which will offer 3,000 to 4,000 titles for true VCR aficionados) is also located in the Twin Cities area. Video Update has also pioneered a unique form of movie information and marketing support, *The Video Update Show,* a 30-minute weekly television program that is syndicated to various Video Update markets throughout the United States.

The success of Video Update has taken Potter and Bedard from memories of the sixth grade to multimillion-dollar sales on three continents, all from a base of operation in St. Paul.

for a time were in the St. Paul Hotel. Now on University Avenue, they straddle the city line dividing St. Paul and Minneapolis. KSTP, the first television station between Chicago and the West Coast, began television programming in 1948. With four other stations, in New Mexico and Florida, Hubbard Broadcasting is associated with a number of other companies. Of major interest for KSTP, in this world of high tech, is the development of a communications network of television stations, satellite transponders, and transportable and fixed earth stations.

There are more than fifty radio stations in the Twin Cities. In a class by themselves as educational and nonprofit stations are Minnesota Public Radio (MPR) and KTCA-TV (Channel 2). MPR began life as KSJR, a small campus radio station established in 1967 at St. John's University at Collegeville in central Minnesota. It soon moved its base of operations to St. Paul. MPR is the home of Garrison Keillor's famous radio

Garrison Keillor brings the mythical world of Lake Wobegon to life at the newly renovated World Theater in St. Paul. Courtesy, Minnesota Public Radio

show, "A Prairie Home Companion." With its twelve interconnected stations spread across Minnesota and reaching into Michigan, Iowa, and North and South Dakota, MPR is the only community-sponsored, noncommercial statewide radio network in the nation, and it became the springboard for the Minnesota-based American Public Radio (APR) network. In 1980 MPR's Twin Cities station became one of only seventeen public-radio operations in the country capable of receiving and transmitting program-

175

CONTINENTAL CABLEVISION OF ST. PAUL

When the stirrings of rebirth began in St. Paul in the late 1950s, television was a strange new phenomenon—and a black-and-white one at that—but one that had already demonstrated its amazing ability to bring the events of the city and the world right into the living rooms and lives of its viewers. Choices were limited. Test patterns began and ended the day. But the potential of this new communications and entertainment medium was indisputable.

Today the potential of the medium to inform and entertain is a reality, and yet still it continues to

In just over two short years Continental Cablevision began full coverage of St. Paul, from installation of the cable itself to creation of Citivision, its own city-based programming arm.

grow. Black-and-white transmission gave way to color. Scratchy sound has become stereo. Small, flickering images have become big-screen, larger-than-life action. A few limited choices have been replaced tenfold and more. And for 50,000 metro-area households, those choices are available today, presented by Continental Cablevision of St. Paul.

Continental Cablevision, the nation's largest privately held cable company, was awarded the franchise to bring cable to St. Paul in 1983. It also provides service to seven communities in northern Dakota County—West St. Paul, South St. Paul, Inver Grove Heights, Mendota Heights, Mendota, Sunfish Lake, and Lilydale—and has a 50-percent investment in the cable systems serving the city's northern suburbs as well as Burnsville and Eagan in Dakota County. The first St. Paul subscribers came online April 29, 1985, gaining access to a state-of-the-art, 62-channel system offering the full array of national, regional, and local television viewing opportunities.

Between 1984 and 1986, when construction of the St. Paul system was completed, Continental Cablevision created one of the most sophisticated cable communications systems in the nation, consisting of more than 1,000 miles of cable and a fully equipped, $2-million office and studio complex in St. Paul's historic Union Depot. The Union Depot is also home to the Cable Store, a retail outlet where new subscribers can sign up, current subscribers can get information on Continental Cablevision programming and services, and anyone can buy cable hardware and other related merchandise.

However, Continental Cablevision is more than a program distribution source. Citivision, Continental Cablevision's local origination channel, debuted in May 1986, a special service dedicated to covering St. Paul personalities, places, neighborhood life, and special events. From arts and entertainment to politics and sports, Citivision gives Continental Cablevision subscribers a unique window on the life of the city through a combination of field- and studio-produced programming. The firm also has developed a unique management and programming partnership with Minnesota Public Radio.

The firm also has committed its resources to serving the St. Paul area in other ways. In 1987 a second local-access network will link institutional subscribers in the St. Paul: Schools, government facilities, large nonprofit institutions, and businesses will be able to hold video meetings, conduct training sessions and information seminars, televise meetings and public hearings, and otherwise meet their own special information distribution needs.

From one employee in 1982 (Randall Coleman, now regional manager), Continental Cablevision of St. Paul has grown to become a well-staffed, multifaceted cable communication system with nearly 200 employees and a growing number of subscribers in the St. Paul metropolitan area.

DISTRICT HEATING DEVELOPMENT COMPANY

Heat, like food, clothing, and shelter is one of life's basic necessities in St. Paul. Although the need for heat is not unique to St. Paul, the city does have a unique system to provide its heat—hot water district heating. The system, the first of its size and kind in the nation, is owned and operated by the District Heating Development Company. DHDC provides reliable and efficient heating service to the State Capitol complex and more than 100 downtown and 298 residential customers.

District Heating Development Company was founded in 1979 by the City of St. Paul, the St. Paul Building Owners and Managers Association, and the State Energy Agency with the support of organized labor and the local utility company. The energy crisis had hit hard, and those groups were concerned about rising energy costs and increased dependence on unstable foreign fuel supplies. To help alleviate that dependence, DHDC's founders charged the firm to investigate the feasibility of a hot water district heating system for St. Paul. After affirming the viability of such a system, DHDC changed its charter to enable it to develop and operate a full-scale district heating system.

After several years of planning, feasibility studies, and financial negotiations, bonds were sold to finance the company, and DHDC purchased its seven-story heating plant and office building at 76 West Kellogg Boulevard. Construction of the piping system and heating plant renovation was completed one year ahead of schedule and $1.3 million under budget. On September 27, 1983, the first hot water for heating flowed from DHDC's Third Street Plant. Once only a vision, DHDC had become an operational utility.

As an operational utility, DHDC's first priority is its customers. By using district heating, customers experience both short- and long-

District Heating Development Company's Third Street Plant, location of the main heating facility and offices. Photo by Kay Shaw

term advantages. DHDC has proved itself reliable and efficient by supplying uninterrupted heat and making it possible for most of its customers to reduce their energy needs by an average of 20 percent.

Customers also benefit from the fuel flexibilty of DHDC's heating plant. The plant currently burns domestically abundant low-sulphur coal, but can also use oil or natural gas. This way DHDC is able to burn the lowest-cost fuel available and pass the saving on to its customers to ensure them long-term, stable energy prices.

Safety is another advantage for DHDC's customers: They do not need a boiler, and its inherent dangers, to heat their buildings. Instead, customers receive their heat from water that has been heated at DHDC's central plant and then piped through a system of more than 50,000 feet of twin piping beneath the streets and sidewalks. When the hot water reaches a customer's building, a

clean, safe heat exchanger extracts the heat and uses it for the building's space heating, water heating, and processing needs. The water is then returned to the plant to be reheated and recirculated.

The district heating concept using steam as the heat medium was created in New York State in the 1870s. It was widely used in the United States until natural gas became plentiful and less expensive after World War II. As district heating lost popularity in the United States, it gained popularity in Europe where energy was scarce after the war. The Scandinavians adapted the technology to use hot water as the heat medium. Since then, the hot water district heating has been transferred back to the United States and has been proved successful by DHDC.

The District Heating Development Company story is a testimony to how foresight, proven technology, and sound management created a company with a reliable and energy efficient system to provide heat—one of the necessities of life—to the people of St. Paul.

DHDC provides the heating service to the State Capitol. Shown here are the pipes under construction in 1984. Photo by Timothy Francisco

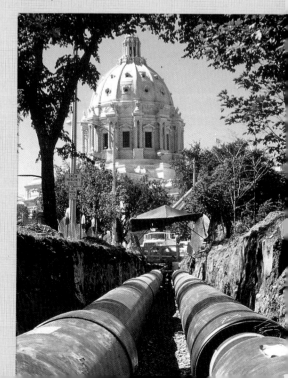

The District Heating System provides energy-saving steam heat to customers through over 50,000 feet of twin pipes below the city streets. Photo by Timothy Francisco. Courtesy, District Heating Development Corporation

ming by satellite. It was this satellite technology that made possible the creation in 1982 of APR by MPR and four other major stations: WNYC of New York, WGUC of Cincinnati, KQED of San Francisco, and KUSC of Los Angeles. APR serves 303 public-radio affiliate stations in 252 communities around the country with programming that is predominantly classical but also includes analytical news, and Keillor's whimsically warm portrait of life in his mythical Lake Wobegon.

APR is a distributor of programs. Because of APR, Minnesota's cultural organizations have received broad exposure. Concerts by the St. Paul Chamber Orchestra and the Minnesota Orchestra are carried by nearly 100 stations. APR distributes a daily news program by Canadian Broadcasting Corporation, an area of news coverage that has been sadly neglected in the United States. Keillor's "A Prairie Home Companion" reaches 3.5 million listeners a week, and another MPR program, "St. Paul Sunday Morning," is carried by more than 100 stations.

The technology involved in telecommunications is behind the development of all the met-

ropolitan region's television stations, including its public-television station, KTCA-TV (Channel 2). Public television arrived in the Twin Cities in the early 1950s. In those years public television was seen primarily as a teaching medium: set up the camera in the classroom, point it at the professor, and let the lecture begin. Today, with "Masterpiece Theatre," with the Public Broadcasting Service's documentaries and dramatic series, with locally produced interviews and news-analysis programs involving state and local leaders, KTCA has moved light years away from the classroom. It is also positioning itself for another move, to downtown St. Paul, where its new studios will be located in Lowertown, a block away from the Union Depot. Twin Cities Public Radio is seen as a catalyst in filling the telecommunications needs of the World Trade Center, as well as those presented by the region's education systems. The technology of satellite uplinks, microwave, and cellular systems is seen as the key to training skilled work forces of the future.

Already there is Continental Cablevision which has its regional offices and studio facilities in Union Depot Place, close to KTCA's site. Continental holds the franchise for cable television programming in the St. Paul area. "Citivision," its local-origination channel, will provide coverage of St. Paul events, including arts, entertainment, politics, and sports.

Many of the advances that are so much a part of daily life in the 1980s have been a century in the making. Their glimmers could be seen during the Golden Age, the last fifteen years of the nineteenth century. By that time much of the technology that created the modern city was in place. Telephone wire had been strung, streetcars had been electrified, and gas lamps were being replaced by electric lights on St. Paul's streets.

The city's energetic early citizens had welcomed gas for lighting because better indoor light extended both their working days and their leisure hours. On March 1, 1856, Alexander

Ramsey, Joseph Hoy, William L. Banning, Edmund Rice, and Charles H. Oakes incorporated the St. Paul Gas Light Company under a charter from the territorial legislature. The pioneering firm became the parent of St. Paul's electric and utility business, eventually edging out smaller-scale local competitors as generating and transmission technology moved forward.

By the early 1920s, however, St. Paul Gas Light had run out of generating capacity and was buying much of its power from H.M. Byllesby's Northern States Power Company (NSP) of Minneapolis, which was also operating in St. Paul. In 1925 St. Paul Gas Light Company agreed to a friendly acquisition by NSP.

By mid-twentieth century, NSP's major challenge was to stay ahead of growing demands for energy. In 1924 NSP's High Bridge plant near downtown St. Paul had been generating sixty megawatts of electricity; by the 1940s NSP plants were producing hundreds of megawatts. By the early 1950s the company had started the biggest building program in its history, including the pioneering use of uranium in nuclear generators at Monticello, Minnesota, and Prairie Island near Red Wing. Power also is imported from Canada, flowing from the Nelson River, near Hudson Bay, over a line that terminates north of St. Paul.

Today's NSP prices for electricity rank among the lowest one-quarter of the nation's investor-owned utilities. As successor to the St. Paul Gas Light Company, NSP also distributes gas to St. Paul and its suburbs. Natural gas pipelines bring it in from wells in the southwestern United States. A new NSP project will turn a civic liability into an asset. Minnesota communities are now prohibited by law from burying municipal solid waste (MSW) because of the danger of polluting groundwaters. A $21 million plant under construction at Newport, south of St. Paul, will convert MSW into "refuse derived fuel." Ferrous material, glass, and aluminum will be removed for recycling and the remainder (mainly paper and plastic) shredded into a light, fluffy fuel for NSP boilers. The plant will be the state's first such facility.

Energy has always been a crucial element in the economy of a northern city. No one, perhaps, understood this better than James J. Hill who was one of Minnesota's early energy czars before he rose to prominence as the builder of a railroad empire. In partnership with Norman W. Kittson, Hill logged off part of central Minnesota's Big Woods, the great deciduous forest that settlers already were clearing for farmland. Hill sold the firewood to the region's growing population. So critical was the need for this early form of energy that firewood dealers in outlying towns began to withhold their dwindling supplies from the city markets. Hill then became the first to import mineral coal into the area.

With the energy crunch of the mid-1970s, a new energy program was developed called District Heating. Both Minneapolis and St. Paul were examined for the program by the Department of Energy at the state and federal levels. The decision was that St. Paul, because of the age and inefficiency of its existing steam-heating system and its high number of degree days under 65 Fahrenheit, was a good candidate for a District Heating program.

The downtown section of the system was built a year ahead of schedule and one million dollars under budget. It could not have been accomplished, reports Mayor George Latimer, without a $7.5-million UDAG grant, the Port Authority's low-interest loans to building owners who wished to connect to the system, and an insured revenue bond package. Crucial to the program was the support of the Saint Paul Area Chamber of Commerce and the Saint Paul Foundation.

According to Mayor Latimer, District Heating is expected to produce energy savings, although it may be years before users see huge savings. In the meantime the people of St. Paul are beginning to move away from dependence on fossil fuels.

PART IV

MIND AND SPIRIT

A rich cultural mosaic has formed part of the city's fabric since the 1850s when Charles W.W. Borup, his violin tucked under his chin and accompanied by family members on the two grand pianos he owned, conducted musical soirees in his elegant villa in Lowertown.

At Fort Snelling in the 1830s, Joseph N. Nicollet, the distinguished French scientist, whiled away long winter evenings playing his violin, accompanied by Indian Agent Lawrence Taliaferro's wife on her piano. When he was a drummer boy at the fort, newspaper editor Joseph R. Brown belonged to the Old Fort Snelling Dramatic Club, and Harry

Artist Seth Eastman captured the wilderness setting of St. Paul's early days. The white cliffs upon which the city was built can still be viewed today. Courtesy, Ramsey County Historical Society

Painted by S. Holmes Andrews, this panoramic view illustrates St. Paul as it appeared in 1855. Thomas Newson wrote of life in St. Paul at this time as "gloriously exhilarating on hearing the whistle of a boat, to rush down to the levee..." Pen Pictures of St. Paul, 1885. Courtesy, MHS

Watkins, a well-known nineteenth century actor, made his debut there while a member of the Fifth Infantry.

The area attracted such artists as the renowned Western painter George Catlin. Edward K. Thomas, a soldier-artist, painted Fort Snelling. Ferdinand Reichardt painted the Falls of St. Anthony, and S. Holmes Andrews was one of the first to paint St. Paul from the now-familiar vantage point of Cherokee Heights on the West Side. Seth Eastman, Fort Snelling commandant and one of the great painters of the Mississippi valley, left behind what many experts believe to be the most nearly complete picture of Indian life in Minnesota portrayed by any artist. Robert O. Sweeny, pharmacist and artist, created with his charming ink sketches a remarkable record of early St. Paul. Sweeny had other interests. He would later found the St. Paul Academy of Natural Sciences, forerunner of the Science Museum of Minnesota. At about the same time Sweeny was sketching St. Paul, his fellow pioneers were establishing the Minnesota Historical Society to preserve the record of their settlement of the wilderness.

St. Paul citizens saw their first professional theatrical performance in Minnesota on August 12, 1851. Seven players from Placide's Varieties in New Orleans began a two-week engagement at Mazurka Hall, near Seven Corners. By the mid-1850s St. Paul had three or four music halls. Singing societies had been organized. An informal string quartet formed in 1858 grew into the St. Paul Music Society. In 1863 this orchestra of twenty-two members performed a Haydn symphony that may have marked the first hearing of an eighteenth-century composer in Minnesota.

The Music Society, which evolved into Minnesota's first symphony orchestra, moved its concerts to St. Paul's Opera House, erected in 1867 at Third and Wabasha, the site today of the Radisson Hotel garage. Although the first opera performed in St. Paul was presented at Melodeon Hall in 1859, the opera house did not present "grand opera" so much as it did a lively mixture of musical comedy, burlesque opera, "Living Art Statues," "Female Minstrels, Can Can dancers," and scenic spectacles such as "Around the World in Eighty Days," which featured a "snow storm on the Union Pacific" and "a fight with the Indians."

Thus began St. Paul's love affair with musical theater. Other such theaters would follow: the Metropolitan Opera House on Sixth Street near Cedar, and the Ford Music Hall and the Garrick, both on Sixth and St. Peter. They were part of the city's theater district, revived today by the move of Actors Theatre into the old Capitol (later the Paramount) on Seventh Street.

Meetings, recitals, and concerts held in private homes would coalesce by the 1880s into the Ladies Musicale, forerunner of today's Schubert Club. A young violinist named Emil Oberhoffer, playing with the Beethoven String Quartet which was founded in 1890, would become the first conductor of the Minneapolis Symphony Orchestra, now the Minnesota Orchestra. The opera tradition would be carried on by the St. Paul Civic Opera and the Minnesota Opera. A number of citizens, seeking a conductor for a group of free-lance musicians, would found the orchestra that has become the

Emil Oberhoffer inspired the growth of the Minneapolis Symphony Orchestra (forerunner of the Minnesota Orchestra) as its first conductor. Courtesy, MHS

world-renowned St. Paul Chamber Orchestra. And the visual arts would be represented by the Minnesota Museum of Art.

Without question, however, the jewel in St. Paul's artistic crown is the magnificent Ordway Music Theatre. Like the restoration of Landmark Center across Rice Park from the glittering Ordway, the creation of this $46-million glass, copper, and mahogany concert hall designed in the tradition of the classical European opera house represents the best that a special group of people can do for their city. No state, federal, or county money was tapped for the theater. Most of it came from the private fortunes of St. Paul families, from the corporations that helped produce those fortunes, and from the foundations those fortunes created.

It was an enormous effort, led by men and women who are descendants of Minnesota's

Above: *Sally Ordway Irvine initiated the development of St. Paul's resplendent Ordway Music Theatre. Courtesy, Ordway Music Theatre*

Above: *Carl B. Drake, Jr., served as president of The St. Paul Companies from 1973 to 1982 and chairman of the board from 1977-1984. Photo by Fabian Bachrach. Courtesy, The St. Paul Companies*

oldest families or linked to its major businesses— G. Richard Slade, great-grandson of James J. Hill; Carl B. Drake, Jr., a descendant of Elias Drake, who came to Minnesota to build the railroads Hill later owned; Elizabeth Musser, who helped restore Landmark Center and whose husband was a Weyerhaeuser Company executive; David Lilly, formerly Toro Company's chief executive officer; and Frank Marzitelli, former city administrator and state highway commissioner who, with Henry Blodgett, Jr., became a project manager.

But above all, the project was triggered by Sally Ordway Irvine, granddaughter of 3M investor Lucius Pond Ordway, who donated seven million dollars to the project. She persuaded other family members to join her in contributions now totaling close to fifteen million dollars, then challenged the Twin Cities metropolitan community to match that money. A new performing-arts theater located in St. Paul had been a dream of Mrs. Irvine's for some years, and the need was all too apparent. The cavernous 2,701-seat St. Paul Civic Theater, built in 1906 on Fifth Street, was not only deteriorating struc-

turally but was also outmoded technically. In 1980, after almost ten years of study by the city's civic and professional leadership, the old theater was condemned.

Now Mrs. Irvine stepped forward, offering to support a new theater. Long a theater advocate and an active board member of Chimera Theater, one of the Twin Cities' best-known full-time professional theater companies, she had in mind a theater that would serve all the performing arts. The architectural firm selected to design the new theater, quickly named the Ordway, was Ben Thompson & Associates of Cambridge, Massachusetts, in association with El-lerbe Associates of St. Paul. Thompson, a St. Paul native, possesses an international reputation based in part on his rejuvenated waterfront marketplaces in Boston, Baltimore, and New York.

Opened in January 1985, the Ordway is seen by Carl Drake, chairman of the Ordway's board and the man who has been chief fund-raiser for the project, as "probably the single most important development" for St. Paul since the city itself was founded. Certainly the music theater with its romantic ambience reminiscent of the gilded past of opera houses, theaters, and concert halls in Paris, Vienna, and Salzberg enhances St. Paul's European feeling and symbolizes the renaissance that has taken place in the city over the past two decades. The design team's creation, a "sparkling prism of glass and light" on Rice Park, has drawn national attention to St. Paul.

Inside, a sweeping spiral staircase rises three levels to the upper promenade surrounding the main hall's three curving balconies. The hall itself—horseshoe-shaped, with a proscenium stage—seats 1,800 to 2,000 people. The theater's thrust stage, unusual for its ability to be moved about, gives it a versatility that allows it to become, in turn, a setting for a small orchestra, for a full-size symphony with chorus, for grand or light opera, for a soloist or small ensemble. The hall actually can be tuned for these

Left: *Mayor Fraser of Minneapolis (at microphone) and Mayor Latimer of St. Paul (right) officiated at the grand opening ceremonies for the new Ordway Music Theatre. Other participants pictured include, left to right: Carl B. Drake, Jr., John G. Ordway, Richard D. Snyder, and Sally Ordway Irvine. Photo by Jerry Miller. Courtesy, Ordway Theatre*

Below: *Amos Martin (center), director of the Saint Paul Area Chamber of Commerce, visits with John G. Ordway (left), and Norman Lorentzsen, the 1976 chairman of the Chamber at the Ordway's opening. Photo by Jerry Miller. Courtesy, Ordway Theatre*

many uses.

The smaller Studio Theater, which seats 315, is linked to the Main Hall by a spacious lobby. Designed to help fulfill the Ordway's mission of providing top-quality performing space for community-based groups, the Studio Theater is a scaled-down version of the Main Hall.

Another jewel in the city's crown is the newly restored World Theater, the home of Garrison Keillor's "A Prairie Home Companion" radio show, produced by Minnesota Public Radio. The 925-seat theater at Wabasha and Exchange streets is St. Paul's oldest surviving theater space and a candidate for listing on the National Register of Historic Places. It is one of the few two-balcony dramatic house proscenium theaters still in existence. Opened in 1910 as the Sam S. Schubert Theater, it cost $165,000 to build and it featured legitimate theater and vaudeville. Purchased by MPR in 1980 to house Keillor's show, it was restored by the architectural firm of Miller Hanson Westerbeck Bell at a cost of $3.5 million. It was a project that not only revived the theater's original splendor but also added advanced technical systems to serve a modern era. The theater's main entrance was reestablished on Exchange

Street, a glass-roof atrium was added on the east side of the building to provide space for receptions, and the intricate plasterwork that runs in bands along the ceiling, side walls, and proscenium was reconstructed.

Within this elegant setting Keillor delivers Saturday broadcasts in which humor is laced with music so diverse that it has included jazz and bluegrass, folk and ethnic tunes, and even opera, on occasion. There have been performances by Emmylou Harris, Chet Atkins, Willie Nelson, Scottish folklorist Jean Redpath, and Atlanta's First Presbyterian Church Choir. But the highpoint of each show is Keillor's monologue about "Lake Wobegon," his mythical hometown

Above: *The Ordway Theatre is the city's crown jewel. Courtesy, City of St. Paul, Planning and Economic Development Office*

Right: *The romantic ambience of the Ordway Music Theatre is reminiscent of the gilded past of opera houses, theaters, and concert halls in Paris, Vienna and Salzburg. At the same time, the latest innovations in acoustical technology assure listening enjoyment for all. Courtesy, St. Paul Convention Bureau*

The Ordway Theatre's sweeping spiral staircase rises three levels to the upper promenade. Courtesy, St. Paul Convention Bureau

The Ordway Theatre aglow, with Winter Carnival ice sculptures standing guard. Photo by Kay Shaw

EMBASSY SUITES HOTEL

Each of Embassy Suites Hotel's 210 guest rooms opens onto the colorful central atrium.

At first glance, the warm, reddish-brown brick building at the corner of Jackson and 10th streets, just off I-94 in St. Paul's historic Lowertown, has the look of a business that may have been on that location since the heyday of rail baron James J. Hill. In actuality, the St. Paul Embassy Suites Hotel is one of the city's newest and most popular hospitality attractions.

Since its completion in the summer of 1983, the hotel has played host to more than 1.5 million guests, from business travelers visiting 3M, Burlington Northern, Stroh's, and other St. Paul companies to pleasure travelers and families staying close to patients at nearby Gillette Children's Hospital and St. Paul Ramsey Medical Center. The setting and the style nicely complement Lowertown's colorful history. Built on the site of the original Farmers' Market (and originally opened as the St. Paul Granada Royale Hometel), the St. Paul Embassy Suites is a study in contrast.

From the outside, the post-Modernist exterior design—the work of Twin Cities architects Frederick Bentz, Milo Thompson, and Robert Rietow, Inc.—was developed to help the hotel blend into the surrounding area. It uses elements of historic forms and materials indigenous to the city's Lowertown, an area still dominated by late nineteenth-century archi-tecture.

Masonry details emphasize the classic building pattern: bottom, middle, and top levels. A decorative stone belt course wraps around the base of the building and its entryways. The middle section features large windows opening onto balconies with wrought-iron railings. At the top, arched stone window openings are topped by keystones, with offsets at the corners to give the massive, seven-story structure the look of a cluster of buildings rather than one.

Inside, however, the subdued exterior gives way to an open atrium and courtyard reminiscent of a Central American piazza. The design, by California's Arthur Valdez, emphasizes warm earth tones and ample greenery, highlighted with colorful murals. Every one of the hotel's 210 suites opens onto the glass-domed, sunlit atrium; at ground level, Woolley's restaurant, the cocktail lounge, the indoor pool, and meeting rooms also access the courtyard.

A wholly owned subsidiary of Holiday Corporation (which also owns Holiday Inns), Embassy Suites reflects a major trend in the nation's lodging industry: a move toward larger and more hospitable accommodations. Each guest room is actually a suite consisting of a bedroom, bathroom, and living room, complete with a galley/kitchen bar. Guests receive a complimentary, full-course breakfast each morning and complimentary cocktails at the close of the day.

The St. Paul Embassy Suites represents a significant amount of cooperation between the hotel's owners, the developers, the city, and Lowertown Redevelopment Corporation, a private developer and financier. Through two years of joint planning, design, financing, and implementation work, they assured that the successor to the Farmers' Market site would preserve and enhance the urban scale and texture of Lowertown.

The Alexander Ramsey House, located in the Irvine Park Historic District, was built in 1872 for Alexander Ramsey, Minnesota's first territorial governor. Today, the Minnesota Historical Society conducts tours of the house that interpret the life and times of the Ramsey family. Photo by Kay Shaw

in central Minnesota that "time forgot and the decades cannot improve." Program "sponsors" include Bertha's Kitty Boutique, the Chatterbox Cafe, Ralph's Pretty Good Grocery, and Powdermilk Biscuits, "the biscuits that give shy persons the strength to get up and do what needs to be done."

The World Theater may well remain best known as the home of a show business phenomenon that has been called the single most significant tourist attraction in the state in years. However, the World Theater Corporation, which owns and operates it, expects the theater to fill a real community need for mid-size performing space that also offers first-class communications systems.

The Ordway was also planned for a wide variety of musical dance and theater groups, local and national and including touring Broadway productions, but it is, in addition, the principal performing hall for three of Minnesota's most prestigious musical organizations: the Schubert Club, the St. Paul Chamber Orchestra, and the Minnesota Opera. Another major user is the Minnesota Symphony Orchestra. All have roots deep in Minnesota's past, but the Schubert

Club is the state's oldest musical organization. What is most remarkable about the Schubert Club, however, is not just its continuing high quality over the years but the fact that it was formed by and run by women for the first eighty-six years of its existence.

By the 1880s the informal musical soirees of earlier years had become ladies' matinee musicales held in the homes of such women as Mrs. Frederick Driscoll on Summit Avenue and Mrs. Charles E. Furness (Marion Ramsey) in Governor Ramsey's "Mansion House" on Exchange Street in the Irvine Park neighborhood. In 1882 the informal meetings, during which the women did fancywork while listening to music by their talented friends, took on a more formal organization as the Music Society. The next year the name was changed to the Ladies Musicale and five years later to the Schubert Club in honor of the Austrian composer.

Gradually the serious purpose of the club emerged. Recitals were interspersed with lectures. The women heard Red Wing's Frances Densmore on "Music of the American Indians" and New York's Walter J. Damrosch on Wagner's *Die Meistersinger.* Since the 1890s hundreds of

The Schubert Club's Keyboard Instrument Museum in Landmark Center displays one of the finest collections of historic pianos in the country. Recordings are also made on these instruments. Courtesy, the Schubert Club

nationally and internationally known artists have appeared in St. Paul under Schubert Club auspices. They have included Arthur Rubinstein, James Melton, Helen Traubel, Vladimir Horowitz, Myra Hess, Lotte Lehman, and Jascha Heifetz. Four have appeared four times: pianists Robert Casadesus and Alicia de Larrocha, violinist Isaac Stern, and soprano Beverly Sills.

In 1968 the club passed from an all-volunteer organization run mainly from the president's dining room table to professional management. Today the Schubert Club presents a many-faceted program. Its International Artist Series brings to St. Paul such famous recital performers as Leontyne Price, who presented the Ordway's opening concert. The Chamber Music Series brings in concerts by such ensembles as the Juilliard Quartet, the Guarneri Quartet, and the Beaux Arts Trio. A festival of music by the visiting Baroque Orchestra, using authentic early instruments, was cosponsored with the Ordway.

Weekly recitals by professional and amateur artists in the Twin Cities region are presented in Landmark Center, where the Schubert Club has its offices and where it presents "Live from Landmark," broadcast over Minnesota Public Radio. Schubert Club scholarships help promising young artists, a musical therapy program helps the handicapped, and project CHEER brings music instruction to some 100 disadvantaged children in an inner-city neighborhood.

In its Keyboard Instrument Museum in Landmark Center, the Schubert Club has assembled one of the finest collections of historic pianos in the country. Recordings on these instruments are being produced. The club's collection of musical manuscripts, including letters of Beethoven, Mendelssohn, Schubert, Brahms, and other composers, is displayed at the Ordway Music Theatre. A highlight in Schubert Club history came in 1975 when its first commissioned work, a song cycle, "From the Diary of Virginia Woolf" by Dominick Argento, won the Pulitzer Prize for music.

One of the Schubert Club's earliest cooperative programming efforts was with the St. Paul Philharmonic Orchestra. America's first full-time professional chamber orchestra, it is known today as the St. Paul Chamber Orchestra. It began modestly as a descendant of several groups of professional musicians who, like the Beethoven String Quartet, banded together to make music. In this case, twenty-four musicians with music instructor Leonard Sipe as conductor founded the St. Paul Philharmonic to provide educational programs for young musicians and present new works.

Nine years later, after a successful New York debut, the Philharmonic had become the St. Paul Chamber Orchestra. In 1969 Stephen Sell became managing director and initiated a marketing program, "Music on the Move," that

took the orchestra to churches, shopping centers, and school auditoriums, establishing the tradition of outreach neighborhood performances.

The years between 1972 and 1980 belonged to Dennis Russell Davies, who had led the Juilliard Ensemble and was named the Chamber Orchestra's music director after Sipe's resignation. By the early 1980s the orchestra's "on-the-move" performances had stretched into tours of western and eastern Europe and the Soviet Union, and 140 American communities. The orchestra's recording of "Appalachian Spring" won a Grammy award in 1979.

The next year, with Davies' move to the Stuttgart Opera, a new era opened. The orchestra's board, chaired by St. Paul business leader and philanthropist John H. Myers, chose as its new music director the internationally famous Pinchas Zukerman, violinist, violist, and a conductor of ten years' experience. Zukerman attracted other major international artists to perform with the orchestra, tripled orchestra subscriptions, increased its size from twenty-six to thirty-four full-time musicians, and placed it within the ranks of the country's thirty-four major orchestras.

As with the Schubert Club, the orchestra's need was for a home, a concert hall that would effectively showcase the delicate chamber music sound. The Ordway Music Theatre provides that special setting, although the orchestra's "on-the-move" concerts continue with tours of the United States and Canada and the major music capitals of Europe.

The orchestra's repertoire spans four centuries of music, from the baroque to the contemporary. Its main series, the Ordway Music Series, is its most popular, with sixteen programs that attract major artists. The Baroque Series, offered in several different neighborhood locations, continues the orchestra's tradition of outreach performances throughout the Twin Cities. The Friday Morning Series, with low prices and free coffee, is designed to appeal to senior citizens.

191

RADISSON HOTELS

The Radisson Hotel St. Paul, the city's largest hotel, began serving the needs of business and pleasure travelers, especially conventioneers, as the St. Paul Hilton in 1965. Located on Kellogg Boulevard on the riverfront side of the downtown area, the hotel from its very beginning offered a combination of modern convenience and traditional hospitality to visitors to the city.

When the $5.5-million remodeling of the Radisson is completed in late 1987, it will mark a new beginning for the hotel that in its own way served as the beginning of downtown St. Paul's renaissance. It will also bring new luster to the city's flagship hotel, a member of the fast-growing family of Radisson Hotel Corporation, a key part of Minnesota's only home-grown international hospitality firm.

The corporation was just three years old when what is now the Radisson Hotel St. Paul opened its doors. Minnesota entrepreneur Curt Carlson first ventured into the hotel business in 1962 by purchasing the historic Radisson Hotel (named for the state's first explorer, seventeenth-century French

The Radisson Hotel St. Paul's lobby, with its rich Early French Empire decor, reflects the warmth and comforts befitting the fine hotel.

voyageur Pierre Esprit Radisson) in downtown Minneapolis. The business had grown to four other properties in the region by 1976 when the company joined the St. Paul property's original owners, SPH Hotel Corporation, as a part owner of the hotel. The Radisson Hotel St. Paul was born.

Today the Radisson continues to be the city's finest, a major convention and business host whose beautifully appointed guest rooms and suites are complemented by fine restaurants and special programs designed for the business traveler. Through the years, the hotel has earned a well-deserved reputation for fine dining, its cuisine enhanced by an ever-varying view of the Mississippi River and St. Paul's skyline.

With the completion of the renovation, its 475 rooms will include 100 two-room suites (guest rooms and parlors) that can be converted back into single rooms to meet the needs of large convention groups. Many suites and cabana rooms overlook the hotel's colorful indoor garden court and pool, while the Plaza Club on the upper floors provides a quiet, luxurious environment and special services for corporate clients. The hotel's ballroom, one of the largest in the Twin Cities, an exhibit hall, and four private dining rooms are in constant use for meetings and

The main entrance of the Radisson St. Paul, on Kellogg Boulevard, annually welcomes thousands of visitors to the capital city.

conventions of all sizes and descriptions.

Radisson Hotel Corporation, a subsidiary of locally based Carlson Companies, Inc., prides itself on offering a collection, not just a chain of look-alike hotels. Under Juergen Bartels, president of Carlson Hospitality Group, and John Norlander, a former manager of the Radisson Hotel St. Paul in its Hilton days and now president of Radisson Hotel Corporation, the current collection of 140 hotels, inns, and resorts worldwide is expected to more than double by the 1990s through a combination of company-developed and franchised properties the world over.

As the idea of a collection implies, Radisson properties come in a variety of shapes and sizes, each uniquely configured to meet the hospitality needs of the community where it is located. Properties encompass five distinctive types: plaza hotels, hotels, suite hotels, inns, and resorts.

As one of America's fastest growing hospitality companies, Radisson Hotel Corporation operates, manages, and franchises distinctive properties in the United States, Canada, Mexico, Europe, and the Mideast.

The New Music Series features musical theater works; a new music pilot series focuses on young composers, and a Sampler Series is presented on Sunday afternoons in Orchestra Hall in Minneapolis.

The St. Paul Chamber Orchestra also joins with other groups in collaborative programming. With Minnesota Opera, the orchestra premiered Dominick Argento's "Casanova's Homecoming," and in 1985 the two organizations presented the American premiere of "Where the Wild Things Are" by Maurice Sendak and Oliver Knussen. Plans call for future collaboration with other performing groups, such as the New Dance Ensemble, the Minnesota Dance Theatre, and the Minnesota Chorale, the orchestra's official chorus, which was founded in 1972 and is now directed by Joel Revzen.

Minnesota Opera grew out of Center Opera, established in 1963 under the wing of Minneapolis' Walker Art Center. By 1971 it had become an independent entity, its name changed to Minnesota Opera. Concentrating on new works by American composers, Minnesota Opera during its early years averaged at least one world premiere a season, one of which, *Transformation,* was later telecast nationally over Public Broadcast System. While Minnesota Opera expanded its traditional repertoire, it also developed a series of works-in-progress productions that, in cooperation with the National Opera Institute Music Theater Workshop, gave composers a chance to work with singers and directors.

Two other programs offer training for young singers: the Minnesota Opera Studio, established with the help of a grant from St. Paul's Jerome Foundation, provides a nine-month training program in all areas of operatic performances, and the Minnesota Opera Institute offers a scaled-down but similar three-week summer program. Through Midwest Opera Theater, its touring and educational arm, Minnesota Opera brings performances to communities throughout the Upper Midwest.

Minnesota Opera is home at last at the Ordway

Above: *Also premiering at the new Ordway, the Minnesota Opera and the St. Paul Orchestra's collaboration of* Where the Wild Things Are. *Photo by Bruce Goldstein. Courtesy, Minnesota Opera*

Top: *Dominick Argento's* Casanova's Homecoming *helped celebrate the opening of the Ordway Music Theatre. Photo by Peter B. Myers. Courtesy, Minnesota Opera*

Music Theatre, after spending over twenty years staging its productions in Twin Cities high schools, churches, college auditoriums, and the Prom Ballroom. Now it has settled into a three-part season, with traditional operas presented in the fall of each year, new and experimental programs in the spring, and classical musicals and operettas during the summer months.

From time to time all three organizations share the Ordway's main hall with the Minnesota Orchestra, founded in 1903 as the Minneapolis Symphony, the eighth major orchestra to be established in the United States. The orchestra's career was launched when Emil Oberhoffer assembled a group of professional instrumentalists from Chicago and from the Twin Cities Orchestra under Frank Danz. In its eighty-three years the orchestra has been led by some of the western world's most distinguished conductors—

LANDMARK CENTER

Henri Verbrugghen, Artur Bodansky, Walter Damrosch, Bruno Walter, Eugene Ormandy, Dimitri Mitropoulos, Antal Dorati, Stanislaw Skrowaczewski, Sir Neville Marriner, and now Edo de Waart. Its Ordway concerts will continue the subscription series the orchestra has presented in St. Paul for some fifteen years. That the Ordway can accommodate such a wide variety of musical events, from recitalists through orchestras all the way up to that most extravagant of all musical theater, grand opera, is a tribute to its great versatility.

The fact that St. Paul's history is studded with theatrical and musical events indicates longtime private support of cultural activities on the part of its people. By the 1940s, however, private patronage had fallen off, eroded perhaps by the lingering effects of the Depression combined with the great national effort that World War II required. Frank Marzitelli, a city councilman and "Commissioner of Libraries, Auditoriums, Museums, and Stadia" from 1950 to 1957, recalls that presidents and directors of a number of St. Paul cultural organizations, surveying their declining community support, decided something had to be done. With a $5,000 grant from the Louis and Maud Hill Family Foundation (now St. Paul's Northwest Area Foundation), the St. Paul Junior League hired a consultant to study these organizations' needs and how to meet them. The results of the study, which recommended creation of a coordinating agency for an arts and educational center, went to Marzitelli, who was told by the city council that he was expected to play a leading role. It

Landmark Center's Richardsonian Romanesque architecture is detailed in this photograph. Photo by Leighton

took about three years, but the St. Paul Arts and Science Council (now the St. Paul-Ramsey United Arts Council) that emerged from this study revived and restructured broadly based community support for cultural organizations.

By 1964 the Arts Council, with help from a general obligation bond issue approved by St. Paul voters, had completed construction of a new Arts and Science Center building at Tenth and Cedar, the site of the old state capitol, that would house the council and its member agencies. The city agreed to pay for the building's maintenance. There was just one problem: by the time the agencies moved into their shiny new building, it no longer was big enough to house all of them.

But help was at hand. The Old Federal Courts Building (now Landmark Center) was about to be transferred to the city. (Later it would be transferred to Ramsey County.) Much of the push to acquire the building as an arts, history, and education center stemmed from the need for more space for the burgeoning cultural groups to exhibit, teach, practice, and perform.

Today Landmark Center's restoration is complete, the result of a public and private partnership between the Board of Ramsey County Commissioners, which agreed to pay for maintaining the building, and Minnesota Landmarks, the private nonprofit agency that agreed to raise the millions needed to restore the building and now manages it for the county. Landmark Center today is not just one of the most successful restorations in the country but it is also, as Marzitelli puts it, "a civic home for the creative energies of the people of this county."

Among the agencies in Landmark Center is the Minnesota Museum of Art (MMA), founded by a group of artists and students in 1927 as the St. Paul Gallery and School of Art. Today the museum mounts traveling exhibits of regional and national importance in Landmark Center. It also owns the Jemne Building at Kellogg and St. Peter, designed by architect Magnus Jemne and built in 1931 as the Women's City

A common sight in St. Paul are historic buildings adjacent to contemporary skyscrapers. Here the Jemne building, now the Minnesota Museum of Art, is surrounded by Bell Telephone (right) while Amhoist Tower looms behind it. Photo by Kay Shaw

Club building. Now on the National Register of Historic Places as a handsome blend of the art-deco and international styles of architecture of the 1930s, it houses the museum's permanent collection.

MMA's collections and exhibitions focus on late nineteenth-century to mid-twentieth-century American art and non-Western art. Its Museum School offers more than 120 classes for all ages in painting, drawing, sculpture, ceramics, weaving, and photography. Kidspace is a gallery for school-age children who create their own art works.

COMPAS, also housed in Landmark Center, was established in 1974 and is the largest community arts agency in Minnesota with a national reputation for innovative arts programming. COMPAS programs are designed to give Minnesota residents a chance to take active roles in the arts in the communities where they live and under the direction of professional artists. These programs include Accessible Arts, for such special constituents as older adults, the isolated, the handicapped, the hospitalized, or the chemically dependent; Writers & Artists-in-the-Schools, which creates residencies for artists and writers in Minnesota schools; Dialogue, which grew out of Writers-in-the-Schools and brings teachers and writers together; and the Community Art Fund, established in 1983 with the City of St. Paul to provide financial support and technical assistance for local arts projects actively involving St. Paul people.

COMPAS was the incubator for one of the most successful and innovative theater programs in St. Paul in recent years. The Great North American History Theater was founded in 1978 as the St. Paul History Theatre, a COMPAS program. Within a few years it was a renamed independent professional theater that commissions and produces new plays dramatizing American history and folklore. Emphasis is on Midwest and Minnesota history, and careful research into old newspaper stories, photographs, letters, journals, diaries, and public documents, as well as interviews with people who were there, forms the background for the scripts.

In its first two years as an independent theater, History Theater reached a 91 percent attendance record. It received two Kudos awards from the Twin Cities Drama Critics Circle and an Award of Merit from the American Association for State and Local History. Among the theater's hits have been *The Man Who Bought Minneapolis,* about empire-builder James J. Hill and the pursuit of power; *Nina: Madam to a Saintly City,* about the woman who ran a famous bordello in Victorian St. Paul; *Four Hearts and the Lords of the North,* performed at historic Fort Snelling, set in the 1820s and portraying events involving the Indians, fur traders, and soldiers; and *The Deadly Decades,* about the Prohibition era. *A Servants' Christmas* is a perennial holiday favorite, and *Plain Hearts* is a country/folk musical about turn-of-the-century women and their lives.

Most of History Theater's productions are staged in the Weyerhaeuser auditorium in Landmark Center, but the theater has toured the Upper Midwest with *Plain Hearts* and a production based on the life and career of Sinclair Lewis. It has established a professional summer theater, the Great Northern Repertory Theater, in Grand Rapids, Minnesota.

One of the best known among Minnesota's theaters is the sixteen-year-old Chimera Theatre Company, an outgrowth of the earlier Theatre

St. Paul. Based in the Arts and Sciences Center complex, Chimera has attracted some 100,000 people in a single season to its performances in the center's Crawford Livingston Theater. Chimera's major emphasis is on family entertainment with such productions as *Amadeus, Evita,* and *Damm Yankees.* Its educational program is one of the largest of its kind in the country. Under a contract with the St. Paul public school system, Chimera provides 1,250 hours of creative dramatics annually in twelve elementary and secondary schools. The program reaches 11,000 students each year. At the Arts and Science Center another 3,600 enroll in classes ranging from creative movement for preschoolers to advanced acting for adults. Chimera's Youth Theatre Company produces three shows annually featuring child actors and concentrating on historical, social, and educational subject matters.

Actors Theatre of St. Paul is another major professional theater that is an important part of a revitalized downtown St. Paul. Founded in 1977, Actors Theatre and its resident ensemble acting company of eight to ten players produce seven plays each season. After eight years of performing at St. Thomas College's Foley Theater, Actors Theatre has seen its audiences grow from 4,500 to 42,000, and theater supporters launched a successful drive for a new home. This was "St. Paul's million-dollar playhouse," the old Capitol Theater on Seventh Street between St. Peter and Wabasha. It was one of eight theaters that seventy years ago formed an exciting and highly visible downtown theater district that extended along St. Peter and Wabasha between Fifth and Tenth streets.

The Capitol, built within the Hamm building by William Hamm in 1920, was once the largest, most elaborate, and most expensive movie palace in the Northwest. It was an important first-run theater and it was designed for an opulent era. As times slowly began to change, however, the Capitol became the Paramount and then the considerably smaller Norstar, closing finally in

The elegant Capitol Theater, here pictured circa 1920, once presented first-run movies to St. Paulites. Today, the Actors Theater has brought legitimate theatre back to downtown St. Paul. Courtesy, MHS

1978—the last, at that time, of the downtown theaters. Now Actors Theatre, with its $1.4-million renovation of the old theater, has brought back to the heart of the city the rich tradition of what once was known as "the legitimate theater."

The late 1970s was a rich period of ferment for St. Paul's theater community. Not only do History Theater and Actors Theatre trace their beginnings back to those years but so do at least two other St. Paul theaters. Park Square Theatre, whose performances have been staged at Hamline University Theatre and Landmark Center's Weyerhaeuser auditorium, was founded in 1975. Penumbra Theatre was established two years later. Penumbra, whose home is in the Martin Luther King Center on Selby Avenue, concentrates on plays that reflect the black experience in America. These have ranged from *Bubbling Brown Sugar* to the Pulitzer-prizewinning *A Soldier's Story* to the little-known new play, *The Resurrection of Lady Lester.*

Film in the Cities is one of the largest media arts centers in the country, but it is also—perhaps is primarily—a school that began life as a program launched in 1970 to teach junior- and senior-high school students the arts of filmmaking. When the schools dropped their funding for extracurricular programs, Film in the Cities' student base shifted to adults, to would-be filmmakers, video artists, writers, and composers, among others. Students can earn an Associate in Arts degree through Inver Hills Community College, long associated with Film in the Cities, and the course is also accredited by Metropolitan State University and the University of Minnesota's University without Walls.

Film in the Cities has moved into a new and most appropriate home, the theater in the former Burlington Northern building in Lowertown, now restored as First Trust Center. The theater is named for Jerome Hill, himself an Oscar-winning independent filmmaker and grandson of James J. Hill, who erected the Burlington Northern building as headquarters for his Great Northern rail-

road.

St. Paul's cultural community does not by any means exist in a vacuum. Minneapolis' Institute of Art, Guthrie Theater, and Walker Art Center, along with the Minnesota Orchestra, all are world-famous. The many smaller theaters and other performing groups, including those emanating from the colleges and universities, have contributed immensely to descriptions of the Twin Cities metropolitan area as "blessed with good arts and cultural groups." This goes hand in hand with figures from a recent survey of area residents by the Minnesota Center for Social Research of the University of Minnesota. Asked to what degree exposure to the arts contributes to a better quality of life, more than 80 percent of those surveyed ranked it six on a scale of one to ten, while 16 percent ranked it

The colorful Actors Theatre Marquee, looking onto West Seventh Place Mall. Courtesy, Actors Theatre of St. Paul

SHERATON MIDWAY

For nearly 75 years the Brown & Bigelow plant—built on the site of the old Lexington racetrack in the Midway district of St. Paul—employed hundreds of people in the making of playing cards, advertising specialties, and custom-printed calendars for businesses coast to coast. Artists from Norman Rockwell to Vargas and Petty created special paintings for the company's distinctive form of wall hangings.

Today those memories live on in the uniquely St. Paul ambience of the Sheraton Midway, one of the youngest properties in the international Sheraton system, yet already one of the best. The hotel's exterior facade harks back to the earlier business carried on along the I-94 corridor between St. Paul and Minneapolis. Inside, Rockwell paintings and memorabilia from the old Brown & Bigelow plant grace Bigelow's Taverne, Bigelow's Restaurant, and the hotel's four-story atrium courtyard.

Construction for the 200-room hotel and meeting center began in 1981, after Brown & Bigelow's operations had been moved to a new home in St. Paul. City planners hard at work on the new Energy Park development wanted a hotel nearby to serve the new businesses they hoped to attract to the complex. The Port Authority of the City of St. Paul provided financial assistance. Shortly after the hotel opened in 1982, it became part of the Sheraton family.

It didn't take long for the Sheraton Midway to establish an identity as a prime meeting site between St. Paul and Minneapolis. In addition to serving businesses in the growing Energy Park development, it also quickly proved popular with visitors to the many small colleges nearby, among them Concordia, Hamline, St. Thomas, and St. Catherine's.

Neither did it take very long for the new hotel to establish a reputation for excellence within the prestigious Sheraton system. In 1985 the Sheraton Midway was one of just 14 Sheratons among 350 worldwide to win the organization's Awards of Excellence for general management, housekeeping, and maintenance. The following year general manager Robert Gramowski accepted the Award of Excellence for general management for the second straight year—one of just 17 Sheratons to earn the award, given on the basis of friendly and professional service in all areas of the hotel, and high-quality food and beverage operations. The Sheraton Midway also received a second consecutive Award of Excellence for housekeeping in 1986.

The key to the Sheraton Midway's success is its nurturing of repeat business travelers who "Meet Midway." In addition to the

The Sheraton Midway's effective use of skylights brings the outdoors inside.

Guests dine surrounded by greenery, Norman Rockwell prints, and memorabilia from the Brown & Bigelow era in St. Paul.

comfortable guest rooms and the large indoor pool and sauna complex (complete with whirlpool and exercise room) in the hotel's sunlit atrium, the Sheraton Midway features a unique, theater-style auditorium, with inclined seating and permanent stage, that accommodates 148 people in comfortable seats with fold-up writing desks. Other facilities off the hotel's separate meeting entrance and reception area include a ballroom and 15 Executive Parlor Suites, with full catering, audiovisual, and other support services available.

Small wonder then that one of St. Paul's newest hotels is also one of its best.

at number ten. More than half of those surveyed said they had visited Twin Cities arts and cultural institutions and museums in the past two years.

Amos Martin of St. Paul's Chamber of Commerce also sees a commingling of boards of directors as men and women from the Twin Cities leadership join forces to support the region's cultural life. This high level of support has attracted national recognition to the Twin Cities. What is interesting, moreover, is the extent to which arts and culture exert a significant economic impact on the region.

The first real look at this economic impact was taken by the Metropolitan Council's Regional Arts Council, which conducted a survey to examine two sides of the question: audience spending (gas, parking, meals) and direct spending by arts groups themselves (rent, staff, overhead). A total of 173 metropolitan area organizations were surveyed.

Direct spending in 1984 totaled $103.6 million, a figure that translated into a total direct-and-indirect spending figure of more than $303 million. Audience spending, based on estimated annual attendance, totaled $84.3 million. The two figures together added up to almost $388 million that flowed into the Twin Cities economy as a result of the efforts of its arts and cultural agencies. Arts and culture, in short, constitute an industry of major importance to the Twin Cities. A United States government survey, cited by the Metropolitan Council in connection with its own survey report, found that the arts industry spent more money than did the commercial sports teams in the Twin Cities, establishing for the region a reputation as a mecca for the arts.

Other institutions play significant roles as part of the larger cultural community of St. Paul. The Science Museum of Minnesota, established in St. Paul in 1907, today attracts an average of 750,000 visitors a year to its new building at Wabasha and Exchange. The Science Museum traces its origins to 1870, when the Saint Paul Academy of Natural Sciences, the first organi-

zation of its kind in the Middle West, was founded by a number of St. Paul physicians, teachers, and other professionals led by Robert O. Sweeny, the pioneer pharmacist and artist, designer of the state's great seal, and Minnesota's first game and fish director.

The academy's collections and library were housed with the Minnesota Historical Society in the first state capitol at Tenth and Cedar, but all were destroyed when the capitol burned to the ground in 1881. Two years later the academy closed; it was revived in 1890, then closed again for good in 1907. Its collections were turned over to the newly formed St. Paul Institute, the Science Museum's ancestor.

Two St. Paul leaders, Charles W. Ames, soon to become president of West Publishing Company, and Dr. Arthur Sweeny, had established the Saint Paul Institute of Science and Letters to bring to St. Paul's people the benefits of free lectures on a variety of subjects. The success of the lectures, which drew 9,000 people, gave Ames a better idea: an institute that would draw together, under one leadership and supported by the entire community, all of the city's cultural activities—musical, educational, literary.

Ames was among the best in a generation that produced idealists with a strong sense of the practical. Frederick M. Eliot wrote of Ames after his death in 1921 that the institute represented to him "in a sense the idealism of the American City. He believed with all his soul that America is a land where idealism can overcome materialism, and he regarded the St. Paul Institute as one of the outposts of the idealism that must in the end conquer."

The new organization, incorporated in 1908 as the St. Paul Institute of Arts and Sciences, was the forerunner of the St. Paul-Ramsey Council of Arts and Sciences of the 1950s. Its programs, far-ranging in scope, were based on the idea of a people's university and were far ahead of their time. The institute conducted evening schools (that foreshadowed evening college courses, community education exten-

sion programs, and Metropolitan State University); put on lectures and musical programs with the Schubert Club and the Minneapolis Symphony; ran the School of Art and Art Gallery that became the Minnesota Museum of Art; and maintained the Museum of Natural and Physical Sciences that became the Science Museum of Minnesota.

Until 1928 the institute leased the upper three floors of the city auditorium on West Fourth Street. Then it acquired the massive stone mansion built in 1887 by Colonel John Merriam, father of Minnesota's eleventh governor, William Merriam, on a hill overlooking downtown St. Paul. When the Science Museum moved into the new Arts and Science Center in 1964, the center already lacked enough space for the Science Museum's expanding programs. Museum attendance had grown from 7,000 in 1917 to 27,000 in 1928 to 100,651 in 1967-1968. In 1974-1975 museum programs attracted 625,423. It is scarcely surprising, then, that when the block west of the Arts and Science Center was sched-

Above and right: *Park Square Theatre, founded in 1975, performs at Hamline University Theatre and Landmark Center.* Elleemosynary, *above,* and Death of a Salesman, *right, were recent productions. Courtesy, Park Square Theatre Company*

St. Paulites also enjoy the world-famous Guthrie Theater in Minneapolis. Above: *Oscar Wilde's* The Importance of Being Earnest *was produced for the company's 1984 National Tour;* left: *a performance of Cole Porter's musical* Anything Goes. *Courtesy, The Guthrie Theater*

uled for demolition by the St. Paul Housing and Redevelopment Authority, the Science Museum began to plan for a new building on the site. It would open a glittering new era in its history.

In September 1978 lines blocks long formed as the Science Museum opened its new building, the result of a $15-million capital expansion program that included a reshuffling of agencies and space in both the Arts and Science Center and Landmark Center. As the council and Minnesota Museum of Art moved out of the Arts and Science Center into Landmark Center, the Science Museum spread out into the old Arts and Science building.

The centerpiece of the Science Museum is the William L. McKnight-3M Omnitheater with its domed, seventy-six foot-wide-screen and its 70-mm Omnimax projector. The museum, second in the world to build an Omnitheater, has shown such films as *Genesis,* and at the time of the Challenger disaster in January 1986 it premiered the space film *The Dream Is Alive.* The Science Museum now leads in helping to produce new Omni films for viewing all over the world.

Throughout the museum's 59,000 square feet of exhibit space, theater techniques in construction and lighting are used to create displays in anthropology, biology, geography, geology, paleontology, and technology, an interesting blend of a natural history museum with a science and technology center. The museum's 1.5 million scientific objects draw scientists from all over the world, while staff scientists conduct their own research projects. A nonformal preschool and elementary-level science program attracts one out of five Minnesota school children to the museum on school trips in one year alone. The museum's membership of almost 25,000 is the second-largest science museum membership in the country.

Support for the museum is broadly based throughout the Twin Cities and the state, but essential operating maintenance comes from the Board of Ramsey County Commissioners, a unique expression of support on the part of lo-

cal government for its arts and cultural agencies. Ramsey County has continued to provide operational support for the Arts and Science Center building and also for Landmark Center, the home of a number of cultural agencies, including the Ramsey County Historical Society.

Founded in 1949, the society has grown from a localized 100-member group with a $7,500 annual budget and a small museum open two afternoons a week with part-time staff to an organization of 1,200 members, a $471,000 annual budget, and a staff of fifteen. Now one of the largest county historical societies in the country, the society conducts an array of programs designed to help residents and nonresidents alike understand the history of the region surrounding the state's capital and the part it plays in a key Upper Midwest metropolitan center.

The society owns and operates the Gibbs Farm Museum, a 137-year-old farm home in suburban Ramsey County. As an urban fringe farm, the museum represents an important aspect of the history of a county that, with two-thirds of its area consisting of the city of St. Paul, the county seat, is the most urbanized county in Minnesota. In Landmark Center the society mounts exhibits, presents free noontime lectures, publishes books, pamphlets, and a semiannual magazine, and conducts historic-site tours throughout the region.

Other historical groups in Ramsey County are centered in suburban communities whose cores are the venerable villages that once existed outside of St. Paul—New Brighton, Roseville, Little Canada, Maplewood, White Bear Lake. There are also neighborhood history groups within St. Paul. All do for their special history what the Ramsey County Historical Society does for county history and the Minnesota Historical Society for state history.

The Minnesota Historical Society, with headquarters just to the east of the state capitol, is the oldest institution in the state and the second-largest state historical society in the country. It was founded in 1849, the year Minnesota be-

Designed in 1906 by Clarence Johnston, noted Minnesota architect, the Samuel Dittenhofer residence at 807 Summit Avenue preserves the Tudor villa style of architecture. Photo by Kay Shaw

came a territory, by the group of settlers who were endearingly similar to pioneers of any other time and place—they wanted to preserve the record of their own past and of their part in what they sensed was the great adventure of their time, the opening of the West.

Led by such men as Alexander Ramsey, its first president, the society for many years occupied rooms in all of the state's capitols. Beginning in 1917, its administration, its library that had been so carefully collected since the society's earliest years, and its manuscripts, documents, and other collections were gathered together into its own building, a gray granite and pillared Renaissance structure on Capitol Hill. By the 1980s the society had long since outgrown the building that seemed so spacious compared with the "five large rooms" the society had occupied in the state capitol.

The state's "memory," in a very real sense, and certainly its record-keeper, the Minnesota Historical Society has had to spread out its archives into a converted warehouse and its artifacts, now numbering in the hundreds of thousands, into the former Mechanics Arts High School. The society's publications have expanded beyond its original quarterly magazine into books and reprints, and its programs have grown beyond its main building and revolve, to a great extent, around the thirty-one historic sites the society administers throughout Minnesota.

Three of these historic sites are located in St. Paul and include Historic Fort Snelling, the frontier post that has been re-created on its original site, using archeological evidence from excavation of the site and the Army's original plans for the fort. Two other St. Paul sites administered by the society are the mansions of James J. Hill on Summit Avenue and Alexander Ramsey in the Irvine Park National Historic District off Seven Corners near downtown St. Paul. Both have been restored and are open to the public for tours.

Plans are going forward for a new Minnesota State History Center, proposed for the site of the old Miller Hospital on a ridge overlooking downtown St. Paul. The center will include a major museum, which will make it possible for the public to view far more of the society's collections than is possible now; library and archival services; and administration offices. The Minnesota Supreme Court is expected to move into the historical society's present building.

Concern for preservation of historic sites within St. Paul is shared by the state and county historical societies with the St. Paul Heritage Preservation Commission, created by city ordinance in 1976. A function of St. Paul's Planning and Economic Development Department, the commission is made up of St. Paul citizens appointed by the mayor and includes several architects and a representative of the Ramsey County Historical Society. The commission recommends to the city council the designation of historic sites and districts, encourages preservation and restoration, and speaks out against threatened demolition of significant structures. Empowered to protect the city's architectural character, the commission reviews all applications for building permits for demolition of officially listed historic structures, for moving them,

or for new construction involving changes to their exteriors.

The relationship between the city and county arts and cultural agencies, all of which maintain educational programs, and the region's formal educational institutions has been long term and mutually supportive. There are thirteen colleges and universities in the Twin Cities metropolitan area, not including the two-year community colleges, and ten of them are in St. Paul. Except for the University of Minnesota, which is spread between Minneapolis and St. Paul, all are private colleges with strong liberal-arts underpinnings.

St. Paul's private colleges are descendants of a nineteenth-century system of education that, before the widespread establishment of public high schools, often placed post-elementary school instruction in the hands of the clergy or of teachers who sought church support for their private academies the College of St. Thomas, a Catholic liberal arts school that emphasizes career-oriented education, is Minnesota's largest private college. It was founded in 1885 by Archbishop John Ireland as St. Thomas Aquinas Seminary, a Roman Catholic high school, college, and seminary.

The archbishop, a towering figure in regional and national affairs, had acquired the pioneer farmstead of William Finn, sixty acres of "woodland and meadow, possessing hills, brooks, standing lakes and groves," according to early accounts. It was also "far removed from town" and close to the east bank of the Mississippi where the majestic Summit Avenue would eventually end at the river. The seminary opened its doors in September 1885 with six faculty members and sixty-two students enrolled in either the classical or theological departments. In 1894, when Ireland built the Saint Paul Seminary across Summit Avenue from the college, the classical department became the college and its first four years eventually became St. Thomas Military Academy, now located in Mendota Heights. All three—college, seminary, and

COLLEGE OF ST. THOMAS

Founded more than a century ago by Archbishop John Ireland, the third bishop of St. Paul, the College of St. Thomas is the largest independent college in Minnesota. A Catholic liberal arts school with a tradition of value-centered education, St. Thomas is also an innovator that in recent years has placed a strong emphasis on community outreach, both in the Twin Cities and the surrounding region.

About two-thirds of the institution's nearly 8,000 students are enrolled in undergraduate programs leading to bachelor of arts degrees in 44 major fields of study. At the graduate level, seven programs lead students toward master's degrees in business management, business communications, software design and development, manufacturing systems engineering, pastoral studies, international management, and education and community services.

St. Thomas' excellent faculty includes both full- and part-time educators, visiting professors, alumni scholars, and—especially at the graduate level—practicing professionals. They can draw on the growing resources of the colorful campus at the western end of Summit Avenue near the Mississippi River, as well as satellite campuses in Owatonna and Chaska.

The modern College of St. Thomas is a far cry from the rustic school that opened in 1885 on what was once Finn's Farm. The St. Thomas Aquinas Seminary of that era was a combination high school, college, and seminary with a rector, a faculty of five priests, and 62 students—all housed in the former Industrial School for Boys. The first baccalaureate degrees were awarded in 1910.

In contrast to its current setting in the pleasant residential neighborhoods of the city, St. Thomas then was considered "far removed from town." Just as the city has grown toward the college's former

The diverse student body at the College of St. Thomas is a combination of traditional younger students and older students, many of them working, united in their quest for high-quality education with practical career benefits.

60 acres of woodland and meadow, St. Thomas also has grown toward the city in developing programs designed to meet a wide variety of lifelong educational needs.

Through the institution's membership in a consortium of five private colleges in the Twin Cities, St. Thomas students may take classes for full credit at any of five campuses. New College, an evening and weekend division for working and other nontraditional students, was initiated in 1975. Two years later St. Thomas ended its all-male enrollment tradition; today nearly half of the college's students are women. In 1986 the institution resumed its affiliation with The Saint Paul Seminary, a major theological seminary located across from the college campus.

In addition to the offerings in the college's catalog, many noncredit programs, courses, and seminars are provided through 10 centers: the Management Center, the Community Education Center, the Economic Education Center, the Center for Religious Education, the Senior Citizen Education Center, the Small Business Development Center, the Small Business Institute, the Campus Life-Care Center, the Center for Jewish-Christian Learning, and the College of St. Thomas Conservatory of Music.

Beyond St. Paul, the Daniel C. Gainey Conference Center in Owatonna brings the institution's educational resources to southeastern Minnesota, and many of St. Thomas' undergraduate and graduate programs are offered at its Peavey Center in Chaska.

More than a century after its founding, the College of St. Thomas offers its students the best of two worlds—a well-rounded, liberal arts education and offerings tailored for practical career development.

military academy—celebrated their centennials in 1985.

By the 1980s St. Thomas was offering bachelor of arts degrees in forty-four major fields of study, as well as five graduate programs in business administration and communications, international management, and a number of other areas. Its 212 faculty members are supplemented by successful professional men and women as adjunct faculty, underlining the college's commitment to liberal arts with a practical application.

The college has been coeducational since 1977. Eighty-six percent of its 6,500 students are from Minnesota and 56 percent of those are from the Twin Cities. St. Thomas also maintains several off-campus centers—the Peavey Center and the College of St. Thomas Enterprise Center, both in suburban Chaska, and the Gainey Conference Center near Owatonna, south of the Twin Cities.

With St. Thomas organized and Saint Paul Seminary established, Archbishop Ireland turned his attention to a college for women. Far from subscribing to the prevailing theory that the average woman's brain was physiologically deficient compared to a man's brain, the redoubtable archbishop had a healthy respect for the intellectual abilities of women in general and of his own two sisters and cousin in particular, members of the Order of St. Joseph of Carondelet that had sent four courageous women into St. Paul in 1851 to establish a school in a shed behind the log Chapel of St. Paul. As Sister Seraphine (Ellen Ireland), Sister St. John (Eliza Ireland), and Sister Celeste (Ellen Howard), they became pioneers in Catholic education for women.

The institution these women played a major role in founding was the College of St. Catherine, still on its original site at Randolph and Cleveland avenues but now spread over a 110-acre campus. Its first building, Derham Hall, opened in 1904 and was named for Hugh Derham, a Rosemount farmer whose $20,000 gift had made it possible. Like St. Thomas, the College of St. Catherine was first a boarding preparatory school drawing students and faculty from the older St. Joseph's Academy established in 1863 near the present St. Paul Cathedral. Classes began in January 1905 with seventy boarding students and twenty-seven sisters. Within ten years the school's collegiate department had achieved the stature of a full-fledged college. Derham Hall, for two years the only building on the campus and housing sisters, students, classrooms, a library, and a chapel, still stands and is a designated National Historic site. The college that surrounds it is now a first-ranked Catholic liberal-arts institution.

If St. Thomas exists primarily for Minnesotans, Macalester College, just a few blocks away and with roots in Minnesota's territorial past, has a strong global orientation. Its 1,700 students come from all fifty states and seventy other countries, a diversity that might have astounded its founder, the Reverend Edward Duffield Neill—Presbyterian clergyman, educator, Civil War regimental chaplain, one of President Lincoln's secretaries, and something of a religious entrepreneur.

Like St. Thomas, Macalester celebrated its 100th anniversary in 1985, but its origins go back even further to the Baldwin School, which Neill established in downtown St. Paul in 1853. Neill had raised the money for his school from Matthew W. Baldwin, the Philadelphia manufacturer of locomotives. In 1874 Neill prevailed upon Charles Macalester, another wealthy Philadelphian and owner of the Winslow House in what is now Minneapolis' East Side, to turn over this once-fashionable hotel to him for a college named, understandably, in Macalester's honor. Six years later the Presbyterian Church's Minnesota synod adopted the college.

In 1883 a real estate syndicate purchased the college's present site on Snelling and Grand avenues, a neighborhood now known as Macalester Park. Again like St. Thomas, Macalester's trustees had their eyes firmly on "location, location, location." The site they bought was the

Above: *The College of St. Catherine, founded in 1904, extends over a 110-acre beautifully landscaped campus. Photo by Kay Shaw*

Left: *Designed by sculptor Paul Granlund, "Constellation Earth" adorns the campus mall at the College of St. Thomas. Photo by Kay Shaw*

Right: *Derham Hall, today a National Register Historic site, was built in 1904 to house the College of St. Catherine's first students and faculty. The building is named for Hugh Derham whose donation ensured the establishment of the college. Photo by Kay Shaw*

Below: *The O'Shaughnessy Auditorium at the College of St. Catherine once housed the Minnesota Opera. Photo by Kay Shaw*

radiate the pure light of Christian culture and scholarship through the Twin Cities to the region beyond.

By 1890 the population of the two cities was 298,000; St. Paul's western boundary was the Mississippi, and streetcar lines linked Macalester Park with downtown St. Paul and Minneapolis.

Macalester opened its doors in September 1885 with thirty-six students. The others were enrolled in the preparatory department. Critical years lay ahead, and it fell to Dr. James Wallace, Macalester's president from 1894 to 1906, to guide the fledgling college through a period of "debt and despondency." Some of these years Wallace shared with his son, DeWitt, who would found *The Reader's Digest* and who would maintain a lifelong commitment to the welfare of the college.

The student body of the 1980s is light years removed from the earnest young people of the 1880s who bent their minds to mastering Mental Science and Logic, Greek and Anglo-Saxon, Latin, Biblical Instruction, and Moral Science. The college now has twenty-six academic departments offering thirty-seven majors, the most

farm settled in the 1860s by Thomas Holyoke. Its "first-rate soil" was studded with oak, elm, ash, linden, maple, and cottonwood trees. In promoting the location, Neill himself told the trustees that:

The cities of Minneapolis and Saint Paul, in 20 years, at the present rate of increase, will contain not less than 250,000 souls, and their suburbs will touch. Between them is the need of a center which with its library, museum, gallery of art, laboratory, observatory and faculty of professors will

MACALESTER COLLEGE

Measuring the quality of a college is no easy task. The dimensions are often intangible—a reflection of the students, faculty, alumni, and community who both serve and are served by the institution.

Macalester has long been ranked among the nation's finest undergraduate liberal arts schools. Its reputation for quality in all aspects of the educational experience has been deepened and strengthened in recent years; the college enters its second century with a renewed commitment to academic excellence and challenge.

Located in one of St. Paul's beautiful and historic residential neighborhoods off Summit Avenue, Macalester is a small world in its own right—one that reflects both the character of the city that surrounds it and the larger world from which many of its 1,700 students and 130 faculty members are drawn. The 55-acre campus includes 19 academic buildings, nine residence halls, and several special buildings, all within 10 minutes of either downtown St. Paul or downtown Minneapolis.

Students from every state and some 70 nations make up the Macalester student body, and international programs attract about 40 percent of its U.S.-born students abroad during their studies. Students can choose from among 27 departments that offer nearly 40 majors and 30 minors, from the arts to natural sciences, business to political science.

The college is an integral part of the city, using surrounding neighborhoods and businesses as a living laboratory for academic, volunteer, and internship programs. Urban geography students survey city streets and neighborhoods. Psychology students make their own animal behavior observations at the Minnesota Zoo. Each year approximately one student in five devotes time to a volunteer or internship program that involves a core of some 300

businesses, service agencies, churches, government offices, and cultural organizations.

The tradition of service continues after graduation. Thousands of Macalester alumni live and work in greater St. Paul, and contribute actively to their churches, schools, neighborhoods, cultural groups, and other community groups.

Although the first classes began in 1885, Macalester was officially founded in 1874. The Reverend Edward Neill, a Presbyterian minister, began laying the groundwork for the college in 1853 by starting a grammar school (on the site of what is now Landmark Center) that he hoped might serve as a preparatory institution. In 1874 he reopened the school in the Winslow House at St. Anthony Falls, an abandoned tourist hotel owned through foreclosure by fellow Philadelphian Charles Macalester, a millionaire businessman and philanthropist. Macalester's will deeded Winslow House to the school; the money raised from its sale funded construction of the first building on the Macalester campus.

On the site of that original build-

A small liberal arts college of national standing, Macalester draws its more than 1,700 students from every state in the U.S. and from 70 nations. Macalester students are very involved in the community; each year 400 to 500 serve as volunteers or interns in more than 300 businesses and agencies. Photo by Ed Bock

Macalester College's faculty and students enjoy the best of both worlds—the serenity of a tree-shaded campus within a historic residential neighborhood, and proximity to the rich educational and cultural resources of St. Paul.

ing, a new central library complex is being designed to serve the needs of Macalester students well into the twenty-first century. Under president Robert M. Gavin, Jr., Macalester continues to encourage the same spirit of inquiry that has characterized it for a century.

It is an environment of quality in learning and living that continues to rank Macalester College among the nation's finest liberal arts colleges—one where students from around the country and the world share a tradition of academic rigor, community involvement, and international understanding.

popular of which is economics. Eighty percent of the faculty members have doctorates. Macalester ranks fourth among liberal-arts colleges in the number of Rhodes scholarships its students have received. Since the college stresses internationalism, more than half its students study overseas at some point before graduation.

Hamline University on Snelling Avenue, just north of University Avenue, is the oldest college in Minnesota. It was founded in 1854 in Red Wing, Minnesota, by a group of Methodists who had been persuaded by real estate speculator William Freeborn that the tiny village of 300 souls would one day become a city of "wealth and intelligence." Hamline was named for Bishop Leonidas Hamline, a wealthy retired Methodist clergyman who backed up his interest in frontier education with a gift of $25,000 worth of real estate to launch the new institution of higher learning. And it was truly that. As early as 1857 Hamline had established a full college course.

Hamline, however, did not prosper in Red Wing. The university closed in 1869, and its trustees, their sentiments leaning toward an urban location, began the search for the site the

ment, library books in the trunk of a student's car. But in 1974 the school moved onto Hamline's campus and by 1980 a new $5-million Law Center had been opened. Annual enrollment now averages 500.

Like other Twin Cities colleges and universities, Hamline offers graduate programs for working adults, one of the bright new trends in American education of the 1970s and 1980s. Hamline's liberal arts and law faculties join with community experts to offer a Master of Arts in Public Administration (MAPA). Courses provide leadership training with an emphasis on the legal/ethical aspects of public management and on state and local issues in public administration. Another program, Hamline's Master of Arts in Liberal Study (MALS), focuses on the historical perspective of present-day issues. Interdisciplinary studies are team-taught in evening seminars, and students design their own courses of study.

A pioneer in postgraduate education for working men and women may well be William Mitchell College of Law. Founded in 1956, William Mitchell grew out of two earlier law schools, the St. Paul College of Law, established in 1900 in downtown St. Paul to offer students a chance to attend law school at night, and the Minneapolis-Minnesota College of Law, which represented a merger of several law schools established in Minneapolis between 1912 and 1920.

William Mitchell, for whom the college is named, was a Winona, Minnesota, lawyer who became one of the most respected associate justices of the Minnesota Supreme Court, serving from 1881 to 1898. Mitchell, his son, and his grandson also helped build one of Minnesota's best-known law firms, Doherty, Rumble and Butler, along with Pierce Butler, the first Minnesotan to sit on the United States Supreme Court.

With its 1,100 students, William Mitchell College of Law is the largest law school in Minnesota. Its emphasis on practical lawyering skills has helped earn it a reputation as a "lawyer's

university still occupies. At that time it was a prairie north of the old Territorial Road (now University Avenue) that linked St. Paul and Minneapolis, and halfway between the two growing cities.

University Hall, now known as Bridgman Hall or "Old Main" and the first building on the new campus, was finished in 1880, and the university reopened with sixty students. University Hall, an excellent example of Victorian Gothic architecture, still stands as one of St. Paul's National Historic sites.

Hamline today, with its thirty-acre campus, nine academic buildings, and six residence halls, bears about as little resemblance to its own hopeful beginnings as other colleges do to their nineteenth-century origins. Hamline's School of Law is one of three in Minnesota. It was founded in 1972 as the Midwestern School of Law by thirty-three students and seven practitioners, who saw that the demand for legal education in the Upper Midwest region was increasing.

The law school's early years were humble, to say the very least—classes in a church base-

law school,'' a reputation enhanced by graduates who hold about half of the judicial positions in the state's district, probate, and county court systems. Warren Burger, the retiring United States chief justice, is a graduate, as are several of the state's supreme court justices and members of the newly formed Minnesota Court of Appeals, based in St. Paul.

The college has pioneered in opening doors to a legal education for women and minorities, who, for much of the twentieth century, could

not attend law school in Minnesota. Its seven-acre campus extends along Summit Avenue. A faculty of thirty-three law professors, supplemented by some 100 judges and practicing lawyers as adjunct faculty, teaches the college's three-year day and four-year evening programs that let students work full-time or part-time.

Metropolitan State University, headquartered in St. Paul as an upper-division member of the Minnesota State University System, recognizes that education as a lifelong learning process

Hamline University offers diverse courses of study for both undergraduate and postgraduate students. Among the campus buildings is the modern Bush student union, right. The Science Building, with Old Main Tower in the distance, is pictured below. Photos by Kay Shaw

Left: *This President's House is on the campus of Minnesota's oldest college, Hamline University. Photo by Kay Shaw*

Concordia College's Luther statue fronts Poehler Hall; to the left is Luther Hall. Photo by Kay Shaw

does not always take place in the classroom. A unique program designed for working men and women allows students to claim credits from college-level experiences through work, community activities, and travel.

The university, which is accredited by the Commission of Institutions of Higher Education of the North Central Association of Colleges and Schools, offers three degree programs—Bachelor of Arts, Bachelor of Arts in Nursing, and a Master of Management and Administration. Students design their own education plans based on their own goals, interests, and educational needs. The entire Twin Cities area serves as Metro University's campus. Classes are held in libraries, community centers, businesses. More than half its 3,500 students are women, and the average age of its students is thirty-four. A faculty of thirty-two professional educators includes another 350 professional men and women as adjunct faculty, a hallmark of many innovative programs that stress academic training combined with practical experience.

The University of Minnesota is one of the great American universities and one of the largest. The need for a university was uppermost in the minds of Minnesota's farseeing territorial legislators, who, 135 years ago, understood the importance of education on the frontier, as well as its ability to lure new settlers. The university was organized in 1851 by an act of the legislature, and part of its present site, on the east

bank of the Mississippi halfway between Minneapolis and St. Paul, was acquired three years later. Then the cause of higher education limped along through a number of reorganizations until September of 1869, when the fledgling university opened again with 175 students, forty of them women.

Student life that first year was vividly described by Samuel W. Pond, Jr. He was the son of the famous missionary who, with his brother, Gideon, ministered during the 1830s to Chief Cloudman's band of Dakotah at their village on Lake Calhoun in what is now south Minneapolis.

Above: *In the 1880s and 1890s the University of Minnesota expanded its campus under the leadership of Cyrus Northrup, who remained president for twenty-seven years. Further expansion occurred during the 1920s when the university constructed a series of buildings creating a modified campus mall from earlier Cass Gilbert plans. Courtesy, MHS*

Facing page: *A study in contrasting architecture: the St. Paul Cathedral, designed by Emmanuel Masqueray, forms the backdrop for the Vocational Technical Institute, designed by Ellerbe Associates, Inc. Courtesy, Ellerbe Associates, Inc.*

In letters home, Pond writes:

Saturday I went down to the grocery and purchased some cranberries and sugar as a kind of Sabbath luxury. I am not by any means in a good humor tonight, having been obligated to wait two hours for bread to be baked at the bakery this afternoon, some time when a fellow is out of bread and is somewhat hungry. The stuff which we buy for bread at the bakery has become of so questionable a character of late, we should be almost at a loss what to call it were we to bestow a name from the principal ingredients . . . among other ingredients carpet tacks, pine shavings, cock roaches (sic) and various other similar articles [figure] largely.

The Morrill Act of 1862 had entitled Minnesota to receive 120,000 acres of federal land for the support of a state university, but it also required the university to offer courses in which "agriculture is taught as a science." The university first established a "farm campus" in what is now the Minneapolis residential neighborhood of Prospect Park, a district of rolling hills east of the university's main campus. By 1888, however, the agricultural school had been moved to its present site in the St. Paul neighborhood of St. Anthony Park.

Now the University of Minnesota's St. Paul campus, the school is a major United States land-grant college that includes the School of Veterinary Medicine and the United States Department of Agriculture's experiment station and extension service. Distinguished scientists have emerged from its walls, among them Norman E. Borlaug, world-famous plant pathologist and winner of the 1979 Nobel Peace Prize for his leadership in the Green Revolution, a plan for solving world hunger problems.

The Hubert H. Humphrey Institute of Public Affairs on the main campus is named for another world-famous Minnesotan and University graduate—the state's longtime United States senator who also served as vice president of the United States. The center is dedicated to furthering Hubert H. Humphrey's belief in the need to train men and women for leadership in public service.

The institute offers a master of arts in public affairs and a master of planning in public affairs programming; it also has an important research function in four areas: strategic planning and management, social policy and distributive justice, regional economics and development, and environmental policy. A Reflective Leadership program helps people in mid-career broaden their perspectives.

Located in the new Humphrey Center dedicated in 1986, the institute also serves as a resource to encourage students, citizens, communities, and organizations to participate in public policy.

Concordia College and Luther Theological Seminary are both affiliated with Lutheran church denominations, and Bethel College in suburban Ramsey County with the Baptist church. The interdenominational United Theological Seminary in New Brighton trains students for Congregational, Presbyterian, Methodist and other church assignments.

Luther Theological Seminary, situated in St. Anthony Park, is the largest Lutheran seminary in the United States. It grew out of a Lutheran seminary established at Madison, Wisconsin, in 1876. Today it represents the 1917 merger of three Lutheran church bodies, each with its own seminary, and their joining a year later in a single seminary in St. Anthony Park. The seminary's original building at 2481 Como Avenue is now listed on the National Register of Historic Places, as is Old Muskego Church, a little log church and meeting house also on the seminary's campus. The first Norwegian Lutheran church built in the United States, it was constructed in 1843-1844 at Muskego, Wisconsin, by Norwegian settlers. It was dismantled in 1904, moved to St. Paul, reconstructed on its

present site, and restored. The church is open to the public by arrangement with the seminary and used for weddings and other special events.

St. Paul Academy/Summit School is a private middle school/high school that is a merger of two schools—St. Paul Academy for boys and Summit School for girls, established after World War I. Breck School, owned and maintained by the Minnesota diocese of the Episcopal Church, was founded as a private high school for boys in southern Minnesota, then reestablished early in this century on a hilltop west of Luther seminary in St. Anthony Park. The growth of both institutions dictated a move by Breck, first to a campus on the West River Road in south Minneapolis and then to the Minneapolis suburb of Golden Valley. Now coeducational, Breck continues to draw many of its students from Ramsey County.

In addition to its colleges, universities, private schools, and public and parochial school systems, the St. Paul area has several vocational-technical institutes (AVTIs) that are part of Minnesota's thirty "Vo-tech" institutions. Also, two St. Paul suburban community colleges offer two-year programs leading to an associate of arts degree and, for many of their graduates, the first half of a four-year college course.

A substantial amount of support for educational, health, welfare and social services, com-

UNIVERSITY OF MINNESOTA

Among the varied components of the vast University of Minnesota system, the St. Paul campus (part of the Twin Cities campus) is unsurpassed in its embodiment of the spirit and the letter of the university's original mission as a land-grant educational institution. From its front-line research programs spanning scores of disciplines to its educational outreach offering practical advice in daily living, the St. Paul campus of the University of Minnesota is a proud partner in fulfilling the call to serve persons of all walks of life throughout the state.

A picturesque expanse of open fields, tasteful gardens, stately older buildings, and contemporary architecture, the campus emerged from humble beginnings as the university's official "experimental farm." When the original 155-acre hilltop site was purchased in 1882 with proceeds from the sale of agriculturally poor but developmentally lucrative land near the Minneapolis campus, few would have predicted that it would one day be an internationally acclaimed center for education and research.

Today that original hilltop site has grown to a 514-acre complex of educational facilities and life-lab fields. Nearly 5,000 of the university's more than 55,000 students are enrolled in the undergraduate

and graduate programs of the five colleges located on the campus. They benefit from all the resources and advantages of a major university and the Twin Cities metropolitan area, yet in a friendly, small-campus setting that harks back to roots in St. Paul that go back more than a century.

In its first years the campus housed only a few students and faculty involved in programs focused exclusively on farming and related disciplines. The emphasis in those years was on "hands-on" experience—it was not uncommon for faculty members to be found somewhere in a field behind a plow and a team of university horses. But as the needs and ambitions of Minnesotans changed over time, the campus rapidly expanded to meet the call for education and research in a variety of areas.

Today the St. Paul campus is home to a number of academic and related units. The century-old College of Agriculture is the largest of the five in terms of total undergraduate and graduate enrollment, but only marginally so. Its course offerings cover the full spectrum of modern technical, social, and economic issues related

Students in the Food Science Laboratory.

St. Paul Student Center. The campus' physical environment creates a serene yet stimulating atmosphere for the pursuit of knowledge.

to agricultural production, processing, marketing, and consumption.

Almost equal in size (in fact, slightly larger in terms of undergraduate enrollment) is the College of Home Economics, which today provides education and research in home, family, and community issues. Research and education in the diverse areas covered by the life sciences occur under the aegis of the College of Biological Sciences. The College of Forestry offers programs dealing with renewable resources—wildlife and fisheries, as well as forests and forest products.

At the graduate level, the College of Veterinary Medicine is the state's focal point for research, teaching, and other activities related to animal health management. And in addition to the five colleges, the campus is home to the Minneapolis-based College of Education's Department of Vocational and Technical Education, which offers programs for future teachers of agriculture and home economics.

The St. Paul campus' competitive academic atmosphere and amiable environment attract under-

of science complement these educational efforts. A century of applied research has yielded innumerable agronomic crops and horticultural varieties adapted to Minnesota's unique climate. Many St. Paul campus scientists today use sophisticated equipment and techniques to conduct front-line research in such diverse areas as plant and animal genetic engineering, economic analysis, food science, and forest products. Others work at the leading edge of the social sciences, studying youth problems, family interactions, and other areas of human concern.

Enhancing the value of its first-rate academic offerings and research programs, the campus' physical environment creates a serene yet stimulating atmosphere for the pursuit of knowledge. A sense of appreciation for open spaces and natural features permeates the groves of trees and graceful gardens planned and planted by resident horticultural experts. Tastefully designed buildings combining old and new on the campus' central hill overlook gently sloping fields that serve as both laboratory and classroom. The inherent beauty and delightfully welcoming atmosphere do much to brighten the lives of the many who choose to make it home, whether for a few months of study or decades of academic endeavor.

The teaching role of the St. Paul campus involves far more than classroom settings and research. Headquarters of the Minnesota Agricultural Experiment Station, a network of research facilities statewide, and the Minnesota Extension Service, which serves as the front door to the university in every county of the state, are also located there.

Some 300 faculty members are involved in more than 370 research projects managed through the Experiment Station. They serve as both principal investigators and supervisors for the teams

of graduate research assistants, technicians, and postdoctoral research associates who work on programs that involve everything from soil, water, and animal management to the development of new crop varieties.

The Minnesota Extension Service is dedicated to helping Minnesotans of every age, background, and profession learn in the communities where they live and work. While its historic concentration has been on the needs of rural Minnesotans, especially agribusinesses and farm families, its mission to

A technician makes crosses in oat breeding in a genetics program.

aim at the central issues facing the lives of people throughout the state also embraces Minnesotans in nonfarm and urban settings.

Since it was founded in 1861, the University of Minnesota's 5 campuses, 10 specialized research facilities, and 92 county extension offices have grown to reach across the face of the state—a network of educational opportunity that stretches from the North Woods to the Iowa border. Scholastically and physically, the St. Paul campus is a harmonious blend of the best of the university's past, present, and future—a century-long tradition of academic excellence and service to the people of Minnesota, the nation, and the world.

A sunflower research field with the St. Paul campus in the background.

graduate and graduate students and faculty from around the world. Many of its programs are considered among the best in the country. Over the years the campus has been a wellspring of talent, producing able graduates who have unselfishly worked to improve their world—alumni like Green Revolution pioneer Norman Borlaug, winner of the Nobel Peace Prize.

Superior research programs and staff working at the cutting edge

219

St. Paul Vocational Technical Institute trains students for a variety of professions. Photo by Shin Koyama. Courtesy, Ellerbe Associates, Inc.

munity affairs, religion, science, and the arts and humanities programs flows from the more than 500 foundations in Minnesota. Among them are at least eight with strong St. Paul connections: the McKnight and Bush Foundations, which stem from the fortunes of 3M's Archibald G. Bush and William L. McKnight; the Saint Paul Foundation, one of the largest community foundations in the country; the Northwest Area Foundation, established by Louis W. and Maud Hill, James J. Hill's son and his wife; the F.R. Bigelow Foundation; the I.A. O'Shaughnessy Foundation; the Charles and Ellora Alliss Educational Foundation; and the Andersen Foundation in Bayport, Minnesota.

St. Paul, like Minneapolis, is a city of parks and playgrounds. When its board of park commissioners was created in 1887, it set about improving Como Park, established in 1873 after the city bought Como Lake and the land around it for $100,000. A lily pond was created in the park, a pavilion built where bands played weekly, and a Japanese garden planted in the "cool and beautiful retreat." The conservatory, its

domed rotunda flanked by two wings in the tradition of English Victorian buildings, was completed in 1915. The Como Zoo benefited from the periodic flooding of Harriet Island by the Mississippi which threatened the island's menagerie. The animals were moved to Como Park where an animal house was built by the WPA in 1936. In recent months an extensive program of renovation of the animal houses, as well as contruction of new quarters, has been completed. The magnificent flower shows held in the park's conservatory attract visitors from all over the region.

The city also bought up land around Lake Phalen for another city park and added improvements to Harriet Island, which boasted at one time an outdoor gymnasium, a refreshment pavilion, and, in an interesting contemporary note, a free day nursery where working mothers could leave their children.

St. Paul is also a city of festivals. The oldest of them all is the St. Paul Winter Carnival, which celebrated its 100th anniversary in January 1986. The carnival owes its existence to the de-

THE SAINT PAUL FOUNDATION

Since it began in 1940, 20,000 donors have given more than $100 million to The Saint Paul Foundation to enable the Foundation to help address the changing charitable needs of the citizens of the Greater Saint Paul area. Over the same period of time, The Saint Paul Foundation has made grants of more than $70 million directly back to the community. The Foundation has also guaranteed its ability to participate in meeting future needs, through the establishment of permanent endowment assets that have grown from nothing in 1940 to more that $70 million today. Total assets of the Foundation exceed $90 million.

The Saint Paul Foundation is the community foundation of the citizens of the East Metro area. It is one of 320 community foundations in the United States, having combined assets in 1985 of more than $3 billion. The first community foundation was established 72 years ago. Since that time, growth of community foundations nationally and growth of The Saint Paul Foundation locally demonstrate broad public acceptance of an exceptional idea. The idea is this: A community foundation is a single organization consisting of an open-ended number of permanent unrestricted and restricted trusts and funds contributed by many unrelated donors interested in a defined community. These donors, either by establishing new funds or by adding to existing funds, ask the Foundation's Board of Directors to accept, administer and make grants from funds contributed in accordance with the specified terms of each gift. The Foundation's Board of Directors, in turn, agrees to accept these contributions and use funds contributed to benefit the community as specified.

This repeated process of gift acceptance and execution through grants reflects the two main missions of The Saint Paul Foundation: grantmaking and development. The Foundation's Board of Directors must see to it that funds contributed are used as wisely as possible in meeting existing and emerging community needs. While making grants is the Foundation's primary mission, it is only through funds acquired through contributions that we can carry out this mission. Hence our second mission: To tell the people and organizations interested in the citizens of the Saint Paul Area about The Saint Paul Foundation and invite their participation in our work.

Ultimately, all the activities of The Saint Paul Foundation are the work of the Foundation's Board of Directors. It is the reputation and credibility of this Board that donors look to in making gifts to The Saint Paul Foundation. It is the willingness of this Board to work hard at understanding community needs and to make grants to address these needs that produces the intended benefit to our community. As can be seen in the list of Board members, The Saint Paul Foundation has had an excellent, hard working Board since its creation.

Through the vision and commitment of its Board and the hard work of its staff, The Saint Paul Foundation has been able to help the Greater Saint Paul community grow. We look forward to continued growth and participation in the life of our community in the years to come.

THE SAINT PAUL FOUNDATION
BOARD OF DIRECTORS (1940-1986)

Elected

Year	Name	Year	Name	Year	Name	Year	Name
1940	F.R. Bigelow	1952	T.A. Phillips	1962	Harold J. Cummings	1975	Jean V. West
1940	Homer P. Clark	1952	Howard Seesel	1962	Walter Gardner	1975	Timothy P. Quinn
1940	Rabbi H.S. Margolis	1952	J. Allen Wilson	1962	Reuel D. Harmon	1976	Norman M. Lorentzsen
1940	Wilfrid Rumble	1952	Ray Cummins	1963	John M. Musser	1977	J. Thomas Simonet
1940	I.A. O'Shaughnessy	1952	Paul Schilling	1963	Harry L. Holtz	1977	**James W. Reagan**
1940	Dr. H.E. Binger	1952	H. William Blake	1963	John F. Nash	1978	**Ronald M. Hubbs**
1940	W.S. Moscrip	1952	Charles J. Curley	1967	Cecil C. March	1981	**Richard A. Klingen**
1940	E.A. Roberts	1952	Clarence A. Maley	1971	John A. McHugh	1982	**Richard H. Kyle, Jr.**
1940	E.R. Reiff	1956	B.A. Weiss	1971	**Sam Singer**	1983	**Reatha Clark King**
1940	F.K. Weyerhaeuser	1956	Rollin O. Bishop	1972	Charles R. Murnane	1983	**Frederick T. Weyerhaeuser**
1940	Alex Highland	1957	John S. Holl	1972	**Richard A. Moore**	1984	**Virginia D. Brooks**
1940	Louis S. Headley	1957	Jerome Hoffman	1973	Benjamin G. Griggs, Jr.	1984	**David M. Craig, M.D.**
1940	H.B. Humason	1958	J. Neil Morton	1973	Charles L. Rafferty	1985	**Willis M. Forman**
1945	Ben H. Ridder	1959	Joseph Paper	1974	Robert W. Downing	1985	**John D. Healy, Jr.**
1952	Frank Anderson	1960	Richard H. Bancroft	1974	Dwight L. Martin, M.D.	1985	**Barbara B. Roy**
1952	Archibald G. Bush	1960	William H. Lang	1974	G. Richard Slade	1986	**John M. Eggemeyer III**

Current Board of Directors members are listed in bold-faced type.

Right and below: *Established in 1873, Como Park offers serene paths and beautiful winter scenery. Right photo by Leighton; below photo by Kay Shaw*

Above: *Only the tracks of passersby disturbs a blanket of snow over the Como Park Golf Course. Photo by Kay Shaw*

Left: *The Como Park Conservatory hosts a variety of shows year-round, including the popular "Mum Show." Photo by Kay Shaw*

Right: *The 1915 Como Park Conservatory glows in a winter sunset. Photo by Kay Shaw*

Below: *St. Paul's Winter Carnival ice palace tradition was initiated with this castle in 1886. Courtesy, MHS*

risive remark of a visiting New York newspaperman who in the 1880s described St. Paul as "another Siberia, unfit for human habitation in winter." The necessary funds soon arrived for organizing a winter carnival that would establish ice and snow as assets to a vigorous, healthful community.

The most spectacular feature of the 1886 carnival was its ice palace, a much-fancied symbol that appeared on everything from sheet music to stereopticon views to postcards to silk scarves. An ice palace—a medieval castle 189 feet long and 160 feet wide with a massive, 106-foot central tower—was erected in Central Park, the site today of the Capitol Approach area. More than 20,000 blocks of ice cut from the Mississippi were used in constructing the palace. Within its walls were skating rinks, ski slides and toboggan runs, and a Sioux Indian village. The 1887 ice palace was even more elaborate and the 1888 palace was the largest ice structure in the world. All glowed from inside, lighted by electric lights newly installed in St. Paul.

However, the carnival and its ice palaces waxed and waned through the years as unseasonably warm weather, financial crises, wars, and depressions interrupted the carnival's orderly year-after-year progression. Since the end of World War II the carnival has been a yearly event, the great ice palaces represented by smaller versions and the parade very much a part of it all. For the carnival's centennial year, to the delight of the city, the county, the state, and even to the nation which received daily televised progress reports, the ice palace was re-created in the tradition of the massive structures of a century ago and lighted once again in a rainbow of colors.

Other festivals and fairs are held throughout the year: June offers Grand Old Days along historic Grand Avenue, as well as the St. Paul Derby, in nearby Shakopee at the Canterbury Downs race track; during July there's Riverfest on Harriet Island, Taste of Minnesota in the Capitol Approach, and the Ramsey County Fair; September brings the Minnesota State Fair; and the Grand Meander closes the year in early December.

The civic pride that supported a carnival to celebrate winter in a city in the center of America's northern tier of states was typical of the 1880s. The nation was in an expansionist mood; the West seemed to have been won. In about ten years American troops would land in Cuba in what many looked upon as a glorious adventure, and in a few more years President Theodore Roosevelt would send the Great White Fleet around the world.

By the 1880s St. Paul had emerged from its cocoon as a frontier village, spreading its wings, this side of the Civil War, as a full-blown nineteenth century American city. An earlier renaissance, a period of redevelopment and renewal, was under way as part of the great building boom of that era. The face of the city was transformed. Stone and brick replaced the frame structures of the 1850s, and the elevator made multistoried business buildings possible. The city's population tripled, from 39,000 to 120,000, in the six years between 1880 and 1886. With sixteen rail lines, St. Paul was the third-largest rail center in the country.

A century later it is heartening to witness the growth and renewal, rebirth and renaissance that are taking place all over again and to realize that they are not unique to any one time or place. They seem to be a constant for a city renewing itself, and for a community that is led with wisdom, commitment, and a careful blending of the private and public forces that make that happen.

The jury may still be out on the question of public subsidies. Certainly, observers point to supply exceeding demand for hotel rooms; to a struggle by downtown retailers to recapture sales that, despite Town Square, flow to the suburbs; to a World Trade Center whose space is filling more slowly than anticipated; to defaults on tax-exempt bonds that financed the restoration of the Saint Paul Hotel and the construction of the Amhoist Tower.

However, similar problems plague other American cities. St. Paul may have fewer than most, and the renaissance in the downtown district is still unfolding as more people move into the new housing that is being built, as more job-holders staff more offices in more downtown buildings. A mid-1986 survey of fifty American cities reveals that St. Paul was one of only four with vacancy rates of less than 10 percent in its downtown office and apartment space.

And so the renaissance is by no means over. In many respects, it has scarcely begun.

AMHERST H. WILDER FOUNDATION

The Wilder Foundation Administration Building at 919 Lafond Avenue in St. Paul.

Amherst Holcomb Wilder was a contemporary of the legendary St. Paul railroad baron, James J. Hill. He came to the city in 1859 from his native New York and over the next 35 years built a small fortune in the development of the Northwest. Less colorful and well known than Hill and other entrepreneurs of that era, he was no less successful—his wide-ranging business interests included trading, freight and stagecoach transportation, railroading, lumbering, banking, insurance, real estate, and merchandising.

Almost a century later the influence of Amherst H. Wilder on the city is far beyond what he himself could have imagined. When his wife, Fanny Spencer Wilder, and their only child, Cornelia Day Wilder Appleby, died within months of each other in 1903, provisions of their wills, in addition to his own, took effect, which resulted in three separate charitable corporations. In 1910, by a special act of the Minnesota Legislature, the three were merged into one: the Amherst H. Wilder Charity, since renamed the Amherst H. Wilder Foundation. At the time the three

corporations were consolidated, the family estate was valued at a then-impressive $2.6 million. Beneficiaries of the charity were to be the poor, sick, aged, and needy people of St. Paul.

Since its founding the Wilder Foundation's initial $2.6 million has been multiplied many times over to the benefit of the city and its people. Over the years nearly $100 million of endowment and investment income has been spent to carry out the charitable intent of the Wilder family. At the same time, through careful stewardship and sound management, the market value of the trust itself has grown to more than $130 million, assuring that generations still to come will continue to benefit from the Wilder family's unique gift to the city. In 1974 its geographic service area was widened to include the greater St. Paul metropolitan area (Ramsey, Washington, Dakota, and Anoka counties), reflecting the growth of St. Paul through the years.

The modern-day Wilder Foundation is one of the largest single social service organizations in the state of Minnesota. Each year more than 40,000 people benefit from the foundation's diverse range of more than 40 human service programs. In recent years income from its endowment has been leveraged through funding from outside sources, including private fees and rents, funds from the State of Minnesota, county contracts, grants, and gifts.

Unlike the typical private foundation, whose primary activity is the provision of grants to aid particular causes, the Wilder Foundation operates each of the programs it funds. Its two largest areas of activity are services to children and families, and services to the elderly. In addition, the foundation provides housing management services and services to organizations, and funds a limited number of special programs. Direct care services focus on the primary purpose of the Wilder Foundation—to directly help people in need.

Services to children and families include operation of a Child Guidance Clinic to provide comprehensive outpatient mental health

Two members of the Wilder Foundation staff meet with a director of a Hispanic program in the metro area.

The Wilder rehabilitation staff provides services to elderly persons who live in the foundation's skilled-care nursing home.

services, and branch Child Guidance Centers in Burnsville, Maplewood, and Mounds View. The Eisenmerger Learning Center provides diagnostic treatment and rehabilitation services for children with special education and mental health needs. The Learning Disabilities Research Project, funded jointly by the 3M Foundation, the St. Paul School District, and the Wilder Foundation, is exploring an electronic communication system for classroom use.

Other services to children and families include a Children's Placement Service that works with foster homes, group homes, and residential treatment centers; a Social Adjustment Project for Refugees staffed by bilingual/bicultural community care workers; the Thomas-Dale Day Care Center; a Prevention Planning Project that works to develop preventive programming in areas such as child maltreatment; the St. Croix Camps and programs, designed to help juveniles and their families; and the Community Assistance Program, which specializes in group and individual counseling for adult offenders and their families, and

couples in violent relationships.

Health-oriented services to the elderly include three Adult Day-health Centers, a Senior Health Clinic, and Transportation Services to help those who need transportation to and from these programs, plus a Home Health Agency and In-Home Services. The Wilder Foundation also operates three residential facilities for the elderly in settings ranging from 24-hour skilled nursing care to independent living.

In addition, the Senior AIDES Program—funded primarily through the National Council of Senior Citizens—assists low-income older people in securing employment, while the downtown Senior Citizens Center provides activities and support services.

The Wilder Foundation's Division of Housing Management Services manages a variety of apartment and condominium complexes, some built and owned by the foundation, some owned by their residents, and some owned by other developers. Most specialize in meeting the housing needs of low- and moderate-income families and individuals, and the elderly.

Finally, in recognition of the tremendous community resource represented by its more than 80 years of experience in providing social services, the Wilder Foundation also provides services to nonprofit organizations and groups. Services range from training and program management consultation to the operation of conference and meeting facilities at Wilder Forest, 30 miles northeast of St. Paul.

In addition to direct involvement, the Wilder Foundation also has evolved innovative ways to multiply its impact on the community. Noteworthy in this area is Altcare, a partnership with General Mills, Inc., that is exploring ways to improve the delivery of long-term services for the elderly, and the Senior Health Plan, offered in partnership with St. Paul-Ramsey

Medical Center and Health Central Corporation.

The Wilder Foundation's most ambitious partnership is with the City of St. Paul and the Port Authority of the City of St. Paul through AHW Corporation. A wholly owned subsidiary formed in 1980 as a nonprofit corporation, AHW is involved in the development and construction of residential housing in Energy Park and the renovation and development of activities for the historic Burlington Northern Railroad buildings on the site.

Throughout its history the Wilder Foundation has been governed by a board of directors drawn from the St. Paul community. The continuity they have provided is mirrored in the service of the three men who have served as executive director: Charles L. Spencer, from 1910 to 1940; Frank M. Rarig, Jr., from 1940 to 1971; and Leonard H. Wilkening, from 1971 to the present.

While its breadth of activities has grown into new forms of direct and partnership services, the mission of the Amherst H. Wilder Foundation has remained unchanged—to help St. Paul and its people in need.

The Bandana Square water tower between two historic railroad buildings in Energy Park. A partnership the foundation entered into with the City of St. Paul, the St. Paul Port Authority, the federal government, and Control Data Corporation resulted in more than 700 housing units and renovation of the historic railroad buildings in Energy Park.

Rice Park offers a colorful fair to celebrate spring. Photo by Kay Shaw

Top: Rice Park marks the Winter Carnival with its display of remarkable ice sculptures. Photo by Kay Shaw

Above, and below, left: *St. Paulites gather on Harriet Island to celebrate St. Paul's riverfront heritage through the sights and sounds of the Riverfest. Photos by Leighton*

Above, left: *The 1986 Winter Carnival ice palace replicated the original palace from 100 years ago. Courtesy, Ellerbe Associates, Inc.*

LOOKING TO THE FUTURE

"2001: Can We Get There From Here?" was the title of a study made by a special Leadership Task Force of the Saint Paul Area Chamber of Commerce several years ago. The study addressed a number of important issues concerning the city's ability to attract and maintain jobs, and to preserve its high quality of life.

The Chamber recently adopted a Long-Range Plan, which emphasizes the need for the chamber and its members to make economic development its top priority. Thus the Chamber is working closely with the Saint Paul Port Authority in formulating a cooperative Saint Paul/East Metro area economic development plan.

St. Paul surely cannot continue its remarkable renaissance unless all areas of the community share in its redevelopment. Many of the city's historic neighborhoods, both commercial and residential, have successfully overcome the problem of urban blight. Yet many sections remain to be redeveloped, in particular the University Avenue area, one of the city's important commercial arteries.

Another issue the city must face is that of transportation. St. Paul and the Twin Cities Metro area must consider light rail or other alternative mass transit means. Accessibility and cost of parking downtown must also be addressed to ensure the viability of private and public investments made downtown and in Lowertown.

The private sector leadership and the city's Riverfront Commission have a unique opportunity to make a profound impact on the city's economic, cultural and recreational future. Any plan, however, must give continued emphasis to the river as a major transportation artery.

Meanwhile, the World Trade Center promises to provide an ideal base for growth, expansion, and new marketing opportunities for Minnesota and midwestern companies. Mid-America's only international trade center, it will be the fortieth member of the World Trade Federation and the tenth center in the country. Not only should the center help alleviate the state's trade imbalance, but it should also create new job opportunities: When it opens in 1987 it will bring the world to St. Paul.

And so as St. Paul faces the year 2001, it is with promise, while it also has some real challenges to be met in order to realize its full potential. Our ever-changing world will undoubtedly present new problems. I feel confident, however, that St. Paul will be an even more viable and vigorous community than it is today—as the renaissance continues.

Amos Martin
President
Saint Paul Area Chamber of Commerce

St. Paul's skyline, with First Bank's renowned "one" lit up, reflects in the waters of the Mississippi River. Courtesy, City of St. Paul, Planning and Economic Development Office

PATRONS

The following individuals, companies and organizations have made a valuable commitment to the quality of this publication. Windsor Publications and the Saint Paul Area Chamber of Commerce gratefully acknowledge their participation in *Saint Paul: A Modern Renaissance*.

American Bakeries Company*
American Hoist & Derrick Company*
American National Bank*
Arthur Andersen & Co.*
BCED Minnesota Inc.*
Bethesda Lutheran Medical Center*
Blue Cross and Blue Shield of Minnesota*
Children's Hospital of St. Paul*
College of St. Thomas*
Continental Cablevision of St. Paul*
Control Data Corporation*
Dart Transit Company
Deluxe Check Printers Inc.*
District Heating Development Company*
Ellerbe Architects Engineers Planners Builders
Embassy Suites Hotel*
Farm Credit Services*
First Bank System*
H.B. Fuller Company*
Gillette Children's Hospital*
The Gillette Company*
Harris Mechanical Contracting Co.*
HealthEast*
Hunt Electric Corp.
Land o'Lakes, Inc.
Lowertown Redevelopment Corporation
Macalester College*
McGill/Jensen, Inc.
Mann, Green, Hayes, Simon, Johanneson and Brehl*
Medtronic, Inc.*
Midwest Federal Savings and Loan Association*
Minnesota Mutual Life Insurance Company*
Multi-Arc*
New York Tea/SYSCO
North Star Ice, Inc.

North Star Steel Company*
Northwest Airlines, Inc.*
Northwestern Bell*
Norwest Bank St. Paul, N.A.*
Padelford Packet Boat Co., Inc.
Peat, Marwick, Mitchell & Co.*
The PEDRO Companies*
Pentair, Inc.*
Plastics, Inc.—Anchor Hocking Corporation*
Port Authority of the City of St. Paul*
Radisson Hotels*
Ramsey Clinic*
Road Rescue, Inc.
The St. Paul Companies*
The Saint Paul Foundation*
St. Paul Pioneer Press and Dispatch*
St. Paul-Ramsey Medical Center*
Samaritan Hospital*
Shaw Lumber*
Sheraton Midway*
Sisters of St. Joseph of Carondelet*
Sperry Burroughs*
SuperAmerica*
3M*
Toltz, King, Duvall, Anderson and Associates, Inc.*
Touche Ross & Co. St. Paul*
Tracy Oil Company, Inc.
The Tyson Companies
United Hospital*
University of Minnesota*
Video Update, Inc.*
Waldorf Corporation*
Amherst H. Wilder Foundation*
Wilkerson, Guthmann & Johnson, Ltd.*
Yorktown Investment Co.

*Corporate profiles in *Saint Paul: A Modern Renaissance*. The histories of these companies and organizations appear throughout the book.

BIBLIOGRAPHY

Below is a list of the major sources consulted.

Books, Journals, and Periodicals:

A Century and Beyond; A History of Macalester College. St. Paul: Macalester College, 1985.

Baker, Robert Orr. "James C. Burbank: The Man Who Used Coach and Boat to Link the Northwest to St. Paul." *Ramsey County History* 9, no. 2 (1972).

_____. *The Webb Company—The First Hundred Years.* St. Paul: The Webb Company, 1982.

Bracelin, Frank. "Two Little Telephones and How They Grew." *Minneapolis, Metropolis of the Northwest* (December 5, 1929).

Brueggemann, Gary. "St. Paul's Historic Family Breweries." *Ramsey County History* 16, no. 2.

Castle, Henry A. *A History of St. Paul and Ramsey County.* Chicago and New York: Lewis Publishing Company, 1912.

Connors, Joseph B. *Journey Toward Fulfillment; A History of the College of St. Thomas.* St. Paul: College of St. Thomas, 1985.

Corporate Report Minnesota. December 1984; February, March 1985; May, June, July 1985; September, October, November, December 1985; January, March 1986.

Corporate Report Minnesota Fact Book. 1985 and 1986.

Dalglish, Cathy. "Henry Schroeder's Dairy and His 'Safe for Baby Milk'." *Ramsey County History* 20, no. 1.

Dillard, Kendra. "Farming in the Shadow of the Cities: The Not-so-Rural History of Rose Township Farmers, 1850-1900." *Ramsey County History* 20, no. 3 (1985).

Dunn, James Taylor. *Saint Paul's Schubert Club—A Century of Music—1882-1982.* St. Paul: North Central Publishing Company, 1983.

Froiland, Paul. "Liberal Arts, Inc." *Twin Cities* 8, no. 11 (November 1985).

Galvin, Kevin. "The Necessities of Life—Available Early on the Frontier." *Ramsey County History.*

Grotts, Patricia. "A City Reborn." *Twin Cities* 8, no. 1 (January 1985).

Huck, Virginia. *Brand of the Tartan—The 3M Story.* St. Paul: Minnesota Mining and Manufacturing Company, 1955.

Inquiry. "Our Red Wing Roots: Hamline's Move Sparked Passions." (June-July 1985).

Johnson, David W. *Hamline University—A History.* St. Paul: North Central Publishing Company, 1980.

Kain, Sister Joan. *Rocky Roots—Three Geology Walking Tours of Downtown St. Paul.* St. Paul: Ramsey County Historical Society, 1978.

Kane, Lucile M. and Alan Ominsky. *Twin Cities—A Pictorial History of Saint Paul and Minneapolis.* St. Paul: Minnesota Historical Society Press, 1983.

Kennelly, Sister Karen. "The Dynamic Sister Antonia and the College of St. Catherine." *Ramsey County History* 14, no. 1.

Kennon, Peggy Korsmo and Drake, Robert B. *Discover St. Paul.* St. Paul: Ramsey County Historical Society, 1979.

Koeper, H.F. *Historic St. Paul Buildings.* St. Paul: St. Paul City Planning Board, 1964.

Kunz, Virginia Brainard. "Promoters Waxed Lyrical in 'Selling' St. Paul." *Ramsey County History.*

_____. *St. Paul—Saga of an America City.* With addendum, "St. Paul: 1977-1980." Woodland Hills, California: Windsor Publications, Inc., 1977.

Lettermann, Edward J. "Student Protests, Marches—100 Years Ago at the University." *Ramsey County History* 6, no. 2 (1969).

Lowry, Goodrich. "Tom Lowry and the Launching of the Street Railway System." *Ramsey County History.*

Mack, Linda, ed. "New Places for Old Saint Paul." *Architecture Minnesota* 10, no. 2 (March/April 1984).

Martin, Albro. *James J. Hill and the Opening of the Northwest.* New York: Oxford University Press, 1976.

Marvin, William W. *Origin, Growth, Leadership.* St. Paul: West Publishing Company, 1969.

Michels, Eileen. *A Landmark Reclaimed.* St. Paul, 1977.

Murphy, Denis. "Colorfully Critical: Newspapers and the Horsecars of the 1870s." *Ramsey County History.*

Our Story So Far—Notes from the First 75 Years of 3M Company. St. Paul: Minnesota Mining and Manufacturing Company, 1977.

Phelps, Gary. "Health Care Crisis of the 1920s—A 'National Epidemic' Launches Blue Cross and Blue Shield." *Ramsey County History* 20, no. 3 (1985).

Pond, Samuel, Jr. "The Letters of Samuel Pond, Jr.—Students Cooked their Food, Built their Fires." *Ramsey County History* 6, no. 2 (1969).

Rajkowsky, John. "*Who was* William Mitchell?" *William Mitchell Magazine* (January 1986).

Ramsey County History 15, no. 1 (1979).

Roach, Inez. *A History of the Science Museum of Minnesota— 1907-1975.* St. Paul: Science Museum of Minnesota, 1981.

Russell, Thomas W. III. "The State: Housewarming Overtures." *Twin Cities* 8, no. 1 (January 1985).

Swanson, Edward. "Macalester and its First Forty Years." *Ramsey County History* 11, no. 1.

"The Revitalization of the Jacob Schmidt Brewery." *Brewers Digest* 56, no. 12.

Tice, D.J. "A Theater in a Park on a River." *Twin Cities* 8, no. 1 (January 1985).

Uphoff, Mary Jo and Walter, with Russell K. Lewis. *Group Health—An American Success Story in Prepaid Health Care.* Minneapolis: Dillon Press, 1980.

Williams, J. Fletcher. *A History of the City of Saint Paul to 1875.* 2nd edition. St. Paul: Minnesota Historical Society, 1983.

Woxland, Thomas A. "Forever Associated with the Practice of Law: The Early Years of the West Publishing Company." *Legal Reference Services Quarterly* 5, no. 1 (Spring 1985).

State and Local Government Reports:

Annual reports. City of Saint Paul Department of Planning and Economic Development, 1981-1985.

Downtown Survey Report. City of Saint Paul Department of Planning and Economic Development, December 1984.

Minnesota Health Profiles. Minnesota Department of Health, 1984.

Minnesota Health Statistics, 1983. Minnesota Department of Health, 1985.

Minnesota State Rail Plan, 1984. Minnesota Department of Transportation.

Saint Paul Heritage Preservation Commission Report. City of Saint Paul Department of Planning and Economic Development.

Saint Paul Tours. City of Saint Paul Department of Planning and Economic Development and Saint Paul Port Authority, January 1985.

Regional Studies and Reports:
A Description of Activities and Services. Minnesota Public Radio, 1985.

Annual Report, 1985. Metropolitan Council.

"Birth Statistics for Health Planning Areas in the Twin Cities, 1983." *Metropolitan Health Planning Board Vital Statistics Report,* publication no. 18-85-102. Metropolitan Council, September 1985.

Community Arts Survey. Community Research Associates, October 1950.

Consumer's Guide to Health Plans, Twin Cities Metropolitan Area. Metropolitan Council, 1984; January 1985.

"Death Statistics for Health Planning Area in the Twin Cities." *Metropolitan Health Planning Board Vital Statistics Report,* publication no. 18-85-103. Metropolitan Council, August 1985.

"Hospital Specialty Services Use in the Twin Cities Metropolitan Area, 1979-1983." Metropolitan Council, October 1984.

Corporate, Industry, and Foundation Reports and Publications:
A Brief History of Sperry Corporation. Sperry Corporation.

Economic Impact of the Lowertown Redevelopment Program. Lowertown Redevelopment Corporation, 1979-1985.

History of American National Bank and Trust Company. American National Bank and Trust.

Johnson, Roger T. *Historical Beginnings . . . The Federal Reserve.* Federal Reserve Bank of Boston, December 1972.

KSTP History. Hubbard Broadcasting, Inc.

Lowertown. Lowertown Redevelopment Corporation, January 1986.

Metro Monitor. Metropolitan Council, 1984-1986.

Metropolitan Fiber Network. Northwestern Bell, July 29, 1985.

Metropolitan Transit Commission. Annual reports, 1984-1985.

Minnesota Motor Transport Association.

Minnesota Trucking Industry. Minnesota Motor Transport Association.

Northwestern/Saint Paul. Northwest Bank.

One Hundred Years—Looking Ahead to Look After You. Minnesota Mutual Life Insurance Company.

Ordway Music Theatre. Commemorative program, 1985.

Reflection from History: The Minneapolis Federal Reserve Bank. Federal Reserve Bank of Minneapolis, February 1973.

Retail Sales. Metropolitan Council, 1982.

Saint Paul Area Chamber of Commerce. Overview of St. Paul area hospitals.

_____. Community profile, 1984-1985.

Sperry in Minnesota. Sperry Corporation.

Stanley E. Hubbard—The Pioneer's Pioneer. Hubbard Broadcasting, Inc.

The J.L. Shiely Company in the Decade of the '80s. J.L. Shiely Company.

West Publishing Company—A New Age in Book Manufacturing Technology. West Publishing Company, 1985.

William Mitchell College of Law. Bulletin/catalogue, 1985-1987.

World Theater. Booklets, April 1986.

Newspapers:
City Pages, 1985
Downtowner, 1985-1986
Grand Gazette, 1985-1986
Minneapolis/St. Paul City Business, 1985-1986
Minneapolis Star and Tribune, 1968-1986
St. Paul Pioneer Press Dispatch, 1956-1986
St. Paul Skyway News, April 17, 1985

INDEX

This book was set in Helvetica, Avant Garde Gothic & Cloister open face. It was printed and bound at Walsworth Publishing Company.